BECOME AN EVENT PLANNER

Secrets for Getting Hired
from Employers, Recruiters, and Event Professionals

MATTHEW JAMES

PLAN B
PUBLISHING

Become an Event Planner
Secrets for Getting Hired from Employers, Recruiters, and Event Professionals
www.becomeaneventplanner.org

This edition first published in 2016 by Plan B Publishing
www.planbpublishing.com

A CIP catalogue record for this book is available from the British Library

ISBN 978-0-9934976-0-5

ACKNOWLEDGEMENTS

I am indebted and grateful to all the event professionals who generously contributed their time, wisdom, and experience to make this career guide representative of the many different sectors of the events industry. You taught me a few things too.

Thank you to Scott Buckland and Annie Ashdown for encouraging me to write, and Kevin McGuire, Mark Davis, and Zoe Mack for your continued support.

A special thank you to my unbelievably patient and supportive partner, Trevor, who learnt the hard way that event planners are control freaks. Finally, to my mother, who inspired me to do things my own way, sorry that I never became a doctor.

CONTENTS

Education and Training

My Route into the Industry: Starting in Travel

From working in a hardware store, to running global meetings and incentive travel programs

Planning Your Route into the Events Industry

My Route into the Industry: Starting in Project Management

From sales promotions at Christian Dior, to Global Head of Events for an international law firm

How to Get Experience

My Route into the Industry: Starting as Event Support Staff

*From temping for an event staffing agency, to working as a
senior corporate event manager for Goldman Sachs*

Resumes and Interviews

My Route into the Industry: Starting as a Volunteer

*From volunteering at the American Film Institute, to producing
the reveal of the largest LEGO model ever built in Times Square*

My Route into the Industry: Starting in Catering

*From selling printer cartridges, to working on events for HRH
Charles, Prince of Wales*

Additional Content

For additional content, visit this book's companion websites at:

Become an Event Planner

Includes information about the different ways to work as an event planner, the pros and cons of the job, and an introduction to the different sectors of the industry—with first-hand accounts from professionals who offer insights into what the job really involves on a day-to-day basis

www.becomeaneventplanner.org

Event Planning Courses

Includes information about the many different event-planning courses available, including campus-based, distant learning, short/part-time, and online.

www.eventplanningcourses.org

1

About the Author

Matt James is an award-winning event planner and owner of Left Field Productions. With 20 years' experience in corporate, charity, brand experience, and special events, Matt has produced events for Elton John, Sarah Jessica Parker, Stella McCartney, Kevin Spacey, David LaChapelle, Canon, Mattel, Montblanc, Chopard, Christie's, The British Red Cross, Wella, and Credit Suisse.

The winner of 30 event awards, Matt is often invited to speak at industry events, such as ILEA conferences and lectures, International Confex, and RSVP; judge awards and competitions, including The Eventice, Corporate Event Association Awards, and Incentive Travel & Meetings Association Awards; and guest lecture at university event-management degree courses.

Matt has contributed to both consumer magazines, such as *Instyle*, *Esquire*, *Sainsbury's Money Matters*, and *Ocado Life*, and trade publications including *Conference & Incentive Travel*, *Event Magazine*, and his own monthly column, *Matt's Planet*, in *RSVP Magazine*.

Prior to founding his own event production company, Matt worked for leading Middle East advertising agency Publicis Graphics. He began his event-planning career working on fundraising events for AIDS charity London Lighthouse, before joining the corporate events team at the investment bank Credit Suisse.

He lives in London, United Kingdom, with his partner Trevor and their mischievous Jack Russell Terrier, Bruce.

www.leftfield.productions   www.becomeaneventplanner.org

2

Meet the Professionals

Throughout this book, professionals working across the different sectors of the events industry will share their experiences and advice for becoming an event planner. For their full biographies, see the companion website at www.becomeaneventplanner.org

Marie Davidheiser

Marie Davidheiser is Senior Vice President, Director of Operations for Jack Morton Worldwide. Based in their New York office, she has worked on experiential campaigns and brand experience events throughout North America for clients including Bank of America, Samsung, Kimberly-Clark, American Airlines, Verizon, LEGO, and Walmart.

Farida Haqiqi

Farida Haqiqi is the former Events Manager for The British Red Cross. Events she worked on included the annual British Red Cross London Ball; a gala fundraising dinner for 600 people, a "major donor" event at Clarence House with HRH Charles, Prince of Wales, challenge events such as the London Marathon, and an annual British Red Cross Skills Share conference for 200 delegates.

Nathan Homan

Nathan Homan is Creative Director and Co-founder of special events agency Rouge Events, which specializes in brand communication events, product launches, parties and festivals for clients including Nissan, Jamie Oliver, Ikea, Sky, Ernst & Young, and Cartoon Network. Prior to co-founding Rouge Events, Nathan worked in banqueting at The Dorchester and Four Seasons hotels.

Chad Hudson

Chad Hudson is President, Creative Director and Owner of Chad Hudson Events, a full service event design, production and management company with offices in New York and Los Angeles. Past events include Guess North American Conference, ABC's Comic-Con booth, Major League Baseball's All Stars Gala, movie premieres including *The Twilight Saga*, *Enders Game*, and *Justin Bieber: Never Say Never*, and numerous Academy Awards, Golden Globe Awards, and Super Bowl events.

Bill Jones

Bill Jones is Vice President and Managing Director of Events for The Channel Company (formerly UBM Tech Channel, part of UBM plc) a global live media and business-to-business communications, marketing services, and data provider. Bill's event expertise spans on-demand conferences, virtual events, live events, conferences, road shows, and partner events.

Fiona Lawlor

Fiona Lawlor is HR Director and Senior Vice President of the EMEA region of global brand experience agency Jack Morton Worldwide. Based in the London office, Fiona is responsible for attracting, developing, motivating, and retaining the talent needed to be an ideas-led agency.

Christopher Lee

Christopher H. Lee, DMCP, is CEO of ACCESS Destination Services. An award-winning destination management company with offices throughout North America, ACCESS Destination Services provides creative program design, event production services, travel logistics, and recreational activities for meetings, incentives, and conventions. Clients include Wells Fargo, Nestle, and Energizer.

Jennifer Miller

Jennifer Miller, DMCP, is a Partner of ACCESS Destination Services and President of its offices in San Diego, Los Angeles, Las Vegas, and Arizona. She originally joined ACCESS San Diego in 2000 as a Program Manager working on meetings, special events, and incentive travel programs for *Fortune* 100 companies such as Microsoft, Exxon Mobil, Toyota, and AT&T.

Grace Nacchia

Grace Nacchia is an Event Director at George P. Johnson where she works on multiple conferences and exhibitions for clients that include IBM and GSMA (Global Systems for Mobile Communications Association). Prior to George P. Johnson, Grace worked for Imagination on the Shell/Ferrari global exhibitions program and EMS Worldwide on roadshows and events for Sony and Royal Bank of Scotland. Grace has delivered events throughout Europe, Asia, and the Middle East.

Dori Rodriguez

Dori Rodriguez is a Senior HR Associate for global brand experience agency Jack Morton Worldwide. Based in the Boston office, Dori's role includes recruiting and filling entry-level positions at Jack Morton offices throughout the United States. She also leads Jack Morton's Summer Internship Program.

Nicola Mosley

Nicola Mosley is the UK HR Manager for George P. Johnson, the #1 ranked experience-marketing agency in the world. As part of her role, Nicola manages GPJ's recruitment efforts in the United Kingdom.

Charlotte Saynor

Charlotte Saynor is the former Vice President of Brands and Events for FremantleMedia Enterprises (FME), one of the world largest creators, producers, and distributors of TV programs such as *The X Factor and American Idol*. Managing the global events program, including trade shows, conventions, festivals, brand launch events, conferences, and sponsorship events, Charlotte has produced events in locations such as New York, London, Las Vegas and Cannes. Prior to FME, Charlotte was the Head of European Events for Apple and has organized events for TV brands such as *Lost* and *Desperate Housewives* whilst at Disney ABC.

Sharyn Scott

Sharyn Scott is Global Head of Events for the law firm Linklaters, which has 28 offices throughout the United States and Latin America, Europe, Asia Pacific, the Middle East and Africa. Sharyn's role encompasses the full spectrum of corporate events from corporate hospitality, dinners, and staff holiday parties, to overseas conferences, global partners' meetings, and client receptions. Prior to working at Linklaters, Sharyn has organized events world-wide for Citibank, Barclays Capital, Credit Suisse, BNP Paribas and the travel company Going Places, a division of Thomas Cook.

Lisa Simmons

Lisa Simmons is Project Manager, Europe, Asia, and Middle East (EAME) Events at Goldman Sachs. Prior to Goldman Sachs, Lisa worked as a freelance event manager for Microsoft, British Telecom, and Credit Suisse before becoming Assistant Vice President in Corporate Events for Barclays Capital and Event Team Leader at Linklaters.

Liz Sinclair

Liz Sinclair is Co-founder and Managing Director of ESP Recruitment, the leading recruitment consultancy for the events industry. A specialist agency founded in 1999, ESP Recruitment have offices in London and Dubai covering all sectors of the events industry both in the United Kingdom and overseas. Prior to co-founding ESP Recruitment, Liz worked for a number of conference and exhibition companies including Centaur and UBM

Charlotte Wolseley Brinton

Charlotte Wolseley Brinton is the former Head of Events at Rhubarb Food Design, one of the UK's top five catering companies, where she worked on high-profile events such as HRH Prince Charles' 50th birthday at Windsor Castle, Elton John's *Annual White Tie & Tiara Ball,* and Stella McCartney's wedding.

Martin Turner

Martin Turner is the former Global Head of Events for the investment bank Credit Suisse. He began his event-planning career in Australia and spent 16 years managing international group travel, conferences, and incentive programs for clients such as Toyota, Pepsi, Xerox, and American Express before joining global brand experience agency Jack Morton. Since leaving Credit Suisse Martin has worked for UBS, Barclays Capital, MJM Creative, and NetJets. Martin also teaches Event Management to Post Graduate students at Birbeck, Kings College, and UCL Institute of Education in London for Event Academy.

Rachel Vingsness

Rachel Vingsness is a Senior HR Manager for Jack Morton Worldwide and works with the New Jersey, Connecticut, and California teams. The Jack Morton HR team is focused on engaging talent, growing careers and fostering culture and community.

3

What You Need to Know before You Get Started

The vast majority of people looking to get into the events industry go about it in entirely the wrong way—which is what prompted me to write this book. Unlike most professions, you don't need formal training or qualifications to become an event planner; you can't just take a course, graduate and start applying for entry-level positions. In this industry, employers are looking for experience rather than qualifications. So how does one get industry experience when first starting out? A lot of that comes down to how you approach potential employers and the preparation you do beforehand. Which is what I hope to teach you in this book.

The Two Mistakes You're Likely to Make When Starting Out

The first is making 'cold' approaches to potential employers. You can't just sit at home passively sending out resumes hoping that someone will just give you an opportunity. As an employer myself, I get inundated with resumes from people asking for entry-level positions, work experience and internships. Most of the time these just get buried in my inbox and I never have time to look at them. On the rare occasion one stands out enough for me to read the attached resume, I'm usually left completely underwhelmed. In truth, the chances of me hiring someone in this way—even for work experience—are probably slim to none.

The events industry, perhaps more so than others, is all about networking, contacts and personal relationships. Ninety-nine percent of jobs—the good ones at least—never even get advertised; they're filled by word-of-mouth recommendations or people already known to the employer in some way. The reality is, most employers prefer to hire people that they know, have worked with before, or come recommended. Often, they just don't want to take the risk of hiring a complete stranger. The majority of event companies are small businesses without formal internship programs, so when they need extra help they generally ask friends and colleagues if they know of anyone suitable. Alternatively, they'll think about who they've encountered onsite at events that might have stood out and showed promise; someone who demonstrated some initiative and went beyond what was expected of them. Employers typically don't have the time to invite random strangers in for an interview on the off-chance they might be a good fit. Therefore, that resume you've emailed in asking for work experience—assuming it hasn't been buried in an inbox unopened—is likely to always take second place behind candidates that the employer knows, or knows of.

This doesn't mean the industry is a closed shop, only for those with friends who can make introductions. What is does mean however, is that you have to get out there and put the effort in to develop your own contacts and relationships; and that can't be done sat at your computer firing off anonymous resumes to people you've never met. You need to work onsite at events where you'll meet people and make contacts—which is the approach I'll guide you through in this book.

The second mistake you're likely to make is not helping yourself sufficiently before asking a potential employer to help you. I mentioned previously that I'm often underwhelmed when I read the resumes of people asking for entry-level positions, work experience or internships. This is because very few have impressed me with the level of effort they've already put in to getting experience, prior to approaching me. In order to convince an employer to take a chance on you, you first need to show them what you've already done to help yourself. If I look at your resume, will I see evidence of your drive and commitment to getting into the events industry? If your cover letter tells me that you are passionate about events, will that be reflected on your resume—in the effort you've made to get experience?

I'll let you in on a secret; most employers resent it when they're faced with a passive 'please give me a job' attitude—no matter how nicely you ask. We don't want you to plead and beg to be given an opportunity—as if you are hoping we're just going to do you a favor. As a job seeker, even one looking for work experience, you need to view the situation from the employer's perspective; show me why I need you. Show me that you're driven and committed, show me the skills and experience you're going to bring to my organization, and show me what you're going to contribute to my business. Don't just ask an employer to hand you an opportunity. Instead, sell yourself based on the benefits to them; why do *they* need *you*?

I set out to write this book to show job-seekers the right way to go about it. Along the way I hope to help you decide whether taking an event-planning course is right for you, and how to:

- make contacts and network,
- get the experience employers are looking for,
- present that experience on a resume,
- approach potential employers, and
- shine in an interview.

All of this advice is based on interviews with other industry experts—employers, recruiters and experienced event professionals—who also offer their own tips and advice. At times this advice might sound harsh and it might not be what you want to hear; the contributors to this book and I have been pretty blunt. But it is given with the best of intentions; to give you a better chance of getting started—and being successful—in this industry. Employers want the job seekers we interview to be the best they can be, as that will only strengthen our businesses and contribute to our success. This book is about giving you the inside track on exactly what employers are looking for, to help you stand out from all the other job-seekers still passively sending out resumes and pleading to be given a chance.

Introduction to Case Studies

I'm sure that, like me, you've probably seen the biographies of successful event planners or read interviews about how they got started. They always say something like, "he began his career organizing events for MTV", or "she started her own events company in 1992." It always sounds so easy doesn't it? Like one day, you just become an event planner. Simple.

The reality is that biographies only focus on the high points and successes. The real 'nitty-gritty' of how he or she got his or her foot in the door, then struggled to work their way up and eventually made a name for themselves, always gets glossed over. Biographies never mention the junior or support roles a planner took at the beginning of their career, the countless rejections, and failures along the way, the months in between jobs with no work or, perhaps most significantly, how exactly—with no experience— they got that very first opportunity that set them on the right path. I know, because my biography is guilty of exactly the same thing.

Throughout this book, I've included a number of case studies that chart—in detail—the route that some of the contributors to this book took to get into the events industry and then work their way up in. In particular, I've focused on the very early stages of their career and their first few steps on the career ladder; highlighting the effort they put in, the sacrifices they made, and what they did right. It's a common misconception that to get a job in events, you have to keep sending out resumes until you get a break. The case studies in this book show that not only do you rarely go straight into a job planning events, but that you often have to be proactive in creating opportunities for yourself along the way.

.

My Route into the Industry

Starting in Charity Events

From college drop-out, to organizing events for Elton John in three years

Matthew James, Owner, Left Field Productions

Let's start by looking at my biography, the one that is often used in interviews and on websites. Then I'll take you through the reality of how I got those early opportunities and all the gaps in my resume that are never mentioned. My biography often reads:

'Matt began his event-planning career while working for AIDS charity London Lighthouse. In 1998, he created and produced the Canon Designs for Life fashion show, bringing together one hundred of the top names in fashion—from Armani to Versace—to design a one-of-a-kind garment inspired by the AIDS red ribbon. During this time, Matt sold sponsorship of the event to Canon and it went on to be a phenomenal success, raising much-needed funds for people living with HIV, and generating global TV and press coverage. Following Canon Designs for Life, Matt went on to found his own event production company. His first client was Sir Elton John, which resulted in the creation of his now famous AIDS fundraiser, The Annual White Tie & Tiara Ball.'

It might look like a lot of good luck, right? You do one charity event, start your own company, and your first client is Elton John. In reality, there was a whole lot more that went on behind the scenes to get to those milestones. It definitely wasn't easy, and for most of the time, I was struggling just to make ends meet and pay the bills. But most importantly—and this is something I really want to drive home—I created all those opportunities for myself. I didn't just send out resumes and hope that someone would give me a job organizing events. I didn't have any contacts in the industry, nor did I have a wealthy family to support me financially while I took unpaid work. I had to be proactive and make it happen myself—and that's something I really want to inspire you to do with this book. Because the really successful people are the ones that stand out from all the others by being proactive, making things happen and creating their own opportunities. And those people are exactly the ones that employers want to hire.

Matt James: Biography—the Full Story

As you can see, my first significant step on the career ladder was working on events for an AIDS charity, London Lighthouse. But I had to do a lot of work even to get to this stage. I'm going to go into a fair amount of detail because I want you to understand that it was a very gradual process.

College Dropout

I actually had no intention of working in events. I'd always intended to be an actor. After working for a couple of years in advertising to raise the money to pay for acting school, I found when I finally got there that I hated it! Eventually, I dropped out before the end of the course, with no clue as to what I was going to do next.

Leveraging Every Opportunity

While I was figuring things out, I took any job I could get just to pay the bills. I ended up doing data entry at a small London magazine, a 'free-sheet' given out in bars and clubs, entering classified ads. I soon managed to persuade my employers to let me do some writing for the magazine—albeit unpaid—and I started to review new theatre and movie openings. The magazine already had someone who wrote all their arts reviews, but I'd noticed that he always seemed really busy. He would spend most weekday evenings going to see shows, but he always felt bad that he didn't have enough time to review the smaller fringe shows, which are usually held miles away in tiny arts centers on the outskirts of town. So, I offered to go and review those shows for him—for free. Of course, I didn't have any professional writing experience to show him what I could do, so before approaching him, I took myself to the movies and theatre one weekend and wrote some mock reviews based on what I'd seen. I think he was pretty impressed that I'd taken the initiative to go out and do this—and of course, he was more than happy to have a free assistant to help with his workload.

This is a great example of taking any job just to get your foot in the door, then leveraging that opportunity to work your way up. Sometimes you have to take a role that you're overqualified for, just to get into the industry. It's so much easier to work your way up from the inside. Also, if you're trying to create an opportunity for yourself, be strategic about it. Take the initiative to do whatever preparation you need to beforehand, to increase your chances of success—don't just turn up and wing it. In my case, I went and got some—albeit amateur—writing experience to show a) what I could do, and b) that I was serious and committed. Then, when it comes to the pitch, don't just think about what you want to get out of the situation, think about what you can offer the employer. See it from their perspective and highlight what you can bring to the table that's going to benefit them. In my case, although I wanted to write for the magazine, instead of begging for a chance, I pitched it based on the fact that I would work unpaid and help the arts editor with his workload. So it was a win-win situation.

Volunteering

While working my day job entering classified ads, and reviewing shows in the evenings, I decided I also wanted to do something a little more meaningful. So I began to look into some charities while figuring out what I was going to do career-wise.

I replied to an ad by a small AIDS charity that provided HIV awareness to young people. The ad said they were looking for help with fundraising, so I called them up and they told me to come in and see them. In preparation, I spent a lot of time brainstorming and drawing up a list of fundraising ideas that might impress them. Bear in mind I had no experience in fundraising, so I'm sure a lot of the ideas were probably, at best, a bit naïve and at worst, lame. I can't remember exactly what the ideas were but they were all quite basic, such as getting the bars and clubs that distributed the magazine to do collections in their venues. Nothing particularly original.

The key thing here is that I went in armed with ideas. I wanted to show them what I could do for them. I came to the interview ready to contribute something. I wasn't just turning up asking for a job.

When I got to the interview, I found that I was just one of dozens being seen in quick succession. It turned out that when they said they were looking for help with fundraising, what they were actually looking for were 'chuggers'; those people who accost you on the street shaking collection jars and asking for spare change. I was so disappointed that when I was given my allotted two-minute briefing, I just launched into my ideas and pitched them anyway. I raced through all my ideas at break-neck speed and when I finally stopped speaking the interviewer just said to me quietly, "I think you should speak to our fundraising manager." I was then ushered into a separate room where I repeated my pitch to the manager, who was more than happy for me to volunteer in other ways.

Going in for something low-level then over-delivering definitely got me noticed and created more opportunities. Always aim to over-deliver and exceeding expectations— you'll stand out and move up the career ladder quicker.

Having pitched a range of ideas, and generated some interest, I knew I now had to deliver.

Working at the magazine, I was given an opportunity to work at a small one-day music festival. It was a day's work, pretty badly paid, but I said I'd do it if I could take along some collection tins and posters to try and raise a bit of money for the charity at the same time. When I arrived on the day, I was given the job of supervising a mechanical bull fairground ride. All it involved doing was taking £1 off people and timing their ride, so I decided to add my own fundraising angle to it. I put up the charities posters all around the ride and told each paying customer that if they fell off in less than a minute they had to put some change in the charity box. I then told the operator to run it at a gentle speed for the first 45 seconds before increasing it to top speed to ensure they fell off. The ride was really popular and, with it being a hot sunny day and everyone in good spirits after a few drinks, I ended up raising several hundred pounds for charity.

Over the next few months, I worked—unpaid—on several small fundraising projects for charity, during the evenings and weekends. It was pretty low-level stuff; mostly things that anyone could have done. I seem to remember taking collection tins to a lot of nightclubs! Because I worked at the magazine, we were given special press passes to get into all the clubs free. Often at the big nightclubs, they would have separate lines for people on the guest list and I spotted an opportunity. The guest list were getting in for free; often saving themselves a good £10–20 on the door charge, so I thought this would be a perfect opportunity to hit them up for a donation to charity. I approached a few of the big clubs with this idea and they agreed to have a collection tin at the guest list entrance. Each week, whoever was ticking the names off the list would just politely ask people to put £1 in the charity tin. And everyone did. They could hardly say no after just getting the door charge waived. It was a simple idea that ended up creating regular income.

The lesson here is that you have to look for whatever opportunities you can exploit in your everyday life. I took the day's work at the music festival because I was broke and needed the money, but I then leveraged that as a fundraising opportunity. Likewise, I happened to notice the guest list opportunity because I was going out to a lot of nightclubs at the time. My point is, it's not about being privileged or having opportunities handed to you. It's about looking at what you have access to in your own life and seeing how you can use that to create your own opportunities. Be proactive. Had I been working in a supermarket, I probably would have tried to create a fundraising opportunity by getting all the staff together to do something like a fun run. You can create opportunities out of whatever situation you're in. Don't sit around waiting for someone to give you a break. Employers want to see what you've done to help yourself.

My First Paying Job in Events

For almost a year, I juggled a mixture of writing, data entry on the classified ads, and a bit of charity work before I decided to pursue the idea of fundraising as a full-time job. In June 1997, I applied for a junior fundraising role at another AIDS charity, but I didn't even get invited for an interview. When I mentioned this to a friend, he said he knew someone who worked in fundraising at another medium-sized AIDS charity, London Lighthouse, and offered to put me in touch with him. This person lived locally to me, so we met up for coffee and I asked if I could just pick his brains on how to get into fundraising.

Asking friends of friends and other acquaintances if you can get their advice is a great way to start networking. You'll build contacts, get recommendations, and hear about opportunities before others.

During our meeting I told him about all the fundraising I'd been doing. He explained that he was leaving his job the following week, but that if I sent him my resume he'd pass it on because they were always looking for people who were driven. I tailored my resume to highlight all the different things I'd done with the smaller AIDS charity. There were a handful of good talking points there, although to any professional fundraiser they would be considered child's play. Nevertheless, within a few weeks, I got a call and they asked me to pop in for an informal chat.

At this point, you're probably thinking "but you knew someone who pulled strings for you." And yes, he did pass on my resume, which probably served as an informal recommendation. But you know what? That's what networking is all about—and it's how 90 percent of all hiring gets done in the events industry—which is why you have to find—and make—your own contacts.

An introduction, no matter how tentative or vague, sets you apart from the crowd. In most cases, an introduction alone won't get you the job, but it might be the difference between you being considered or not. That's why you can't just send out resumes cold; you've got to put yourself in an environment where you are going to meet people who might be able to help you.

The reality was that London Lighthouse wouldn't have invited me in for a chat if there weren't something on my resume of interest. Also, my contact wouldn't have even been able to suggest passing on my resume had I not filled it with all the volunteer fundraising I had done over the past year. That's why it's important to go out and get experience, however basic, to demonstrate commitment and drive.

Before I went in to see London Lighthouse, I did a huge amount of research on the charity and the types of events they did, and started to put together a list of ideas I could pitch to them. Again, they were all quite basic ideas, such as approaching new theatre shows that were opening to do preview nights in aid

19

of the charity. I knew that, having spent a year reviewing shows and dealing with theatre publicists, I could probably go knocking on a few doors and ask for favors.

Again, I put myself in the mind-set of "what could I do for them?" I didn't have a huge amount of fundraising experience so I couldn't demonstrate a proven track record. Instead, I decided to impress them with lots of ideas to show potential; I was bringing something to the table. That, coupled with the fact they could see from my resume that I'd already put some effort in by fundraising for the other charity, demonstrated a genuine passion and drive. That type of insight into a person's character can count for a lot when employers are hiring.

I have to admit that I was quite surprised when they eventually offered me two day's work a week (paid!) to try to implement some of my ideas.

Early Events

Now, I want to make it clear that although I now had my foot in the door, it was still a major up-hill struggle. It was casual employment, with no fixed term contract, and of course, the money was terrible. So if I didn't start showing results pretty soon, I knew I'd be out.

It can be really tempting once you've landed an opportunity to become a bit complacent; you've got your foot on the ladder, so you start to relax. Fortunately, my circumstances meant I had a limited amount of time to prove myself—and I think that's how everyone should approach their first break. Now that you've got your foot is in the door, what are you going to do to make yourself invaluable?

I started in September 1997 and basically just hit the phones; cold calling people and firing off letters until I made something happen. The first event I managed to secure was a private view of a new Bruce Webber retrospective due to open at The National Portrait Gallery. The gallery was prepared to give us a preview evening for free, which we could then sell tickets to. I think the charity were quite taken back that I'd managed to pull it off so easily, without any assistance. The truth was, I just called up the gallery, spoke to a woman in publicity and proposed a charity night to her. Following that, I'd heard that a new production of the musical *Chicago* was due to open, so I contacted the producer's PR team to see if we could have a preview night for charity, which they agreed to.

The next event I put together was a preview screening of a small independent movie for World AIDS Day, followed by an after-party at a trendy nightclub, The Café de Paris. Again, I literally just called up the film distribution company and asked them if they'd let us have an advance copy of the movie, then I asked a handful of cinema's if anyone would donate a screen for the evening. It really wasn't that hard. I started to realize that if you had a good charity name behind you, and were prepared to do a lot of cold calling and letter writing, you'd be amazed how much people are prepared to do—if you just get out there and ask. The hardest part by far was actually selling the tickets, but I was prepared to do whatever it took to make sure the events were a success. Which meant I would often do a full day's work at the office then, in the evenings, I'd go and stand outside theatres that were showing plays that I thought would attract a similar target audience, and hand out flyers for my events to the audience as they left. I didn't tell anyone at the charity I was doing this, I just got on and did it, because I genuinely believed that it was my responsibility to make sure the event sold out—by whatever means. Then one evening, I came face-to-face with my boss who was leaving a show, who couldn't quite believe I had come out to do this at 10.30 pm on a Friday night. The following week he obviously told other people at the charity because suddenly I became known to the senior management team and people started to take an interest in me and my work.

The qualities employers look for in an event planner include resourcefulness and accountability. Always take ownership of any project you work on and go the extra mile. People will notice and you'll definitely stand out.

The great thing about those first few events that I organized was that, although they were quite glamorous and high profile, behind the scenes they didn't require a huge amount of technical production. Therefore, it wasn't too daunting for someone who had no experience of organizing events, and I could learn on the job. For the movie premiere, I had to find a cinema, design and print some flyers to promote it, co-ordinate the ticket sales, find a venue for the after party, book cabaret artists to perform, and run the event on the night. As the after-party was held at a nightclub, technical elements like lighting and sound were provided by the venue. For *Chicago*, one of the charity's supporters owned a restaurant close to the theatre, so he agreed to host the after-party and provided free drinks and hors d'oeuvres. Therefore, most of the event planning involved producing invitations, promoting the event, selling tickets and program advertising, and securing prizes to raffle on the night. If anything, I learned more about the importance of event marketing and ticket sales during this time, because I had to make sure that, after organizing the events, they actually made a healthy profit too.

Of course, I'm simplifying things a bit. It was all pretty stressful at the time, especially as there's often no budget for charity events, so you've got to get everything donated. But the point I want to stress is that charity events make a great stepping stone into larger events for someone looking to gain experience. They often involve less technical production and use venues with onsite catering, which makes the planning a little more straightforward— so you can learn on the job without being totally overwhelmed.

From September 1997 until March 1998 I was still only working two days a week for London Lighthouse. Being a charity, the pay was obviously very low—and who can live on two day's work? So I had to take other jobs to pay the bills. At one point, I had three jobs. I would work for the charity two days a week, then at an office admin job for a couple of days a week, and on top of that, I took shifts in a bar at evenings and weekends. Sometimes I would finish work at London Lighthouse around 6pm, cycle across London to a bar and work until 2am, and then be up and at my admin job by 9.30am for a full day's work before starting over again. It was exhausting, but when you're starting out and trying to build up experience, you often have to juggle several jobs so that you can keep paying the bills while you learn. The chances of you finding work experience that also pays enough to live on is pretty low. So you've got to be prepared to do whatever it takes— knowing that it will pay off later. Many people think they can just go straight into a junior event role and get paid; but even junior roles require lots of experience. So, be prepared to juggle several jobs at once. To be honest, if you can't see yourself doing that, then you won't be right for event planning anyway. Events require long, anti-social hours working evenings and weekends, often on top of your usual full day in the office, so you need to be flexible.

The Game-Changer

One of the first ideas I thought of when I started at London Lighthouse took a bit longer to take off, but it actually turned out to be a game-changer. I came up with the idea of asking fashion designers to create an outfit inspired by the AIDS red ribbon. I knew nothing about the fashion world back then, so I just went out, bought a stack of magazines, and drew up a list of well-known designers. I researched their publicists and started firing off letters asking them to get involved. After a while, I hit the phones to follow up. When I called Vivienne Westwood's office, they loved the idea and asked me who else was involved. To which I had to admit no one—yet. They very kindly said that I could use Vivienne Westwood's name and tell other designers that she was on board, to see if I could get other people involved. They said that if I could get some other big names interested, they'd do it. That changed everything. As soon as I had one big name involved, it was easy to get others. I started getting a little crafty and played designers off against each other. I faxed Versace's publicist and told them Armani were doing it (they weren't!) then I'd fax Armani and tell them Versace was doing it. From there it just carried on snowballing. By the end of the project, we had 100 of the top names in fashion designing outfits for us including Armani, Versace, Alexander McQueen, Donna Karan, Dolce & Gabbana, Oscar de la Renta, Moschino, Missoni, Philip Treacy, and Jimmy Choo—to name just a handful.

Over the next eight months the fashion show, which I'd named *Designs for Life* just kept getting bigger and bigger. In addition to all the designers, I also managed to attract some of the top hair teams, such as Nicky Clarke, John Frieda, and Toni & Guy. Then MAC came on board to handle the make-up, David Bailey provided photography, top models such as Sophie Dahl, Jodie Kidd, Sophie Anderton, and Marie Helvin got involved. Next, a jeweler, Hennel of Bond Street, created an exclusive Red Ribbon broach, and Liberty—a prestigious London department store—created a series of window displays using the dresses to help promote the show. Along the way, I also managed to sell title sponsorship of the event to Canon, which gave me a production budget to underwrite all the costs. The event was held in September 1998, attended by celebrities such as George Michael and Kylie Minogue, and received international press and TV coverage. Most importantly, it made lots of money for the charity from ticket sales to the event alone, and we then planned to auction the outfits later to raise even more money.

Starting My Own Event Company

After the success of *Canon Designs for Life*, a supporter of the charity got in touch and told me that he had brought David Furnish (Elton John's partner) as his guest to the event. He wanted to set up a lunch so he could introduce me to David. We met for lunch, where David told me how impressed he'd been with the fashion show and that he'd like me to create a similar high-profile event for Elton's own charity, The Elton John AIDS Foundation. He arranged for me to meet the head of their charity, and at that meeting we discussed some ideas for events. I asked whether he thought Elton and David would ever consider hosting a fundraising event in the grounds of their home, because it occurred to me that a lot of people would pay serious money to say they've been to a party at Elton John's home. He went away to speak to Elton and David about the idea, and we agreed to keep in touch. A few weeks later, he came back to me and said they'd agreed to it, and that was the beginning of their now famous *Annual White Tie & Tiara Ball*. We discussed terms and how I would work for them on a freelance basis to organize the event over the next six months. Once I had an offer letter from Elton's charity, I decided to take the plunge, leave London Lighthouse, and set up my own event production company—which of course, consisted of just one employee, me, working out of my bedroom.

That's how I got to the point of starting my own event company. However, it was far from easy from this point on. I learned the hard way that just because you start an event company, doesn't mean you're necessarily going to have any clients. That old saying, "if you build it, they will come", just isn't true. I had huge gaps in between jobs in the first few years, to the point where I ended up going to work in-house, on lengthy contracts, for the investment bank Credit Suisse, in between my own events. There were times when I'd work at Credit Suisse for six months straight because I just didn't have enough other work on—and that's despite having Elton John as a client and a really high-profile event to my name. The reality is, to get clients; you need to have lots of contacts. I've seen so many businesses launch after doing just one event, only to close within a year or so because they don't have enough work. Coming straight from a charity, with just a couple of years' experience, I just didn't have enough contacts to generate regular work for myself. And, like sending out resumes looking for a job, I found out that you can't just send your company brochure out to people and hope they hire you—because they won't. People want to hire people they know, have worked with before, or come recommended by someone they already know. That's an important lesson I want to share with you through this book, because it's the same whether you are an event company looking for clients or an employee looking for a job; it's all about networking and developing relationships.

The truth is, if I did it over again with the benefit of hindsight, I probably wouldn't have started my own event company straight away—because I had so much more to learn than I thought at the time.

4

So You Want to Become an Event Planner?

Imagine a luxurious private mansion in the Hollywood Hills, which has been hired to host a party for *Vanity Fair* magazine. Valet parking attendants greet A-list celebrities as they step out of their stretch limos onto the red carpet, surrounded by flashing paparazzi photographers. Inside, the venue has been transformed with Great Gatsby-inspired 1920s era decadence. 30ft tall Cristal champagne fountains tower over the pool, zebras and flamingo roam the grounds, molecular gastronomy hors d'oeuvre prepared by Wolfgang Puck are passed around by flapper girls wearing Cartier jewels, while Jay-Z performs an exclusive set above Busby Berkeley-style aquacades with hundreds of bathing-suit clad showgirls forming human waterfalls.

Sound amazing, doesn't it?

Well, that's not event planning. That's the event.

Event planning is all about budgets, contracts, and logistics.

The event planner is the one who spent days picking through clause after clause in a legally binding contract, so that *Vanity Fair* could hire the private mansion in the Hollywood Hills owned by a litigious Russian billionaire.

They're the one who compiled a four-inch thick dossier of risk assessments, method statements, fire certificates, and other health and safety documentation in order to erect the aquacades and human waterfalls.

They're the one who spent many a Friday night in the office at 10pm, crying into an Excel spreadsheet because the client had decided at the last minute that they were now "not quite feeling" the sets that were approved and built two months earlier.

They're the one who missed Jay-Z's set because they were running around backstage ensuring his post-performance private chill-out lounge was decorated in "calming shades of taupe" with a selection of cold cuts, Gatorade and a dozen eucalyptus-scented white Versace towels—washed once—on hand.

They're the ones who spent weeks negotiating permits and insurance documents to allow zebras and flamingo to walk around the event. And they'll probably be the ones who will have to deal with the fall-out when they crap all over the Russian billionaire's hand-woven yak-hair carpet.

If you're thinking of becoming an event planner, it's important that you have a realistic understanding of both the industry, and what the job itself really involves. For a start, most events aren't remotely glamorous. They are business meetings, seminars, conferences, trade shows and conventions, or experiential marketing events designed to promote brands and products—and it's in those sectors where the majority of event-planning jobs are. Even if you do end up working on some of the more exciting and glamorous events—the movie premieres, launch parties, awards shows and red carpet affairs that make up a small niche in the industry—the chances are you probably won't get to experience much of that glamor or excitement yourself; because you won't be there as a guest. As the event planner, you'll be too busy juggling spreadsheets and schedules, rushing around backstage with a radio stuck to your ear putting out fires—although not literally, I hope.

Event planning is still one of the most unique, exhilarating, and rewarding professions you can choose. It can see you travel to overseas locations, work (and sometimes stay) in luxury hotels and private venues, grant you special access to people and places—including celebrities and VIPs—and provide you with some truly unique experiences that most people will never be privileged to. My own career in event planning has allowed me to fly on private planes, ski in luxury resorts, party at the Cannes Film Festival and

The Academy Awards, work with legendary performers such as Mary J. Blige and Elton John, and hit the dancefloor with Madonna, Tom Ford, and Gwyneth Paltrow at Stella McCartney's wedding. Contributors to this book also recall their own privileged moments, such as throwing footballs around the pitch with the Carolina Panthers, visiting the Lego factory in the Czech Republic and meeting their 'master builder', and escorting Nelson Mandela to sit with the Queen of England at a state banquet.

These experiences can create amazing moments in a career, but they make up a very small fraction of the day-to-day job. Similarly, the excitement and adrenaline rush of working onsite—when months of planning is finally brought to life—and the thrill you get from seeing the reaction on guest's faces, also makes up only a fraction of the job. This is why it's essential to differentiate between 'the event' and 'the event planning'—so you know what you're getting into. While the event might involve overseas travel, luxury hotels, champagne, gourmet food, entertainment from world famous headline acts, and maybe even celebrity guests. The event planning will be all about number-crunching budgets, drawing up contracts, negotiating with suppliers, creating schedules and lists, and overseeing logistics. For the most part, it's a desk job. The majority of events take several months to organize; some take six months to a year—or even longer. If the event only lasts for one day, but six months has been spent on the planning, that means more than 99.9 percent of the job consists of office-based administrative work preparing for the big day.

If you're comfortable with that prospect, and are attracted to the idea of being the person responsible for all the meticulous and detailed planning, thorough organization, and military-style logistics that goes on behind the scenes. If you relish problem solving, and the thought of juggling multiple events at once excites you. If you understand that while you might be flying to exotic locations, meeting celebrities, or working on high-profile events, you will be there as staff; to work and serve others. Then a career in event planning may just be right for you.

5

What an Event Planner Really Does—The Idea v the Reality

I'm sure that when my friends think about me organizing high-profile events for celebrities such as Elton John or Stella McCartney, they picture my days spent gluing things onto mood-boards, flicking through swatch books debating between 'cream' and 'ivory' napkins, and thumbing through menus pondering Wagyu beef from hand-massaged Japanese cows, or gold-leaf encrusted lobster dusted with Himalayan pink salt. That after a morning spent at the florists shouting "bigger!" and "bring me more orchids!", the afternoon is spent emailing Mary J Blige or Justin Timberlake's people to check whether they're available to perform, before taking my red pen to the guest list to decide who's made the cut.

Now, while I'll admit that there was the odd trip to a florist to view centerpieces, and a menu tasting at the caterers, the rest of the planning was typically far more mundane and admin-heavy work. If a career in event planning is going to be right for you, it's this type of work you need to be comfortable doing day in day out. Below, I've listed the five key areas that make up the event-planning process, to give you a feel for what the job of an event planner *really* involves.

The Event-Planning Process

1. The Brief and Proposal

The first stage of event planning involves taking a brief from the client. As the event planner, you need to ascertain what their needs and objectives are; what is it they are trying to achieve? What needs to be communicated? What budget do they have? How are they going to measure the success of the event? Will it be through an increase in sales, media activity, or just feedback from the guests? Often a client won't have thought about some of these points, so it's your job to ask the relevant questions to help them articulate their goals—before you can go back to them with a creative solution in the form of a proposal.

The initial proposal you submit will typically consist of information such as the event date, location, venue, format, timings, running order, creative concept/theme and ideas for catering, invitations/marketing materials, decor, entertainment, production, set, staging, and transport—along with a budget and timeline. In order to provide all this information, you may need to:

- Devise the creative concept, strategy, theme, and format of the event—and be able to justify how this will communicate the necessary values, identity, message, tone, and feeling, in order to meet the client's objectives.

- Conduct a feasibility study and investigate whether the event concept is viable, what restrictions there might be, and whether permits, licenses, or special permissions are required.

- Research venues and locations, check suitability and availability, conduct inspections, reserve dates and obtain prices.

- Research travel and accommodation options, including prices and availability.

- Draw floor plans and/or visuals to demonstrate the use of space, flow, and staging.

- Decide on timings and create a program of events/running order explaining what will happen and when.

- Research catering options, obtain sample menus, and written quotes from suppliers

- Liaise with technical suppliers to obtain written quotes for lighting, AV, sound, staging, and any ancillary services such as generators, power, heating/cooling, toilets, waste removal, and parking.

- Develop ideas and obtain written quotes for event marketing materials, invitations, tickets, payment processing, websites, social media campaigns, databases, brochures, mailings, joining instructions, conferences packs/event brochures, handouts, giveaways, signage, and branding.

- Create initial designs, set drawings, visuals, models, and mock-ups for the décor, set, and theming, and obtain written quotes.

- Research ideas, check availability, and obtain written quotes for entertainment, activities, and speakers.

- Calculate requirements and obtain quotes for event staff, crew, transport, security, first aid, and insurance.

- Create a detailed budget, often with a number of different optional 'upgrades' or reduced spec alternatives.

- Develop a project plan and timeline to communicate the schedule of activity during the planning process, along with deadlines and responsibilities.

- Create an illustrated presentation to communicate all the above information, with support material that might include photographs, video, music, floor plans, set designs, stage plans, artist's impression visuals, mock-ups, swatches, samples, and 3D models.

A lot of people are attracted to event planning because of the creative side; choosing venues and locations, designing invitations, creating menus, overseeing decor/theming and choosing entertainment—and often that's because they're thinking about events in terms of parties and celebrations. Sadly, the creative side only accounts for a very small fraction of the job—maybe 10-20 percent, usually at the beginning of a project. As an example, for most of the events I organize, I usually have approximately two weeks to submit a proposal to a client at the beginning of a project. Most of the creative work has to be done in that first two weeks; the remainder of the event planning is taken up with other things.

Some types of events, such as meetings, conferences, and conventions, have a different definition of creative altogether. Less emphasis is put on menu planning, invitation design and room décor. Instead, it's about providing creative solutions in the form of the venue, location, format, staging, and the content of the event program—which might include activities, excursions, speakers, and workshops.

If you are attracted to the creative side of event planning, the really bad news is that some event companies even have their own creative directors and design teams who are responsible for these areas. Alternatively, the creative may be outsourced to designers or specialist theming suppliers. Sometimes it will be a collaborative process, so you might be involved in the creative, but chances are it won't make up a very big part of your workload. You need to be prepared for that, and ensure that you are genuinely interested in the other aspects of event planning that make up the other 80-90 percent of the job, before getting into it.

2. Project Execution, Monitoring, and Control

The execution stage of the process is about actioning all the elements that were researched and presented at the proposal stage. It involves drilling down into the details to develop or revise the initial ideas in light of feedback from the client/host. It's where an event planner's attention to detail, problem solving, organizational, decision-making, and time management skills really come into play. This stage of the planning is about making everything happen; fine-tuning plans, finding solutions to problems, negotiating with suppliers, number-crunching the budget, adhering to deadlines, promoting the event and co-ordinating replies, confirming reservations, booking equipment, staff, and resources, paying supplier deposits, and designing, creating, or sourcing the deliverables—such as the sets and décor, or the event marketing/communications materials. This process usually involves hundreds, if not thousands, of calls and emails flying back and forth between yourself and suppliers as you ask questions, make decisions, chase information, and confirm arrangements in order to move the process forward.

During this stage, the planner acts as a go-between for the client and the suppliers as they monitor, control and report on the progress. Some clients will expect daily updates or weekly status meetings, and so a lot of your time is spent re-formatting and presenting information from suppliers in the form of reports, schedules, lists, drawings, plans, itineraries, and presentations.

Some clients need their hand held throughout the entire process; which means you spend a lot of your time walking them through everything, reassuring them and explaining every detail— when actually you'd really much rather just get on and do it. Other clients will make crazy demands, expect you to perform miracles with no budget, or turn things around in unrealistic time frames. Fortunately, there are some nice clients who you'll genuinely enjoy dealing with too—some of mine have even become friends. But many of them, it's got to be said, are 'challenging'. Managing clients can take up a lot of your time, and will often be a test of your patience, diplomacy, and people skills.

3. Budgets and Contracts

Budget management makes up a large part of the event-planning process. You'll need to be a whizz with Excel, because you're going to spend countless hours slaving over a spreadsheet; creating formulas, inputting data in a methodical order, adding, subtracting, sorting it, and breaking it down line by line. Quotes will come in from 10, 20, maybe 30 different suppliers, all in different formats, and you'll have to go through these picking out the items you do and don't want and transferring them into a master budget. Accuracy and attention to detail is important, as it's so easy to miss something out, enter amounts incorrectly, or make errors with formulas—only to discover later that you submitted a budget to the client that only accounted for two-thirds of the actual costs that you owe your suppliers.

You'll also spend days and days trying to balance the budget, because you'll never have enough money to do everything your client wants. This means a lot of number crunching and going back and forth to each supplier, one by one, negotiating them down on price, asking them to re-quote with different specifications, or looking for alternative options. Then, once you've finally balanced the budget, the client will usually change their minds about everything they asked for, and so you'll start the process over again. This pattern will continue several more times over the course of planning the event—in fact probably right up until you confirm final orders with suppliers a few weeks before. Typically, the budget you first start with at the proposal stage, bears very little resemblance to the budget you finish with post-event.

Then there are the contracts to be negotiated. Before you confirm orders you have to really pull apart the contract and make sure you understand exactly what you're committing to; what's included and what isn't, what you're liable for, what happens if the event gets cancelled, or the client decides they don't like something, and what the payment terms are. You might be dealing with 20 to 30 different suppliers, each with different clauses or terms and conditions of supply, so you need to be absolutely sure what you are agreeing to with each one.

You then have to confirm all the orders with your suppliers by raising purchase orders for each one, and ensuring their deposit invoices are paid before they show up at the event (which typically involves chasing your accounts department to process a rush payment).

Even after the event, there's yet more budget work to do. You have to reconcile the final budget post-event to include all the little extra costs that were incurred onsite, or to finalize costs that were estimated then based on consumption, such as drinks, power, and fuel.

Without doubt, budget management and contracts are some of the most stressful and—for me—least appealing parts of event planning. However, they also make up a very large part of the job, so you need to be meticulous when it comes to managing them.

4. Operations and Logistics

Probably one of the most important parts of the job is operations and logistics; managing exactly when something is going to happen, exactly how something is going to happen, and exactly who is responsible for making it happen. This usually involves a lot of admin, such as creating production schedules, itineraries, delivery/collection times, briefing documents, running orders, floor plans and layouts, seating plans, contact lists, information sheets, and safety briefing documents. Everything must be discussed, planned, mapped out, agreed, and communicated to all parties involved. This might involve:

- Booking and confirming flights for guests, production crew, onsite event planners, artists, speakers, and performers—then informing all parties of the necessary arrangements.

- Drawing up a list of all flight arrivals/departures and ensuring someone is there to meet each person.

- Arranging airport transfers for each guest, who often arrive on different flights, at different times, on different days, at different terminals, or even different airports.

- Reserving and confirming hotel rooms for guests and staff, including any ground transfers necessary to take them from hotel to event venue and back each day if necessary, and rooming lists to detail who is in each room.

- Creating a table plan for the room and a seating plan for each table (which always involves last minute changes), an A-Z list of each guests' name so they can locate their table, and a list of dietary requirements which must correspond with the seating plan so waiting staff can identify the location of special meals.

- Writing joining instructions/invitations, distributing these, and managing a registration database to facilitate arrivals.

- Drawing up a production schedule to show each supplier's role during the set-up, event and de-rig stages.

- Planning a delivery schedule for suppliers to load in, including making arrangements for unloading, parking, and storage.

- Arranging air freight/trucking to send equipment to and from the destination city.

- Creating a running order for guests, speakers, and performers
- Creating a technical schedule for AV, lighting and sound cues.
- Creating briefing documents for staff, speakers, and performers.
- Creating information packs for guests with essential information for the event, contact numbers, local amenities, and dropping these in each hotel room prior to arrival.
- Creating a contact list of all staff and supplier's telephone numbers while onsite.
- Creating health and safety documentation with risk assessments, method statements, accident/emergency procedures, and insurance paperwork.

This list is not exhaustive, because every event is different, but as you can see, a lot of your time will be spent on admin, creating lists, and devising schedules. You need to be very thorough at planning because even slight mistakes can have drastic consequences.

5. Post-Event Evaluation

Even after the event, there's still a great deal of admin necessary to close the event. This might include following up with guests, team de-briefs, client de-briefs, budget reconciliation, processing final payments, dealing with any contractual disputes or non-fulfilment, receiving and unpacking any return-shipped equipment, and finally, collecting data, measuring results and compiling reports to demonstrate return on investment to the client.

The five categories above: The Brief and Proposal, Project Execution, Budget and Contracts, Operations and Logistics, and Post-Event Evaluation make up the majority of office-based work conducted by an event planner on a day-to-day basis in the months leading up to an event. Of course, the exciting part of being an event planner is working on the event itself. This is when you get to see all the months of meticulous planning, thorough organization, and military-style logistics that have gone on behind the scenes, finally come together in an exhilarating live event. This pay-off is the reason most event planners love the job they do.

Onsite Event Co-ordination

Being onsite at an event can be quite exciting, but it's often far from glamorous and incredibly hard work. It may well be a very glamorous or high profile event, but you probably won't have time to appreciate that. For a start, the working conditions onsite for staff can sometimes be pretty poor. Most of the time I'm lucky if I even get to eat during the event—and even then, it's usually a basic crew meal (not the same food that the guests eat!) wolfed down while standing up or, at best, leaning against a flight case backstage.

I used to organize an annual event for The British Red Cross, which was held in a tent in winter. As it was an enormous tent, it would have cost a fortune in generator fuel to heat it continuously for the three-day set-up period prior to the event—plus with suppliers loading in, doors were always open, so there would be no way to keep the heat in anyway. For three days, we had to set-up in the freezing cold wearing gloves, scarves, hats, and huge coats—indoors. It was literally like working outdoors in winter, doing 15-hour days. Not something you might associate with luxurious special events.

The hours are also incredibly long; you often have to arrive onsite very early in the morning, say 6am, in order to maximize a whole day of set-up time before the guests arrive. You then work through the day, into the evening, and then once the guests have gone home you have to clear up—which can often continue right through the night. Until you experience it, it's pretty hard to describe the deflated feeling you get at the end of an event when you're exhausted, your feet are swollen because you haven't sat down for 15 hours, and everyone else has gone home; the guests, the clients, the suppliers, sometimes even the rest of your team. Yet you're the one who has to stick around packing up boxes, extinguishing candles, or carrying heavy crates of leftover champagne to a safe storage area because the caterers forgot to. You might leave at 3am if you're lucky, only to be back onsite at 7am to finish the de-rig and load all the equipment out. This is something that people often forget about event planning. Not only are there late nights, but these are usually followed by early starts, as you have to clear up and load out of the venue so that it's ready for the next event.

There's also a customer-service element to the job when working onsite and the guests can be a real pain sometimes— especially after a few drinks. You've really got to be able to think on your feet, and be able to deal with almost any situation in a calm and diplomatic manner without panicking. I've had to deal with investments bankers getting into fistfights after too many drinks, a wealthy woman demanding that the £3,000 dress on loan from a designer be paid for because a waiter had stepped on the train, and a guest insisting a cloakroom attendant had lost £30,000 worth of jewelry that she'd supposedly checked-in inside her bag. I've had to handle drunk guests having sex in bushes in full view of everyone else, guests trying to steal raffle prizes from a table at a charity event, guests trying to walk out with fixtures and fitting, and guests demanding three extra gift bags "for their kids" at a charity fundraiser. Not to mention a man who had a heart attack, an elderly woman who evacuated her bowels while wearing a very expensive ball gown, and a well-known fashion designer with an explosive temper only informing me that she was on a low-sodium diet after being presented with her main course of salt-baked sea bass.

The truth is there are usually so many things to deal with onsite at events, that an event planner spends most of their time running from one situation to another, so they often miss most of the event as seen from the audience's perspective. Instead of gawping at celebrities or watching headline acts, the event planner is busy trying to find out why the air conditioning has stopped working, why the guest speaker has disappeared two minutes before he's due on stage, and why the transport to take the VIP guests home hasn't turned up. That's the reality of onsite event co-ordination.

Onsite Roles

Below are some of the roles that make up onsite event co-ordination during the set-up, the event itself, and the de-rig (based on a meeting, conference or incentive travel program). As the lead event planner, you will usually allocate different members of your team (or freelance event managers) to supervise one or more areas of the event. Earlier on in your career, before you become the lead planner, your experience of working onsite is likely to consist of being delegated one of these areas to manage.

- **Airport Transfers:** Meeting each guest at the airport and arranging transport to their hotel, or directly to the event itself. As guests arrive on multiple flights, at different times throughout the day and night, sometimes into different terminals, this can involve being stationed at the airport from early morning till late at night over one or more days.

- **Hotel Check-In:** Meeting guests at their hotel and overseeing check-in. Like airport duty, this can involve waiting at a check-in desk all day to process staggered arrivals. Managing check-ins might also involve organizing a 'room drop' in advance, so that each guest receives a welcome pack, itinerary, or gift in their room when they arrive. Overseeing 1,000 room drops, in a tight window between when the room has been serviced and when the guest checks in, can itself be a logistical nightmare.

- **Transport:** Co-ordinating transport to and from various different hotels to the event venue and off-site activities. This might start at 7am, with coaches laid on to get guests from their respective hotels to the event venue, and continue right through the day until the early hours of the following morning, when you have to wait around for the last guests to leave after dinner before you can put them on a coach back to their hotel.

- **Food & Beverage:** Supervising the set up and delivery of all food and beverage during the event. Again, this can start with breakfast set-up at 6am and go right through until the end of the evening dinner. It may also involve overseeing off-site catering at various restaurants and venues.

- **Registration/Break Outs:** Registering each guest on arrival at the event, issuing badges, or managing the various break-out rooms surrounding the main conference that are used for smaller meetings, talks, and one-on-one sessions. Checking in 3,000 delegates requires a lot of smiling!

- **Speakers:** Managing the arrival and departure of guest speakers and the delivery of their presentations. You may have a speaker whose flight gets delayed, meaning you have to contact all the other speakers to change the running order at the last minute. That, or they'll want to "just add a few slides to the presentation" five minutes before they're due to speak. Or swap their lapel microphone for a lectern microphone. Or have a laptop on stage to use PowerPoint's 'presenter view.' The list goes on…

- **Conference Set-Up:** Supervising the main room set-up, including the room layout, seating, staging, AV requirements, and the distribution of any conference folders and handouts.

- **Activities & Excursions:** Supervising on-and off-site activities and excursions—anything from golf and spa days to beach bonfire parties and swimming with dolphins. This might include arranging tickets/passes, transport, catering, or equipment hire. Sometimes you get to take part too!

One of the great things about working in events, especially corporates events and meetings, is that there's often a lot of travel involved—which is definitely one of the perks of the job. Flying to foreign countries at the client's expense and staying in luxury hotels for a week. Not only do you get to work on an exciting event but you also get to travel and see different cities—with all your flights, accommodation, and meals paid for. Well, sometimes the reality is a little different unfortunately.

When I worked in the corporate events department of the investment bank Credit Suisse we'd often travel to amazing places such as Barcelona, Spain, in the summer and luxury ski resorts such as G'Staad and St Moritz, Switzerland, in the winter months. Which sounds glamorous. However, the truth is you work your butt off when you're there, often putting in 15-hour days. Sometimes there's no free time to get out and see the city, and on the rare occasion there is, you're usually so exhausted and sleep-deprived that you'd rather just order room service, take a hot bath, and then fall into bed for a good night's sleep. Most of the time you're holed up in a windowless hotel ballroom, so you really could be anywhere in the world. You go from airport to venue back to airport. Sometimes you don't even get to stay in the same 5 Star luxurious hotels as the guests—you're packed off to a cheaper 2-star hotel for all the staff. I've even known of event staff being flown from London to Buenos Aires (average flight time 14 hours) in coach, then because they've landed during the day local time, they've been expected to go straight to work and help set up at the venue.

The other thing to remember is that each of the onsite roles outlined above comes with their own set of drawbacks. At one event in Barcelona, my role was to supervise the guest's airport arrivals and ensure they transferred safely to the hotel. For two days, while it was glorious sunshine outside and all my colleagues were telling me that Madonna was staying in our hotel, I was stationed at an arrivals desk inside the airport (airside so I couldn't even go in and out without passing through security) from 6.30am to 10pm waiting for planes to arrive. I'd have to patiently smile at hundreds of demanding investment bankers who'd talk down to me as I tried to co-ordinate a continuous rotation of mini buses and taxis (the drivers of which only spoke Spanish) to pull up outside the airport—where they couldn't park—to shuttle them to their hotels. Not only was it mind-numbingly boring hanging around for hours in between flights, the only company I had was a team of support staff from a local DMC (Destination Management Company) who spent the entire time speaking to each other in Catalan so that I couldn't understand what they were saying. It was a very long three days.

At another event in G'Staad, I was allocated food & beverage duties, which means getting up at 5am to supervise breakfast. Then of course, you're the last one to leave at the end of the day following the evening dinner. And when I say the end of the day, it's actually the early hours of the following morning—because when executives are away at a conference, on the company dime, and there's an evening dinner involved, they're in no hurry to go to bed. They just keep ordering more wine, then cognacs, then coffee, then cigars. Which, as the event planner, you stand around and watch them do, before making sure they get the right transport back to their hotel. Then you finally get back to your room around 2am, if you're lucky, and set your alarm for 5am to start all over again. I remember getting to bed at 1am one night, really excited that I was going to get a full four hours sleep, only to be woken by one of the guests—an investment banker, naturally—insisting that I call an emergency doctor to come out in the middle of the night. Which of course I arranged, fearing it might be serious, only to later find out the guest was diagnosed with indigestion, brought on by the copious amounts of cheese fondue he'd consumed at dinner. I think I maybe got an hour's sleep that night.

Fortunately, it's not always like that. If you're onsite for a day or two before the guests arrive, then there's often time to grab an evening meal out in a local restaurant with the rest of the team— or there might be a team night out on the final evening once all the guests have gone. I've even worked on conferences in Ski resorts where we've packed the guests off home after breakfast and spent the rest of the day on the slopes!

It's Not All Doom and Gloom

Although event planning is not always as glamorous as it might seem from the outside, it's still undoubtedly a very unique, exciting, and rewarding career—and you can have a lot of fun on the job. Despite the endless Excel spreadsheets, boring health and safety paperwork, and 15-hour days hanging around at airports, event planning is an amazing job unlike most others. The chances are you will end up travelling to exciting locations, staying in fancy hotels, working with incredibly talented people, meeting celebrities, sampling fine food and wine, getting VIP access to places, being the first to adopt new trends and technologies, and generally being given unique opportunities that most people just never get to experience—as part of your job!

What Other Event Planners Say

Check out this book's companion website at www.becomeaneventplanner.org to hear other event professionals describe some the most unique, fun, and rewarding experiences that they've had from their career in event planning. These range from the superficial; chartering luxury yachts, visiting private rooms at Windsor Castle [an official residence of The Queen of England], meeting Presidents and working with the Secret Service, to the profound; creating unforgettable experiences for clients/guests, and forming deep friendships by working onsite as part of team. Not to mention the ultimate reward that every planner gets; the adrenaline rush of working in a live environment, the thrill of seeing your work come to life, and the reaction on guests' faces.

45

My Route into the Industry

Starting in Hotel Conference and Banqueting

From casual banqueting staff, to co-founding an award-winning special events agency

Nathan Homan, former Assistant Banqueting Manager, The Dorchester, and Co-founder, Rouge Events

Nathan is a great example of someone who used hotel banqueting as a route into the events industry. Starting at the most junior level, as a casual bar assistant, Nathan worked his way up to Silver-service Banqueting Waiter, then Operations Manager and finally to Assistant Banqueting Manager, before using all that experience to co-found his own special events agency with two of his banqueting colleagues.

While at university studying Middle Eastern History & Politics, Nathan worked during the evenings in a bar. Chatting to a customer, who, it transpired, worked as the banqueting dispense bar manager at The Dorchester hotel, he was invited to interview for a job.

"He said 'how much are you earning here?' and I said '£3.25 ($5) per hour.' He said 'how would you like to earn £6.50 ($10) per hour? Come and have an interview with me at The Dorchester.' I didn't exactly have to think about it for very long."

Hired as a member of the banqueting dispense bar team, he essentially worked as a barman in the various function rooms of the hotel. For each event, Nathan would be responsible for setting up a temporary bar and ensuring the drinks service ran smoothly, before taking down the bar at the end of each night in order to leave the function room empty.

"Very rapidly, within the first three months, I fell in love with the kind of events I was exposed to working in that environment. For

someone at university to be suddenly serving celebrities at one of London's 5 Star hotels and being at all the glamorous events you read about in magazines, was just incredible. I remember phoning my mum from the banqueting kitchens one day and saying "I can't believe it; I've just served Princess Diana!"

During day shifts, Nathan typically found himself working on corporate meetings and conferences. In the evenings, it would be charity balls, fashion shows, corporate dinners, and weddings, so he was able to experience a wide range of different events. For an evening event, he would typically start around 2pm; polishing glasses, setting up the bar and laying out trays ready for the wine waiters to collect for a drinks reception. He'd then work through the event and pack up everything at the end. Over the Christmas period, he would often find himself working 60–70 hours a week.

"Working as casual staff, if you turn down too many shifts then they just don't bother to book you in future. It does actually require quite a bit of self-promotion. There are cycles in banqueting, for example, it's busy in the autumn (fall), but it's dead in August, so I made a point of being proactive and looking at other areas of the hotel that I could work in during quiet periods. I did everything from room service to switchboard. At first, I really just used it as an opportunity to earn money while I was at university, but by halfway through my degree I was so hooked on working in hotels that I had already started my campaign to get a full-time post-graduate job at The Dorchester. It took about a year of knocking on the banqueting manager's door saying 'I really want to do this, please can I have a full-time job?' and they kept brushing me off or telling me to go away. Then, after a year of pestering the banqueting manager, I think she finally realized I was serious and gave me an opportunity to make the transition from casual to permanent staff."

By working as casual staff at The Dorchester for several years, it was easier for Nathan to land a permanent position because he was known to all the staff and management. Although he'd been working as a barman under the banqueting dispense bar manager, he made a point of learning silver service so that he could apply for shifts under the banqueting headwaiter, with the intention of getting his face known by the banqueting manager.

"I was quite strategic really. I knew I wasn't going to get a job as a banqueting manager without doing lots of other little steps in between, so I just made sure I got to know all the different managers and built relationships with them by working in all different parts of the banqueting team."

When trying to break into the events industry, it's important to accept that you need to start at the bottom and work your way up. It's very unlikely that you'll go straight into event planning, or even assisting an event planner, without first having to get some on-the-ground experience. Nathan recognized that, put time into learning skills in the lower ranks, and was strategic about developing relationships so that management could see that he was progressing upwards. You've simply got to put the groundwork in.

Before long, Nathan began working as Head Waiter in banqueting, running events in the ballroom, which helped him develop his people and time-management skills; regularly briefing and motivating 50-plus staff and ensuring each event ran to a tight schedule. He then applied for an assistant banqueting manager position, but they told him they didn't think he was ready yet and that perhaps he needed a few more years' experience. He then left The Dorchester to take up the position of Banqueting Operations Manager at the Four Seasons.

"I spent six months at the Four Seasons, but it just wasn't right for me. The culture was so different there. Whereas The Dorchester was all about being individual, eccentric and personality driven, the Four Seasons had a very 'corporate handbook' approach that dictated how service should be. So I called up my old boss at The Dorchester and told them I wanted to come back. Ironically, those

six months at The Four Seasons, although really tough for me, actually proved invaluable because when I came back to interview at The Dorchester, I was able to share that experience with them. I think they believed that had toughened me up and that I was now ready to go back as an assistant manager."

Back at The Dorchester as Assistant Banqueting Manager, Nathan's role was now focused more on event planning; meeting the clients, showing them around the venue, and all the organizing and administration for each event. In fact, because he was so passionate about events he frequently got more involved than his manager would have liked. A banqueting manager's role is ultimately about facilitating the client's hire of the venue, which generally involves overseeing the food and beverage and the use of the space. However, hotels often up-sell by offering to provide additional items, such as flowers, production equipment and entertainment, which they can make a profit on by sub-contracting out to third parties suppliers.

"Most hotels just want you to keep it simple; sell the client some flowers and a DJ, nothing too time consuming. Whereas, I would always be trying to talk clients into doing more with production and decorations, or making suggestions for the layout and design of the event. I was always getting told off because obviously I wasn't getting paid to get involved in all of that, but I just loved it and always wanted the events to be bigger and better."

An advantage of working your way up through hotel banqueting is that you have the opportunity to get both practical on-the-ground service experience, and also office-based event-planning experience if you progress to a banqueting manager role.

After three years, Nathan realized that it was going to be a slow career progression working his way further up at The Dorchester and, being more ambitious, started to think about moving on. Although he recognized that he still had more to learn about events, his partner encouraged him start up his own business organizing events.

"I loved what I was doing, and I was still only 24, but I started to look at the value of the accounts I was looking after—which brought in about £1.5 million ($2.4 million)—and then I looked at my salary of £22,000 ($36,000) and I just thought, 'this doesn't quite add up. Why should I be responsible for generating so much income for them and still get paid so little?' As a banqueting manager, you meet lots of event production companies; sometimes they are your actual client if they've booked the venue on behalf of the person hosting the event. I observed so many production companies and watched how they'd interact with their clients and I just thought, 'I really could do this better than you.' The training we'd been given at the hotel was so service-oriented; there was a right way and there was a wrong way to do things. Professionalism and the service culture was so important. So I thought, 'if nothing else, I could do a better job than them simply by being more professional.' Forget the creativity or the technical side of things; I can improve on what you're doing just by providing a better service, doing things on time, and delivering what we say we'll deliver. So many of the production companies I dealt with just weren't that good. My partner really encouraged me and just said 'learn the rest on the job, don't wait for that mythical point where you feel like you've acquired enough experience, just get on with it and get the experience as you go along.' So, with two other business partners we set up Rouge Events. I had a good foundation working at The Dorchester, so sometimes you just have to take the step and go for it."

6

Understanding the Purpose of Events

Most people considering a career in the events industry are typically looking at it from the outside. Therefore, they focus on the end result; they see an event from the audience's perspective and appreciate the creative elements, the content, the venue or location, and the entertainment. However, if you're going to work in the industry, you need to understand it from the inside.

Ask yourself:

- Why does a brand such as Louis Vuitton throw a party?

- Why does an investment bank such as Goldman Sachs hold a conference?

- Why does a car manufacturer such as Ford run an incentive travel program?

- Why does a brand such as Dove skincare produce experiential roadshows?

The simple answer is that events are now recognized as an extremely effective marketing and communications channel—to the point where they are rapidly replacing traditional forms of advertising and marketing.

An event gives companies and organizations a way to offer their clients, customers, employees, and supporters an experience; a two-way channel of communication where they can see, hear, touch, taste, feel, learn, discuss, interact, sample, connect, and share. With the application of social media, events now have a far broader reach than just the people who attend on the day; they often exist online, in the form of video, photos, tweets and likes, long after the physical event has ended. Those factors combined make events one of most effective ways to communicate with an audience.[1]

Ultimately, the purpose of every event, whether business or social, is rooted in marketing and communications; to sell, promote, reward, solicit, educate or celebrate. As such, they all have clearly defined objectives and goals. Any company or organization staging an event will have asked themselves, 'What do we want to achieve?', 'What do we want to communicate?' and 'How are we going to use an event to realize those goals?'

As companies and organizations are now using events far more strategically—in order to achieve specific business goals—they are generally spending more of their marketing and communications budget in this area. As such, greater attention is now paid to measuring results and using those results to demonstrate a return on investment (ROI), i.e. what did the event achieve and was it a worthwhile way to spend the budget?

Nowadays, event planners are much more involved in the strategic side of the business. The role no longer just involves planning and executing; employers and clients also expect you to understand the 'why?' What is the purpose of the event? What needs to be communicated? How is that going to be communicated through the creative, format, staging, tone, style, and content of the event? How are the results going to be measured, and how can we then use those results to demonstrate that the money spent has been worthwhile? It's your job as an event planner to understand all of this, and to design and plan events that fulfil these requirements.

Therefore, if Louis Vuitton is throwing a party, the purpose

---

[1] Shaz Smilansky, Experiential Marketing: A Practical Guide to Interactive Brand Experiences [Kogan Page 2009]

might be to announce a new retail location or showcase a product line. The primary objectives might be to reward and entertain existing clients or attract new ones, while generating media coverage and word of mouth 'buzz', and develop relationships with journalists, bloggers, brand ambassadors, and key opinion formers. A secondary objective may be to make some sales at the event. Another might be to reinforce the brand values of luxury, heritage, quality, and craftsmanship. The success of the event will likely be measured by the quality and quantity of media coverage, the caliber of guests who attend, feedback from those guests, and any uptake in sales.

All of these factors will be influenced by the choices made during the event-planning stages. If the party was held on the wrong date and had to compete with several other fashion parties, or the invitation wasn't sufficiently original or attention grabbing, the party might not have attracted the right amount or type of people, which might in turn have an adverse effect on the media coverage. If the food, drink, and entertainment were of a poor standard, it might have resulted in negative comments shared on social media, or if the décor looked cheap and tacky it would have contradicted the values they were hoping to promote—both of which would damage the reputation of the brand. Or if the party was overcrowded and people couldn't experience the products, it might have a negative effect on sales.

Therefore, the event planner would have to ask themselves at the beginning of the process *'What can I do to ensure the event I'm creating will attract the right caliber of people, generate both traditional and social media coverage, demonstrate the product, encourage sales, and communicate the necessary brand values?'*

Similarly, if an investment bank such as Goldman Sachs is holding a conference, the purpose might be to communicate its knowledge and expertise in a particular sector, in an attempt to market themselves to potential clients. Success is likely to be measured by the turnout and caliber of attendees, how they responded to the experience, and what business relationships could be developed at—and following—the event. That means how the event is marketed, the quality of the communications materials and the content of the conference—such as the caliber of the speakers or the program of supporting events and activities—are going to be of upmost importance.

So you can see how the success of an event is very much dependent on the decisions made by the event planner. Every decision you make has to contribute to achieving the business objectives. A client will be looking for you to demonstrate an awareness of all these issues, be able to justify the choices you make, and explain how they relate to the original goals and objectives of the event. You can't just book a headline act to perform at a brand event because they're cool and you like them, you have to consider whether they are a good fit with the brand's image and values, and whether they appeal to the same demographic as their customer base. Similarly, if you're planning an evening dinner after a conference for a group of affluent investment bankers in their 40s and 50s, you've got to choose a restaurant/venue, catering, and entertainment that is going to be in keeping with their tastes and interests. None of the content that goes into an event happens by chance; it all has to serve a purpose and communicate the right message, to the right audience, in order to achieve the desired results.

That's why, if you're just starting out in the industry and you tell potential employers that you're passionate about events because you love the creative aspects, they are likely to just roll their eyes and assume you have no understanding of the business of events. When you meet potential employers, onsite or in an interview setting, you need to set yourself apart from the wannabes and amateurs by showing that you understand the events industry from the inside; not just the how, but the why? What the objectives are, how the creative solutions meet those objectives, how results are measured, and how to demonstrate a return on investment. Demonstrate that you understand that it's not all about creativity and throwing parties—and even when it might seem like it is just a party; there is always an underlying objective. Demonstrate commercial awareness.

7

The Different Sectors of the Events Industry

Most people tend to think of the event industry as divided into two main camps, corporate events, and special events. Under the umbrella of corporate events would be meetings, conferences, trade shows/conventions/exhibitions/fairs/festivals, incentive travel, hospitality, and employee events. Whereas, special events would include public events, parties and celebrations, consumer shows/conventions/exhibitions/fairs/festivals, sporting events, fundraisers, charity, political and educational events. Nowadays, brand marketing and experiential events tend to straddle both categories of corporate events and special events. Traditionally, these were defined as corporate events, given that most brands are owned by corporations and the purpose of these events is rooted in advertising, sales, marketing, and publicity. However, as brand-marketing events have evolved to become more consumer-oriented and social in nature—focusing on providing a customer experience associated with the brand—they often stray into the territory of special events.

Whichever sector of the industry you choose to work in will ultimately come down to your strengths, interests and personality. If you're quite a casual, laid back, or spontaneous person, you probably aren't going to enjoy working in a rigid corporate environment where you have to dress, speak, and behave in a professional and formal manner. Alternatively, if you're not someone who likes the pressure of having to come up with creative ideas, original concepts and 'the next big thing', but are a whizz at organizing, planning and logistics, then corporate events might suit you better than brand marketing and experiential. If your idea of creative involves choosing food, décor and entertainment, then special events is probably going to be a good fit for you. Whereas if you're drawn to the type of creative that involves holding flash-mobs in Time Square one week, followed by creating a pop-up skate-board park in a disused car park the next, then experiential will probably be your thing. You may want to travel and have the type of home-life that enables you to take off for weeks at a time, in which case incentive travel might suit. Event planning offers many options.

You might think at this stage in your career that you already know exactly which sector you want to work in. However, they all have pros and cons attached. You may discover once you start working in your chosen sector that, although you're passionate about the work, the pay is not as high as you'd hoped, the environment is too formal, or that job opportunities are scarce. Alternatively, you might start in a sector that involves a lot of travel, then your personal circumstances change, and you don't want to be away from home as much.

Whether you think you already know which sector you want to work in, or whether you are looking to explore different options, it's important to have an overview of the industry as a whole. This will not only aid your own career choices and development, but will also to demonstrate to potential employers that you understand the entire landscape, where you sit within that, and why you're a good fit for their particular sector. If you haven't done so already, before proceeding, be sure to read the section about understanding the events industry on this book's companion website www.becomeaneventplanner.org. There, each of the main sectors is examined in detail, explaining for each:

- What type of events are involved
- Who organizes these type of events
- The benefits of working in that sector
- What it takes to be an event planner in that sector

First-hand accounts by professionals also offer insights into what the job really involves on a day-to-day basis. These include:

Meetings and Corporate Events
By Sharyn Scott, Global Head of Events, Linklaters

Conferences and Conventions/Exhibitions
Conventions by Grace Nacchia, Event Director, George P.Johnson

Conferences by Bill Jones, VP Managing Director Events, The Channel Company (formerly UBM Tech Channel)

Incentive Travel and Destination Management
Incentive Travel by Martin Turner, former Director of Travel, International Travel Group

Destination Management by Jennifer Miller, Partner & President, ACCESS Destination Services

Experiential and Brand Communications
In house by Charlotte Saynor, former VP Brands & Events, FremantleMedia Enterprises and former European Head of Events, Apple;

Agency by Marie Davidheiser, Senior VP, Director of Operations, Jack Morton Worldwide

Special Events (Public, Sporting, Festivals, Parties, Celebrations)
By Chad Hudson, President, Chad Hudson Events

Charity and Non-Profit Events
By Farida Haqiqi, former Events Manager, The British Red Cross

Catering
By Charlotte Wolseley Brinton, former Head of Events, Rhubarb Food Design

Venue Management and Hotel Conference & Banqueting
By Nathan Homan, former Assistant Banqueting Manager, The Dorchester and Four Seasons Hotels

My Route into the Industry

Starting as an Intern in Publicity

From an unpaid internship in publicity, to producing
The X Factor USA launch

**Charlotte Saynor, former Vice President, Brands & Events,
FremantleMedia Enterprises,
and former European Head of Events, Apple**

Charlotte got into event planning via various jobs in marketing and publicity. Event planning and public relations (PR) are so closely aligned that, if you work in PR, you're almost certainly going to spend some of that time organizing press launches and other hospitality events. Therefore, starting out in PR can be a great way to side step into event planning, which is exactly what Charlotte did. She is a great example of someone who started with no professional experience, but by taking on unpaid work experience, was able to work her way up and carve out an extremely successful career.

After studying History at university, Charlotte graduated at the height of the recession in 1993 when competition for jobs was fierce. Having gone through rounds of interviews, always coming down to the final stages, she was finding it impossible to find a paid position and so made the decision to just take any opportunity to get experience. She visited every public relations agency in Edinburgh, Scotland, (where she was living with her parents to save money) and dropped off her resume with a covering letter offering her services for free. A few days later, she received a call from a woman who owned a small agency consisting of just three people, who invited her in for a chat.

"That woman gave me an opportunity and I actually ended up sharing an office with her—which was just the best break you could ever get—and because it was a small set-up I learned so

61

much. Not only was I getting publicity experience, I was also learning about running a business by observing her; all the stresses and strains, the highs and lows. I also learned about pitching and the way to talk to clients; she didn't really have to teach me, I could've just watched what she was doing and learned like that. But you know back in those days, pre-Internet, you still had to fax hundreds of press releases out to publicize something, so the majority of my days were spent feeding paper into a fax machine and hitting the send button over and over again! The work wasn't glamorous but I learned a lot while I was there and, because it was a small agency, a lot of clients would drop in during the day too and I got to deal with them—which is unusual for a work experience person to have that type of access."

If you have little or no experience, offering to work for free—and being prepared to do anything that you are asked to do, with a smile—is just a necessary part of the process. Don't be too proud about it. If you use the opportunity correctly, you'll get your foot in the door and build up experience far more quickly. It's not always easy to balance this with financial commitments; I realize not everyone can live at home with their parents to save money. So it might mean couch surfing with friends for several months; staying for a couple of weeks with each one before moving on to the next. Alternatively, you might need to hold down an evening job in a bar or restaurant while doing unpaid work experience during the day. It will be hard work, and you will be exhausted, but it will only be for a short period. If you want it bad enough, you'll always be able to find a way to make it work.

"After three weeks of being there she started paying me, and not only did she start paying me but she paid me retrospectively for the first three weeks. Then I started to take on more and more responsibilities and eventually started going to client meetings on my own, commissioning journalists to write articles, and organizing photo-shoots—which was all really great experience."

Although the agency predominantly worked on publicity for professional services, such as lawyers and accountants, because it was a small agency it also did other things such as producing the consumer magazine for ScotRail (Scotland's national rail service), which Charlotte found herself virtually editing within her first month of starting there. She also got her first taste of event planning when the agency handled the launch of a new shopping mall. *"It wasn't exactly a glamorous event, I think we had the Chippendales and Mr. Blobby [a kid's cartoon-like character] perform at the opening! But public relations is a great way to get into events because you often end up working on press launches."*

One of the advantages of working for a small business is that you'll have more opportunities to get involved in different things far more quickly than you might at a larger company. ·

Charlotte stayed with the agency for about a year before moving to London where, thanks to the experienced she'd gained and a glowing reference, she was able to apply for a job as an account executive with a large PR firm. *"I was thrown right in at the deep end!"* Over the next two-to-three years she worked her way up to become an account manager for food and drink clients, which included organizing drinks-tasting events for Champagne brands, dinners with world renowned Michelin starred chefs, and numerous press launches. By organizing press launches, she started to gain valuable event-planning experience managing suppliers, coming up with creative executions, and building those ideas into an overall proposal for the client. Crucially, she began to understand the value of events and how they fitted into an overall marketing and publicity campaign.

"Working for large corporations such as Mars and Seagram, they'd often have multiple agencies working on the same campaign to handle different aspects, such as branding, design, marketing, advertising, and events, so you'd often go to huge

planning meetings and present your part to ensure that it integrated into what everyone else was doing. Working there first made me really think about return on investment—which is important in events nowadays—because as an agency we had to justify the events to our clients and demonstrate how they'd achieved certain goals, to justify the expenditure."

When she left that job Charlotte went travelling, but because she had gained such great experience working for large brands, she was able to get a job for three months at a PR agency in Sydney, Australia, while she was travelling. Interestingly, she went about applying for this job in a creative way.

"I wrote a press release about myself. I presented my resume in the form of a press release and sent it off to various PR agencies in Sydney. The headline was something like "Talented Account Manager Seeks..." and then it went on to present all the usual resume information laid out in the style of a press release. I got lots of phone calls because at the time, people didn't really do it that way. I was bold, and that got me an interview. Then once I was at the interview, I could demonstrate all the experience I had. That got me in the door because they obviously thought, 'she'll be an interesting person to meet' and I knew once I was in the door I could sell myself."

As an employer I get so many resumes sent to me every week by email, most of which I just don't have time to open before they get pushed down and buried in my inbox by more important work-related emails. Once they're out of sight, they just get forgotten. These days, you've got to do something different or creative to stand out. Just emailing a resume isn't going to get you noticed.

As her year travelling was coming to an end, Charlotte started to put the word out among friends and contacts that she was coming back to London and would be looking for work. One of the people she spoke to was a former colleague. As it happened, that person was now working at Disney and she mentioned that they were looking for someone in publicity and offered to put a word in for her. She sent over the job spec and Charlotte applied. *"I still had to apply and go for an interview along with everyone else, but having an existing member of staff vouch for me definitely gave me an advantage. If it had maybe come down to me and someone else, they'd probably be more likely to go for me because I had that extra recommendation."*

This is another example of why networking is so important. Almost everybody I spoke to for this book secured key positions or opportunities in their career by asking around and speaking to friends, family, contacts, and former colleagues. If you've worked with someone and done a good job, people will remember that. So make sure you nurture your business contacts and relationships, and ensure that you always leave every job on good terms.

Charlotte got the job at Disney and became a publicity supervisor for Buena Vista International Television (now Disney-ABC International Television) which involved supporting the sale of TV programming to international broadcasters. Although the role was predominantly about publicity, that included organizing lots of press junket events for shows such as *Lost* and *Desperate Housewives*.

"If international broadcasters wanted to do interviews with the cast of Lost, then I'd have to arrange that with the studio in California. I'd have to liaise with someone to provide craft services, or hair and make up for the talent, and co-ordinate everything needed onsite. Then I'd co-ordinate all the journalists and broadcasters, manage their travel and itinerary from Europe to Los Angeles, and draw up a schedule of appointments to give them time with the talent and producers. It was a lot of logistics and planning, and of course when you're dealing with talent you can never guarantee what's going to happen!"

Over the next seven years, the publicity team at Buena Vista grew from five people to 25. Charlotte's role began to broaden and there were more opportunities for her to work across different areas of PR, marketing and events. She started managing Disney's involvement in trade shows, exhibitions, and conventions (known as festivals in the TV industry) such as MIPTV and MIPCOM held in Cannes. At MIP, all the major TV distributors and production companies get together, twice a year, to showcase, promote, and sell TV programs to international broadcasters. Charlotte's role now involved all the logistics of designing and building the exhibition stand, hiring venues and yachts for parties and entertaining, registering delegates, organizing hotel accommodation, and planning product launch events for individual TV show brands.

"Toward the end of my time at Disney I was mainly just doing events. I'd proved myself in that area by doing an audit of all our presence at the festivals in Cannes. I realized we weren't getting enough of a return on our investment so I came up with various different proposals for how we could do it in a different way; challenging the whole protocol of how the events had been done previously. As a result of doing all of that, I got pushed up the food chain and was given more opportunities to do events. I realized that's where I could really make my mark, because a lot of people in events—certainly at that time anyway—weren't very commercially minded and I knew I was good at that side. Then I saw the job advertised to run the European events team for Apple and I thought 'this is a great opportunity to step up.'"

Taking the initiative to not only plan and manage the events, but to try to improve the financial management of them, is exactly the kind of attitude that most employers are looking for; they want you to go above and beyond your role. This is particularly relevant at a junior level, when you're trying to get your foot in the door. Even at a work experience level, you really need to go above and beyond what's expected. You should be demonstrating initiative in how you go about getting experience, how you approach employers, the research you do before approaching them, how you use each opportunity to learn, the interest you take, and the effort you put in—all those little extra things you can do to make yourself stand out and impress. That's really attractive to potential employers, so apply it right at the beginning of your career when you're looking for those first few bits of experience to help you get on the career ladder.

"*The interview process at Apple was very challenging. I went to Cupertino in California to meet the team there, I did panel interviews in London, I met HR, I met the CEO of Europe, and then I had to do a video conference with Steve Job's second in command who was the Global Head of Corporate Communications—so it was quite a big process for an events role. People often think of events as being quite fluffy, but when you're getting into the corporate brand world it's not at all.*"

For the role at Apple, Charlotte tailored her resume by pulling out and emphasizing all the events she had done at Disney, but most importantly she spoke about them in the context of the broader marketing mix; emphasizing the business objectives and results. For a company like Apple, that was really important because the types of events they do are mainly trade shows, both consumer and business, and also product launches. Therefore, the commercial side is really important; they won't be organizing an event without some sort of business strategy and objective behind it.

"*From my time at Disney I knew a lot about brand integrity, sharing the same brand voice, and the importance of what we're launching. Often the people interviewing you are not events people so you've got to speak the language that they want to hear. I was able to talk to the Head of Marketing, Corporate Communications, Product Development, and HR about how* events fitted in with the marketing mix, about brand guidelines and corporate culture. We spoke a lot about high-level stuff like strategy, budget management, where they should be, and how the brand should be represented, but I remember that what clinched the first round of interviews for me was when I said 'I'm not above vacuuming a carpet if that's what needs to be done to get an event ready.' I made it clear that I am happy to be hands-on if that what needs to be done, but I can also manage million pound event budgets for you too. I could see all the lights went on when I said that. That's the key thing about events; you've got to be prepared to roll your sleeves up."

Demonstrating an understanding of the commercial side of events, what the business objectives are, and how these are measured, is really important. It's easy to focus on the superficial aspects; the catering, the decorations or the amazing venue, but that's just seeing it from the guest's perspective. If you can show potential employers that you have some understanding of the commercial side of events too, you'll really stand out and impress them. Obviously, you might not know a company's objectives for holding an event, as that is likely to be privileged information, but just asking them in an interview what the objectives were, and how they measured the return on investment, will show that you have a deeper level of understanding. It will show that you are serious and not just getting carried away with the idea of events being all fun and excitement.

After some time at Apple, where she presided over launch events for products such as the iPod Nano, Charlotte was headhunted for a role as Global Head of Events for FremantleMedia Enterprises. At the time, FremantleMedia was in the process of merging three divisions; distribution, home entertainment and licensing, into one business and, fortunately for her, the CEO was aware that events could play a big part in integrating the businesses and building the company profile and positioning. He wanted someone to come in and set up a dedicated events team. Interestingly, she got the job after just one interview; for which she took a creative approach to selling herself—something she highly recommends:

"I took in a video of some events I'd done at Disney where we'd had a film crew cover it, so I had something visual to show them. You have to remember that a lot of meetings you have are quite dull, that old phrase 'Death by PowerPoint' is true. I knew I could make my experience more engaging by using video—and it worked."

8

Education and Training for a Career in Event Planning

One of the great things about the events industry is that you don't *need* higher education, formal training, qualifications, or profession certifications to start working in the business. While some of these can be advantageous, they are not a requirement. Which means a career in event planning is accessible to anyone who can develop the necessary skills, and has sufficient commitment and drive to obtain relevant experience.

To understand the types of training available, and which are going to be most suitable for you, it helps first to understand a little about the evolution of the events industry and where it is currently at:

A Transitional Period in the History of the Events Industry

The events industry is still relatively new. It evolved from the entertainment, catering, and hospitality industries on one side and the marketing and communications industry on the other, to create a diverse industry that encompasses corporate events, meeting planning, hospitality, brand marketing and experiential, and special events.

Before event planning became an established profession, events were organized by administrative staff, marketing and communications executives, catering and hospitality staff and travel agents who specialized in group bookings and tours. As those people organizing events came from such different industries and backgrounds, and were organizing events for so many different reasons, there was no formal training available that unified the process of planning an event. They learned by doing. Often it was just a case of trial and error, making mistakes and learning from them.

As events became more common across different industries, and companies began to hire dedicated event planners, basic principles and procedures common to all events began to emerge that could be taught in a classroom environment. This led to programs, modules, and classes on event planning being incorporated into Travel and Tourism, Catering and Hospitality Management, and Marketing and Communications courses. In the early 2000s, entire courses dedicated to event planning began to emerge and, particularly in countries such as the United Kingdom, it became possible to earn both undergraduate and post-graduate degrees in event management from respected universities. In recent years, particularly in the United States where there are still very few bachelor's degree courses in event management, there has been a flood of both online and classroom based 'diploma' and 'certificate' courses emerging— some of which are of questionable value, which I'll examine later.

Because of the fairly recent emergence of training courses and degrees, the event industry is at a unique point in its evolution. The majority of event planners working in the industry— particularly those in senior or management positions—probably didn't have formal training or a classroom-based education specific to event planning. Many of them may not even have a college degree. Instead, they learned on the job through experience and worked their way up. At the same time, we are now seeing the first generation of people entering the industry who have obtained degrees, certificates, and diplomas in event management. This poses an interesting dynamic where the people doing the hiring, who achieved success in their event-planning career without formal training, may not fully value the qualifications of those entering the industry who have studied in the classroom.

In the future, I think it will be the norm for event planners to have some type of formal training, whether that's a diploma, certificate, or degree. However, the value of that formal training might not be fully recognized until the current generation at the top of the industry, those who didn't study, have retired—which could be another 20–30 years or longer.[2]

With that in mind, I think it's worth pausing to consider whether you should take a course in event planning at all and, if so, how much time you should invest in a formal classroom-style education versus how much time you should spend obtaining relevant experience where you can learn on the job.

Choosing the Right Type of Training for You

There are three ways you can train for a career in event planning: study, experience, and certification. However only one of these options, experience, can be pursued on its own.

You can either:

- Learn on the job by getting experience. Then, after a few years, you will have the option to become certified if you wish—although this is not mandatory.

Or

- Choose to study first by taking a course, although you will still then have to obtain a significant amount of experience before you are likely to be considered employable. Doing a course is not a shortcut to getting a job; it won't mean anything on its own. It still has to be coupled with experience.

Regardless of whether or not you take a course, in order to become certified as an event planner, you must first obtain a significant amount of experience. In the events industry, certification is not something you need, or can even obtain, before you start work.

---

[2] Rennette Grace, Event Planning & Event Management, LinkedIn Group

9

Certification
and Why You Don't Need It—Yet

Unlike many other professions, event planning doesn't follow the traditional career path of study, qualify, entry-level job. With event planning, even if you've studied, it doesn't mean you are qualified. That's because there is no formal qualification required to work in event planning. How qualified you are for an event planning job is a discretionary decision made by the person hiring you, and is usually based on the skills you can demonstrate and the experience you have obtained; rather than what you've studied. In event planning, far greater emphasis is placed on experience than education.

Therefore, unlike many other professions that require you to become certified before you can practice, event planning requires you to have worked in the industry for several years before you can apply for certification. The minimum amount of full-time work experience required to apply for certification is two years, and that is when combined with an industry-relevant bachelor's degree, without the degree the minimum is three years' experience. Therefore, at the beginning of your career, certification is not something you need to be too concerned with.

Certificate v Certification

I've noticed that there are quite a few courses available, particularly online, that give the impression that completing their course will make you a 'certified', 'registered' or 'professional' event planner. These courses usually offer some form of certificate/diploma. However, there is a difference between 'certification' and a 'certificate.' A certificate is issued by a school to confirm that you have completed an event-planning course. Whereas, certification is issued by a professional association, such as ILEA, and results in an industry-recognized designation, such as CSEP. Therefore, despite what some schools misleadingly claim, obtaining a certificate issued by an individual school does not mean you are a certified event planner as recognized by the industry—nor does it make you a professional event planner. There is also no such thing as a registered event planner.

Industry-Recognized Event-Planning Certifications

Industry-recognized certifications are those issued by professional associations, not schools, and result in a designation you can put after your name. The three most common, specific to event/meeting planners, are:

CSEP: Certified Special Events Professional

Issued by ILEA (International Live Event Association). Requires three years full-time professional employment in the special events industry. See www.ileahub.com

CMP: Certified Meeting Professional

Issued by the Convention Industry Council. Requires three years full-time work experience (or two years with a bachelor's degree in meeting, event, exhibition, or hospitality/tourism management.) See www.conventionindustry.org

CMM: Certificate in Meeting Management

Issued by MPI, the Meeting Professionals International association. Requires 10 years' experience. See www.mpiweb.org

While the certifications above are the most common for event/meeting planners, others exist that are specific to:

a. sub-sectors of the events industry, such as:

CEM: Certified in Exhibition Management, and
DMCP: Destination Management Certified Professional

b. niche areas of the industry, such as:

CMP-HC: Certified Meeting Professional Health Care, and
CGMP: Certified Government Meeting Professional

c. related roles, such as:

CFBE: Certified Food & Beverage Executive, and
CFE: Certified Facilities Executive (venue management).

Beware of Other Designations

You may come across other event-planning designations, typically offered by online courses and other lesser-known organizations. However, you should be aware that these are often of questionable value.

For example, an organization called The International Society of Meeting Planners, offers designations such as CEP: Certified Event Planner and RMP: Registered Meeting Planner, which can be obtained simply by filling in an application form and paying $210 to become a member—there is no study, coursework, or exam involved. I would question the value of a designation that can be obtained simply by paying a membership fee.

Similarly, many online courses offer their own designations, such as the GCPE: Global Certification in Professional Events offered by the Institute of Event Management, or the IEPP™: International Event Planning Professional issued by the QC Event School. However, these are not industry-recognized designations as they are proprietary to these individual schools, rather than being issued by a professional association. As such, many employers will not recognize these designations and therefore, I would argue their value is questionable.

Most employers in the event industry are all too familiar with the handful of professional industry-recognized designations that exist specifically for event planners, i.e. CSEP, CMP, and CMM. Therefore, I suspect they might treat any job seeker brandishing a non-recognized designation with suspicion. As an employer and an industry professional myself, I know it would make me question whether the candidate is trying to mislead clients/employers, or whether they themselves have been misled into believing that they hold an industry-recognized certification. In my opinion, proprietary designations are a red flag and can undermine the credibility of school's training.

Does an Event Planner Need to Be Certified?

Certification is not mandatory, although many planners choose to obtain it in order to demonstrate their credentials. Once achieved, it's a testament to your expertise—like a badge of honor. It demonstrates to clients and employers that you have attained a degree of authority in the business and learned the standards of best practice. That said, plenty of planners simply don't bother with certification—myself included.

I've worked in event planning for 20 years, producing events for high-profile clients; celebrities such as Elton John, Kevin Spacey and Stella McCartney, as well as global brands such as Montblanc, Canon and Barbie. I run my own company, have won 30 industry awards, been a guest speaker at numerous industry events, given guest lectures at universities and been invited to judge several industry awards and competitions. Yet I've simply never felt the need to obtain the CSEP (Certified Special Event Professional) certification. I'm confident that the work I do is of a high standard and I've always preferred to let the work speak for itself. I've also never had a single client or employer in my entire career ask me whether I had any sort of official qualification or credential—even when I worked in corporate events for the investment bank Credit Suisse. They've always been more concerned with seeing my portfolio of past events, which is the real testament to my skills, experience, and proficiency.

Some employers—particularly in meeting planning—may favor a candidate with a certification such as the CMP (Certified Meeting Professional). It definitely communicates a level of experience and a commitment to your profession. But even then, they're going to be far more concerned with the experience you have. If you have great experience, in all likelihood, they're not going to care whether you've got a certification or not. Experience always trumps qualifications in the event industry. Your resume will already have *shown* them what you can do, rather than a certification *telling* them what you can do. The difference between *showing* and *telling* is quite an important distinction to make. Hence why experience is so much more important than study in this industry.

The other thing to consider is that, in reality, many people obtain certification and then do not continue to uphold the standards and practices they've been taught. Much like when you take your driving test and you're taught to keep both hands on the wheel in a 10 and 2 position. Does anyone really continue to do that after the driving test? I've seen some shockingly poor practices by certified event planners. People often obtain them with the best of intentions, but in some cases they just don't follow through and adopt the best practices they've been taught. If I were the client or employer, I'd much rather someone demonstrated the standards of best practice in their actual body of work, rather than relying on a certification they might have obtained up to five years ago.

Sometimes it can be worth getting certified just to give yourself that extra professional edge. You may find yourself down to the final two for an interview, against an equally strong candidate, where there is little difference between the two of you. In situations like that, sometimes it can be the slightest thing that will push the balance in one candidate's favor—and that might be which one has obtained an official certification.

Ultimately, you shouldn't be too concerned about certification at the beginning of your career. Once you have a few years' experience and understand how the industry, the jobs market, and the hiring process works, then you can decide whether obtaining certification is right for you. By then, your career might be advancing perfectly well and you decide you don't need it. My own situation is testament to the fact that you can have a perfectly successful career in event planning without being certified.

10

Is an Event-Planning Course Right for Me?

"I think if someone wants to study that's great, but a lot of people in the industry don't have an event management qualification. It's not really about the qualification. If you look at very successful employees and freelancers, what they've got is experience. I wouldn't look at someone's resume and think, 'well they haven't got a degree in event management, I won't consider them', absolutely not. A lot of it is about the experience they've got. The good thing about doing an event management degree is that they will have got some practical experience as part of that by doing a placement. Therefore, if you don't have a degree you should work on increasing the amount of experience you have in order to put you on an even footing."

Nicola Mosley, HR Manager, George P. Johnson

Now that we've established that taking an event-planning course does not make you a certified event planner, you need to consider whether formal study is still the right path for you. To do this, you first need to understand what will happen when you've finished your studies. Unfortunately, an event-planning course on its own will not make you qualified to work in the industry. It might make you a little better prepared, in terms of how much you understand. However to an employer, a course or qualification on paper will, on its own, count for very little—until it's combined with experience.

Taking an event-planning course is not a short cut to getting a job. In fact, if anything it might slow down the process. When you've finished studying, in all likelihood you'll still need to seek volunteer opportunities and unpaid work—in order to build up a portfolio of experience—before anyone will hire you for a paid position. So, while there are advantages to learning the theoretical side of event planning before you try to get experience, it's also possible to learn this on the job while simultaneously gaining real-world experience. Therefore, you just need to decide whether you're going to study first, or go straight into looking for work experience.

"I've actually never hired anyone that had any event management qualification. I tend to look for people who have broader experience. I don't think these courses are the only way, or necessarily even the best way, into the industry. Experience is much more important."

Charlotte Saynor, former Vice President of Brands & Events, FremantleMedia Enterprises and Head of European Events, Apple

Why an Event-Planning Course Isn't Necessary

"I think a university degree is a must, but I don't think it need be specifically in event management. If a candidate did have an event management degree then great, but at the end of the day it's having the right experience that will really sell you to an organization. If it was me, and I had the choice of some excellent work experience opportunities over an event degree, then I'd choose the work experience every time."

Farida Haqiqi, former Events Manager, The British Red Cross

It's important to remember that the majority of people working in the event industry today did not study event management or take classes in event planning. That is because formal courses weren't available until fairly recently. Now, just because the industry was founded—and is still largely populated—by people who didn't study event planning, that doesn't mean that's the preferable route to take now that there *are* courses available. What it does mean is that taking an event-planning course isn't *necessary* in order to get started in the profession. As a course won't qualify you to work as an event planner, the purpose of taking one is to get a head start in learning some of the theory and procedures used. As the majority of professionals working in the industry—who didn't take a course—are a testament to, this is something you can teach yourself. If you're prepared to jump straight into the industry and work in 'bottom of the ladder' support roles, use these opportunities strategically—to observe, question and learn—and then supplement this real-world experience with some reading and research, then it's perfectly possible to work your way up and become an event planner without studying first.

"My problem with event courses is that you often aren't getting hands-on experience, and this job is all about experience. You can have the best degree in the world that tells you on paper how to organize an event, but what I want to see is that you understand what to do when things go wrong, that you understand why they go wrong, and you can deal with it. The fact that you've trained for it at college doesn't tell me you're going to be OK onsite, and that you'll be able to pick up an event and run with it, because I don't think you will.

People that I have interviewed that have come straight from college courses have not really been able to demonstrate any of the core skills by showing me 'this is what I've learnt and this is how I've put it into practice.' To me, event management graduates are often much higher risk because they often think they know it all just because they've done a course, but they haven't got enough onsite experience.

If you've done a course, that's great, but you're not going to stand out anymore to me than someone who hasn't. The candidate with more experience is definitely going to be more valuable to me."

Sharyn Scott, Global Head of Events, Linklaters

Why an Event-Planning Course Might Be Beneficial

Now that we've established that taking an event-planning course is not *necessary*, let's examine whether it's *preferable*. I believe that, if you have the choice and can afford the fees, taking a course is preferable to not taking one. Knowing how competitive the industry is, how busy employers are, and how little time and patience they sometimes have to train people, learning the fundamentals before you start out is always going to be advantageous. It will tell employers that, at the very least, you have a basic level of understanding about what the job involves. The better prepared you are, the more likely an employer will be to take a chance on you.

Taking a course will also demonstrate commitment to potential employers, and will indicate that you are serious about working in the industry. Event planning has become a very popular profession over the past decade. If you're trying to break into an industry where there are lots of candidates chasing fewer and fewer job opportunities, then being able to demonstrate your commitment through study is definitely going to give you an advantage over someone who hasn't studied. Even if, in the early days, you're only seeking volunteer roles, work experience, or unpaid internships. It's going to be much easier to compete for those opportunities if you can show you've educated yourself on the subject of event planning. Of course, one of the other advantages of studying is that a good school will offer some form of assistance with internships, placements, or volunteer opportunities to help you get experience and start networking.

Now, while I believe that there is definitely some value in taking an event-planning course, I do not believe a traditional two-, three-, or four-year college or university course is the best option. I'll explain why in Chapter 12 "The Most Relevant Qualifications and How Long to Study for."

If You Don't Take an Event-Planning Course

"30–40 percent of jobs require a degree of some kind, but initially when we're recruiting we look at a candidate's experience first and foremost— and if the skills match we would put them forward even if they don't have the relevant degree."

Liz Sinclair, Managing Director, ESP Recruitment

If you decide not to take an event-planning course, perhaps because of the high cost of tuition fees, don't worry; that definitely won't exclude you from the industry. Remember, in event planning, experience is still far more important than formal study or qualifications. If you don't study event planning, there is another way to learn that is perfectly acceptable—and that's on the job. Learning this way doesn't put you at any disadvantage, in fact many employers find it preferable.

Most of the useful elements taught in a classroom environment are procedure-based; strategic planning, timelines, schedules, budgets, risk assessment, and event safety. A lot of these things can actually be learned by reading books or taking a few online classes/video tutorials, while simultaneously putting them into practice on the job. Whereas, someone who studies in the classroom then has to learn how to apply that knowledge to real-world situations at a later date. Of course, a lot of what goes into event planning cannot be taught in the classroom anyway. It's about how you think on your feet and react to situations, whether you have the confidence to take control and lead, how resourceful you are, whether you can think laterally, visualize, and problem-solve, and how well you can negotiate and communicate with others. Which is perhaps why many employers aren't that impressed by someone taking an event-planning course on its own. It raises doubts about whether they will know how to deal with something going wrong onsite, under pressure, when they cannot have experienced those types of situations in a classroom.

"I'm a great believer in learning onsite. You learn so much more from being onsite than you ever will from a textbook or from being in a classroom. So I always look far more for onsite experience when it comes to hiring."

Chad Hudson, President, Chad Hudson Events

Event planning isn't black and white. You can plan, prepare, and try to implement as much control over a situation as possible in advance, but no matter how well thought-out everything is, an event always takes on a life of its own onsite. There are simply too many variables for you to plan for every eventuality. The test of a good planner is only partly based on what they do in advance to prepare for an event—the procedures that can be taught in the classroom. Perhaps more important is how they think, operate and respond onsite at an event when faced with real situations. If you've learned by working on real events, then you already know the realities of the job; how theory from books and tutorials translates in practice.

Many employers actually have more respect for people who have worked their way up in the business without studying— perhaps because it shows determination, drive, and initiative, or maybe because it's likely to resonate with their own background. However, if you've chosen not to take a course you're still going to have to demonstrate commitment, to prove that you're serious about working in events. If you're going to succeed this way, you must be proactive in order to learn the things you would have if you'd taken a course. This means undertaking as much reading as possible to teach yourself how the industry works and to learn the fundamentals of project management. It means not being too proud to take any opportunity to work—paid or unpaid—no matter whether it's inconvenient, or you consider it too basic or beneath you. It means having the confidence to approach everyone you meet on-site in order to network and seek out further opportunities. And finally, it means maximizing every opportunity in order to get the most out of it; observe and question everything onsite, study it later at home to 'reverse-engineer' it, and always push to take on more than is asked of you.

"They don't necessarily have to have a degree, just a good standard of education. We wouldn't discount someone who hadn't been to university but had decided they were passionate about this industry and want to work in it"

Fiona Lawlor, HR Director, Jack Morton London and Dubai

Don't be put off by the idea of starting at the bottom. If someone has taken a course, he or she will still have to start at the bottom, obtain lots of experience, and work their way up too. So in effect, you're starting in pretty much the same place. They may have done a little more preparation on the theoretical side, but you'll have a head start in getting practical experience on real events. Of course, by doing a course they might have access to more internships or work placement opportunities provided by the school or college. However, you can still go after these yourself. As an employer, I'm far more impressed by a non-college student taking the initiative to seek out an internship.

"Our intern program is opened up to a very wide range of establishments. We do have people from event management degrees, but we also have lots of people from other degree courses as well. We also consider people who haven't been to university for internships; we've had mature students and people who haven't been to college. In fact, we're even thinking about rebranding our internship scheme to call it something else so it doesn't suggest that people have to come from a university background. We have people on our intern schemes that already have a few years' experience, so we're not just looking at people straight from university."

Fiona Lawlor, HR Director, Jack Morton London and Dubai

11

The Different Types of Courses: Accredited and Unaccredited

Nowadays, there are many different types of event-planning courses available offering degrees, diplomas and certificates. Some of these are accredited courses offered by reputable schools and universities, while others are simply commercial businesses that make money from selling courses offering 'diplomas' and 'certificates' which have little or no value. Therefore, one of the most important factors used to distinguish the reputable courses from the less reputable, is whether the course is accredited and, if so, by whom?

> *'Educational Accreditation is a type of quality assurance process under which services and operations of educational institutions or programs are evaluated by an external body to determine if applicable standards are met'. Source: Wikipedia*

Let's first identify the different courses available, both accredited and unaccredited, by the type of course provider. Then, in the next chapter, I'll discuss the most relevant qualifications and the length of time you should spending studying event planning.

1. Public and Non-Profit Private Colleges

These are traditional campus-based universities and colleges (although some may also offer distant learning) that are either state-run or private colleges operating as non-profit organizations.

As they are not operated for profit, money earned through fees is invested back into the school to provide the educational services.

a. The Qualification

These universities and colleges will typically offer a nationally recognized qualification in event planning.

In the United States, only a handful of colleges currently offer bachelor's degrees in event planning. These are typically offered by a university's school of hospitality, for example The University of Central Florida operates the Rosen College of Hospitality Management, which offers a four-year Bachelor of Science in Event Management. Alternatively, some schools offer minors in event planning, which are often combined with majors in communications or hospitality and tourism. Some community and technical colleges also offer two-year associate's degrees or one-year certificate programs in event planning. Many students take these courses part-time, which can be particularly advantageous as it allows them to work in the industry simultaneously, gaining the necessary experience while they study.

In the United Kingdom, there are many bachelor's and master's degrees in event management on offer from dozens of universities—in addition to those that combine event management within a hospitality & tourism degree. There are also quite a few qualifications below a bachelor's degree offered by community and technical colleges, such as Higher National Diplomas (HND) and National Vocational Qualifications (NVQ).

b. Accreditation

In most cases, these courses will have been accredited by national/regional accrediting agencies approved by the country's department of education. If a particular course is not accredited by one of these approved accrediting agencies, it may be accredited by a relevant professional association, for example The Chartered Institute of Marketing (UK). Before considering a course offered by a public or non-profit private university/college, be sure to check that it has been accredited by a relevant agency or association. Assuming the correct accreditation is in place, it's safe to assume these courses are legitimate and trustworthy. However, that doesn't necessarily mean they will teach the most relevant topics to prepare you for working in the industry today. I'll discuss this in Chapter 12: "The Most Relevant Qualifications and How Long to Study for."

2. For-Profit Schools and Colleges

For-profit schools and colleges, also known as academies or institutes, are commercially operated businesses that make money for their owners and shareholders by selling products and services; in this case educational courses and classes. These schools often have physical premises where the courses are taught, although some may also offer distant learning options too. Some will offer accredited courses, while others will be unaccredited. Despite being businesses, they often refer to themselves as schools, colleges, institutes, or academies. However, just because they incorporate school, college, institute or academy into their business name, it doesn't necessarily mean they are an accredited education provider.

a. The Qualification

For-profit event-planning schools typically offer certificate or diploma courses. However, given that any commercial business can start trading as a school and issue its own proprietary certificates/diplomas, it means not all certificates/diplomas are of the same—or any—value. The value in any certificate or diploma issued by a for-profit school is dependent on the credibility and relevance of the organization that provides the accreditation.

b. Accreditation

If a business is positioning itself as a school, college, institute or academy, it's important to look beyond the name of the business to see who—if anyone—is providing the accreditation. Is it accredited by an approved accrediting agency or a relevant professional association? In some cases, these courses are not accredited it all. Which begs the question, why are they not accredited? Is it because what they are teaching isn't considered of a high enough quality to warrant accreditation from a reputable body? Or do the business owners just not care enough about the quality of what's being taught to seek out accreditation? Even more worryingly, some less scrupulous courses will give the impression that their course is accredited, but when you do a little digging, you realize the accreditation is not from an approved accreditation agency.

It's also important to ensure that any accreditation is relevant to the provision of educational courses. For example, both the Institute of Event Management and the QC Event School refer to their BBB (Better Business Bureau) Accreditation, with QC's website saying:

"We know that some students may be hesitant about enrolling in a distance education course. Rest assured that we have the highest possible consumer satisfaction rating (A+) with the Better Business Bureau."

While this is a perfectly legitimate claim on their behalf, the BBB accreditation relates to how the school operates <u>as a business</u> and should not be interpreted as accreditation of educational courses. In fact, a quick look at the BBB website reveals:

"BBB accreditation does not mean that the business' products or services have been evaluated or endorsed by BBB, or that BBB has made a determination as to the business' product quality or competency in performing services."

As a qualification, a certificate or diploma issued by a for-profit school is only of value if the body providing the accreditation is both reputable <u>and</u> relevant.

None of this means that a for-profit school should be discounted just because it's a business. In fact, I believe some of the most relevant and worthwhile courses tend to be offered by for-profit schools. They often attract part-time teachers who are experienced event professionals still working in the industry—and those are typically the best people to learn from, as they know the relevant topics to teach for such a fast-evolving industry.

When it comes to for-profit schools, what's most important is to differentiate the accredited ones from the unaccredited. While an accredited course doesn't necessarily guarantee it will teach the most relevant topics—the course content would still need to be evaluated separately—it does at least mean that the school is a legitimate education provider and the topics contained in the course have been externally verified to meet certain educational or professional standards.

To sum up, if a course is offered by a for-profit school the most important thing to check is the relevance of the accreditation. If you are satisfied with the accreditation, you can then go on to evaluate the rest of the course before deciding whether it's right for you. If there is no accreditation at all, then you need to evaluate the course based on who has created the course content and who teaches it. I'll go into more detail on how to evaluate a course and its content in the Chapter 13 "How to Choose the Right Event-Planning Course." In the meantime, the section below about online-only schools and colleges highlights other issues around unaccredited courses.

3. For-Profit Online-Only Schools and Colleges

"If you take a course where you don't get to organize events as part of this course or there are no placements, then it's going to prove a lot more difficult to get a job after you graduate as this industry is about experience. It's all very well learning the theory of event planning but, until you apply that to an event, it doesn't count for very much."

Liz Sinclair, Managing Director, ESP Recruitment

Online-only schools and colleges generally offer pre-prepared courses and/or videos, which can be streamed, downloaded, or mailed out for the student to study at home, often at their own pace. Sometimes these courses will offer access to tutors who will grade your coursework, while others simply leave you with the course materials to educate yourself. Generally, any organization offering online-only event-planning courses is likely to be a for-profit school. The exception to this is when a public or private non-profit school/college offers distant learning courses online, usually in addition to campus-based courses. The points below do not apply to distant learning courses from public or private non-profit schools. They are intended to deal with course providers that *only* offer training via home study with no classroom-based courses offered.

a. The Qualification

Online-only schools will usually offer certificates and diplomas. So again, one must look at who is providing accreditation to assess the value.

b. Accreditation

What differentiates most online-only schools from other for-profit organizations is that the majority of courses offered this way tend to be unaccredited. I would strongly advise you not to take a course that is unaccredited—unless it is authored by a leading industry expert, and even then, those have pros and cons, which I'll outline below. Remember that unless a relevant and reputable organization has accredited a course, what you are being taught could be irrelevant, incomplete, out of date, or unprofessional.

A Note on Unaccredited Courses

If a school offers a course and it is not accredited, the certificate or diploma issued may be of questionable value <u>as a qualification</u>. However, that doesn't necessarily mean the content of the course doesn't contain any value. It just means that any value is in the knowledge being imparted by the person who wrote the course materials.

For example, a world-renowned award-winning chef, who's an expert in his field and admired by his peers, might decide to open their own school or create a cookery course. If the chef's credentials are sound, then of course there is going to be a great deal of value in learning from them. In fact, you often hear chef's credential's established by whom they trained under. However, you need to be aware that, without accreditation, no external body is verifying what that chef is teaching. No one is dictating the syllabus, ensuring certain standards, or assessing the depth or relevance of what is being taught. Which means the knowledge being imparted could easily be wrong, incomplete, irrelevant, or just out of date. So while you might learn a great deal, the knowledge will only be from that particular chef's perspective and experience, which could include all his bad habits, mistakes, and outdated techniques.

It's the same with event planning; if you take an unaccredited course, what is taught will only be as good as the person who wrote the course. So you would need to look very closely at who authored the course materials and/or who is teaching it. Are they who you want to learn from? Are they experts in their field? What are their credentials? Are they teaching the most relevant, up-to-date information? Are they still practicing in the industry, if so, to what level? Or did they retire years ago? If they did, then how relevant is their knowledge going to be now in such a fast-evolving industry?

Unaccredited courses can sometimes be of value, depending on the caliber of the course provider. However, you should be aware of the potential limitations they come with, both in terms of the 'qualification' and the quality and accuracy of the content.

In Summary

Most public and private non-profit schools typically offer accredited courses with a nationally recognized qualification—although you should always check. Therefore, if considering one of these courses you just need to evaluate the school itself, the qualification, the course content, and the length of the course, to decide whether it is right for you.

For-profit schools can offer either accredited or unaccredited courses. The first thing to do is check the accreditation is reputable and relevant. If it isn't, you need to decide whether you still want to consider the course—my advice would be not to, unless it's authored by a leading industry expert that you feel comfortable trusting with your education. If the accreditation is sound, you can proceed to evaluate the course based on the school itself, the qualification, the course content and the length of the course—the criteria for which I'll discuss in Chapter 13 "How to Choose the Right Event-Planning Course."

For more information, see this book's companion website at: www.eventplanningcourses.org

12

The Most Relevant Qualifications and How Long to Study for

In this chapter, I'll look at the different levels to which you can study event planning, and how long you should spend getting a classroom-based education.

1. Bachelor's Degrees

"For entry-level positions, a college degree often isn't required but it's definitely becoming more common. I would encourage getting one because a college degree says more to an employer than just that candidate has a higher level of education. It also says that they have some level of discipline and they've made sacrifices and dedicated another two, three, or four years to invest in both themselves and their future employer. It's not just the tangible benefit of having more knowledge that they gained in college, but also that they have the disciple and maturity to make that additional commitment."

Christopher Lee, CEO, ACCESS Destination Services

Why You Should Get a Degree if You Can

Generally speaking, having a bachelor's degree is definitely preferable; assuming you have the time and money to invest in one. Many employers—especially those in the corporate world—will *only* consider candidates with a bachelor's degree, simply because it demonstrates a certain level of education. This is particularly the case in the United States, where there is more of a dividing line between having a college degree and not. You will probably find there are more opportunities available to you with a degree. I've known people who, despite having lots of great experience, don't even get considered by overly rigid HR departments simply because they don't have a degree. It's often one of the first things HR look for on your resume, and if it's not there, they might not read any further.

"At the Red Cross, any job application would stipulate that a candidate had to have completed a university degree with a minimum 2:2 grade."

Farida Haqiqi, former Events Manager, The British Red Cross

Fortunately, a lot of companies in the events industry are small businesses without formal HR departments to handle their hiring, which often means they are more open to the idea of considering candidates without a degree. However, even in times of recession, when there are often a lack of jobs for graduates, having a degree will still give you an edge if you're competing against someone who doesn't have a degree.

Having a college degree is also a good thing because it gives you something to fall back on should you not be able to get work in the event industry, or if you find you don't like it, and later decide to change careers. Therefore, if you have the option to get a degree, I would recommend it. However, while having a college degree is definitely a good thing; my advice would be *not* to get a degree in event planning.

Why You Shouldn't Get a Degree in Event Planning

"In the 14 years I've been recruiting, we've probably only been asked specifically for someone with an event management degree maybe four times. It's still very much about experience. Having said that, if you have an event management degree with a one-year placement, it will definitely get you a better first job. Equally, you could just as easily spend that three or four years working your way up from a lower position, getting on-the-job experience, to arrive at the same point."

Liz Sinclair, Managing Director, ESP Recruitment

In the United Kingdom, there are dozens of universities offering bachelor's degrees in event management and, while in the United States there are currently very few, I'm sure more will emerge. However, just because there are bachelor's degree courses available, that doesn't mean they are the best course to take for a career in events. I would advise you not to study for a bachelor's degree in event management, for a number of reasons:

- **Teachable Skills v Innate Qualities**

It's fair to say that many employers—certainly the ones I interviewed for this book—are skeptical of the value in studying event planning to bachelor's degree level. Most of what is taught in the classroom is procedure-driven, such as the fundamentals of project management. While these are useful and necessary skills, they're also somewhat basic. You certainly don't need to spend three years studying them. Employers tend to be much more interested in an event planner's personal qualities, which can't be taught in a classroom, but can often be developed through experience. These include how you think on your feet, react to situations, and use your initiative, or how confident and resourceful you are. An employer wants to know that you can think laterally, visualize, and problem-solve, and that you have good leadership, communication, negotiation, and people skills.

"I personally think that going to university for three years to study event management is an absolute waste of time. You'd be far better off taking a short three or six-month course in the form of evening classes. The industry, and the world in general, evolves and changes too quickly over the course of three years for a course of that length to stay relevant. Courses taught by professionals still active in the business are definitely the way to go."

Martin Turner, former Global Head of Events for Credit Suisse

- ## Course Length

If you take a three-year event-planning course, while *some* of what you learn will be useful, you will still have to obtain a significant amount of experience after graduation before you will be considered employable. Compare that scenario to someone who does a short course just to learn the fundamentals, or someone that goes straight into the industry by volunteering and working their way up. By the time you graduate after three years and set about seeking experience, the person who didn't go to college or took a short course, already has up to three years of real-world experience. Which person do you think is going to be more attractive to an employer in an industry where experience is more important than education? In an industry where the employer probably got to where they are without studying event planning?

"It [an event management degree] is not something I specifically look for in a candidate, but it might help you stand out because, if it's a good course, you will get measureable experience of organizing events. However, if someone who hasn't studied had gone out and got lots of experience then it would level the playing field, so a course is probably never really going to give you that big an advantage."

Nathan Homan, Co-founder, Rouge Events

- ## Course Content

Many event professionals, myself included, believe that there is too big a disconnect between the knowledge and experience gained academically from event-management degrees, and the needs of employers in the industry. There are typically lots of unnecessary 'filler' modules included in degree courses, such as public relations & events, celebration ritual & culture, enterprise & events, events & leisure innovation, green events, and leisure marketing—which I suspect is there to pad out the course to create three years of study. That time would be far better spent getting practical 'hands-on' experience. Also, as I've mentioned previously, the events industry—and its use of technology in particular—is constantly evolving at a rapid pace, so topics taught at the start of a three year course could easily be out of date or irrelevant by the time a student graduates.

"At the end of the day we don't just target event management graduates when we're looking to hire people, we widen the net to pick up from all areas and backgrounds. It's important to have a diverse workforce. Event management degrees are useful, but it's not part of the hiring criteria for us."

Fiona Lawlor, HR Director, Jack Morton London and Dubai

• Limited Applications

An event-management degree is, I believe, both unnecessary and potentially quite limited in its applications. If you later decide event planning isn't the right career path for you, then your degree isn't going to be as useful in pursuing other options. In the United Kingdom, where we have dozens of universities offering event management degrees, there are far too many graduates flooding the jobs market year upon year, all competing for fewer and fewer jobs. Many end up unemployed or seeking work in other professions. A degree in event management won't be as transferable as a degree in marketing or business studies.

"You don't have to be coming from an event degree course, sometimes its business or marketing. It's not really about what degree you have; it's about having the right approach and attitude, and demonstrating a real desire to work in the industry. I would look for someone who has some knowledge about the industry and some interest not just in events, but marketing, communications, and branding; someone who has good background knowledge, can understand how events fit in within the marketing mix, and knows that it's not just about organizing events. Someone with a broader mind-set."

Nicola Mosley, HR Manager, George P. Johnson

Alternative Bachelor's Degrees

"Like myself, many people who got into event management left university with a degree in something entirely unrelated; the important thing is to have transferable skills."

Farida Haqiqi, former Events Manager, The British Red Cross

While I don't believe a bachelor's degree in event management is worthwhile, I do recommend getting a bachelor's degree, if you can. Therefore, as most event-planning skills can be learned on the job, I would recommend using a degree as an opportunity to obtain a broader set of skills and knowledge. You'd be far better off studying another subject then following it with a short/ intensive course to teach yourself the fundamentals of event planning—which is all you really need from a classroom education.

- **Marketing and Communications Degrees**

"Doing a course that shows an interest in this field—so marketing, advertising or communications—is always something that catches my eye, but we are completely open to all sorts of degrees. As long as you show that you have an interest, and we can see that through the experience you've had in the past or the extra-curricular activities, then that's fine."

Dori Rodriguez, Senior HR Associate, Jack Morton Worldwide

Personally, I think studying for a degree in marketing and communications would be of far more use to you. You're also not just limiting your future prospects to a career in event planning; there are so many other potential applications for a marketing and communications degree. Events are essentially a communications tool. Whether it's meeting planning, brand marketing events, special events, or fundraisers, the purpose of events is always routed in marketing and communications. The more you understand about the purpose of events, their objectives, the messages that needs to be communicated, and how to do that in a live—and increasingly digital—space, the more successful and employable you will be. Employers aren't just looking to hire people who can do the mechanics of event planning: creating budgets and timelines, booking venues, and arranging logistics. They want to hire people who understand the theory behind it; the bigger picture of why we are doing this event, what we are trying to achieve, who it is aimed at, and what the best solution is going to be to achieve the results we want.

Therefore, if you're going to study for a degree, I think that having a deeper understanding of marketing and communications—that you can then apply to event planning—is going to be far more beneficial to both yourself and your employers.

"If you are doing to go to university, I think it would be far more beneficial to do a communications degree, because that's what it really all comes down to. Events are "live communication" I absolutely would not recommend to anybody that they spend three years studying events at university."

Martin Turner, former Global Head of Events for Credit Suisse

• Business Degrees

A business degree—perhaps minoring in marketing—would also give you a broader education, while still covering many of the strategic planning, financial reporting, and evaluation skills relevant for event planning. In many ways, every individual event operates like a mini-business; it requires a plan, strategy, marketing, and promotion. It involves income, expenditure, profit and loss, budgeting, accounting, contracts, resources, staff and equipment, taxes, and insurance. In addition, many event planners go on to start their own event-planning business, so a business degree will prepare you for all the issues involved.

"My personal opinion is that if you're going to do a course, you'd be better off doing something broader, like business studies or marketing, so that you understand events within the broader marketing mix. Events do not stand in isolation in a corporate world, or a brand environment."

Charlotte Saynor, former Vice President of Brands & Events, Fremantle Media Enterprises, and Head of European Events, Apple

• Hospitality and Tourism

"For this particular area of the industry, incentive travel and destination management, I would definitely recommend doing a travel & tourism course. That's how we find a lot of our employees. We meet a lot of our entry-level team members through the colleges, because they actively try to help students connect with different companies. We just hired someone in our Las Vegas office that was a direct referral from a college course. In fact, I think in all of our offices throughout the United States we look to travel & tourism courses for entry-level positions."

Jennifer Miller DMCP, Partner & President, ACCESS Destination Services

Degrees in hospitality and tourism can also be a good grounding for a career in certain sectors of the event industry, such as catering, hotel conference and banqueting, incentive travel, sporting and leisure events, and destination management. These degrees can give you a route into the industry by qualifying you for entry-level positions in related sectors, which you can then use to work your way up into more event-specific roles. For example, after studying hospitality & tourism you may go to work for a hotel. That hotel will probably have a conference and/or banqueting department that you could side step into. From there you will come into contact with conference organizers, event planners, and destination management companies that you can develop relationships with. When you've built up sufficient experience, you may be able to approach those contacts for event-planning positions within their organizations. The great thing about the events industry is that you can easily work your way up and move around within different sectors of the industry. A hospitality & tourism degree will definitely provide entry points into the events industry; however, you just need to be aware that this type of degree is more relevant for some sectors of the industry than others.

"Candidates don't have to have an event management degree. We've got people here with English degrees and also someone with a degree in astrophysics, so one degree won't give someone an advantage or disadvantage over another."

Fiona Lawlor, HR Director, Jack Morton London and Dubai

If you decide to study for degree that isn't in event planning, make sure that any part-time work you take as a student is relevant to the events industry, so that it counts as experience. Then, on graduation, you can just start seeking volunteer opportunities, internships, and work experience in order to learn on the job. Alternatively, my advice would be to follow your degree with a short, intensive, or part time/evening course to learn the fundamentals first; it will just give you a little head start in understanding the theory and procedures involved.

2. Certificate, Diplomas and Other Qualifications

Assuming, for whatever reason, you decide not to study for a bachelor's degree, but you'd still like to take an event-planning course before getting experience, there are other options available. However, you need to approach these from a different perspective; it becomes less about the qualification itself and more about the quality, depth, and relevance of the information being taught. You should look for an accredited course that will teach you the fundamentals of event planning, covering the necessary topics (listed in the next chapter), in sufficient depth and in a reasonably short amount of time, e.g. one month full time or three months part time.

I've explained previously that an employer is unlikely to be that impressed by an event-planning qualification on your resume—they'll be more interested in your experience. Therefore, the purpose of taking a short course is just to teach yourself the basic skills and theory, so that you'll be better prepared when you start getting on-the-job experience. A short course will still demonstrate to employers that you are serious, committed, and proactive about starting a career in event planning. You'll still learn the theory and procedures of event planning, but you can move on to getting experience as soon as possible. If the short course is part-time/evenings classes, you can even study while obtaining relevant paid work experience in support roles in the industry, which I'll look at in later chapters.

I strongly recommend, if you have no degree or it's not in event planning, that you take a short, intensive course then start getting experience as soon as possible. Spending a year or more studying event planning is just far too long—it's just not the type of subject that can be taught in the classroom.

Choosing a Short Course

Community/technical colleges—and even some universities— offer shorter 'certificate program' courses in event planning, many of which are part-time/evening classes. However, they often still take one or more years to complete. This, in my opinion, is still too long to spend studying event planning, unless you are working in the industry to gain experience simultaneously. My biggest concern about these certificate programs though, is whether they go into enough depth and cover the most relevant topics. They typically have little or no ongoing input from professionals currently working in the industry and as such, the ones I've looked at appear to be either too basic, incomplete, or out of date.

I actually think some of the best options for short/part-time courses tend to be offered by for-profit schools. These are often taught by events professionals currently working in the industry and, as such, they know the most relevant topics to cover. That said, there are still only a handful I've come across to date that I would feel comfortable recommending. For more information, see this book's companion site at www.eventplanningcourses.org

In Summary

To summarize, I believe that:

- If you can, study for a bachelor's degree as this will likely give you more career opportunities

- Consider carefully before spending time and money studying event management to bachelor's degree level

- Choose a bachelor's degree that will give you a broader knowledge but will also be useful for event planning e.g. marketing, communications, business, or hospitality & tourism.

- While studying, work part-time in support roles in the industry (see later chapters) and on graduating seek work experience, internships, and volunteer opportunities

- Alternatively, if you feel you still want to learn the fundamentals of event planning before seeking experience, do a short, intensive or part time/evening course

- If you're not studying for a degree, do a short/part time course to learn the basics while getting on-the-job experience through paid support roles, volunteering, and work experience

- If you're considering a short course, research and scrutinize both the school and course content thoroughly; there are a lot of 'thin' courses and disreputable schools out there!

- After you've gained a few years' experience in the industry, you can decide whether you want to obtain an official industry-recognized certification.

13

How to Choose the Right Event-Planning Course

As there are so many different courses on offer around the world, with new ones starting all the time, it's not possible for me to research each one in detail and make recommendations or tell you which to avoid. Instead, I will tell you what to look for in order to better assess each course and ultimately make your own judgement about whether it's right for you.

How to Evaluate an Event-Planning Course

Education is always a good thing and should be encouraged. However, put simply, not all education is of the same quality and, therefore, value. The quality of a course can usually be judged by factors such as:

- **Reputation of the School**

For traditional public and private non-profit schools, the reputation can be evaluated by league table statistics and national rankings, which will list their success rates. Therefore, if you're considering one of these schools, be sure to do your research by checking one of the many lists published online.

Similarly, if you're considering a for-profit school, do your own research and ask them:

- How many people apply?
- How many are accepted?

- What is the criteria for acceptance?
- Is everyone who applies accepted?
- How many drop out/graduate?
- If there are different grades available, how many people achieve each grade?
- If it's a pass/fail course, what is the minimum pass criteria?
- Does the school have relationships with employers in the industry and does it provide work placements?
- Does the school have links to or endorsements from professional associations or leading figures in the industry?
- Are there any notable alumni?
- Can they give you specific details of jobs that former students have gone on to? If not, why not?
- Will they put you in touch with former students so you can ask their opinion about the course? If not, why not?

Remember that if a school is successful, and its students go on to get good jobs in the industry, this is something they will want to promote. If the school doesn't promote its success stories, you need to ask yourself, why not?

- **The Qualification**

A traditional public or private non-profit school will offer a nationally recognized qualification, such as a bachelor's degree, associate degree (USA), HND/NVQ (UK), or a certificate program.

If the school is for-profit, then the qualification is likely to be a certificate or diploma. However, given that any business can issue a certificate, it is only really of value as a qualification if it is:

a. Accredited

and

b. Accredited by either a government approved accrediting agency, or a reputable and relevant professional association

- ## Content of the Course

Detailed research into the content of a course is imperative. Not just in terms of which topics are covered, but also to what depth and how much time is devoted to each element.

For courses from non-profit organizations, be wary of filler modules, as discussed in the previous chapter. With courses offered by for-profit organizations, a lot of these tend to put far too much emphasis on the fluffier side of event planning; table-styling or holiday and theme parties, or random niche topics such as 'events in private homes' or 'religious rites and funerals.' Alternatively, they combine event planning with wedding planning in the same course. While these topics might seem quite fun to study, they're not going to prepare you for the realities of the job. Neither is studying wedding planning—which has a completely different emphasis. This type of training is more appropriate for party planning and won't be applicable to the vast majority of positions in the events industry.

The majority of event-planning skills that an employer is looking for are rooted in business, marketing & communications, project management, and digital media—with a little creative design or technical production knowledge thrown into the mix as a bonus. It is this type of education you should be seeking, not how to choose centerpieces or design an invitation. For the most part, that's what an event planner uses suppliers to do for them.

Below, I've made a list of knowledge and skills you should look for an event-planning course to teach you. These are just the essential topics. It's fine if a course includes other topics that I've not listed, as long as these are included. If these topics aren't mentioned in the course description, then you should contact the course administrator and ask them whether these will be taught as part of the course. If they're not, then you might be wasting your time on a course where the emphasis is on all the wrong elements. If that's the case, you're not going to be very well prepared with the right skills when you enter the jobs market.

1. Overview of the Event Industry

- The purpose of events as a communications tool
- Understanding the different applications of events:

  o Corporate communications: meetings, conferences, and employee events
  o Publicity, marketing and sales: conventions/exhibitions, trade shows, and experiential/brand marketing events
  o Hospitality: client/staff entertaining, and incentive/ reward programs
  o Fundraising/education: charitable, political, and educational events
  o Entertainment/leisure: fairs, festivals, public, and sporting events
  o Celebrations: special events, parties, and weddings

- The role of an event planner: pre-event, onsite, and post-event responsibilities

2. Business and Finance

- Financial management: forecasting income and expenditure, fixed v variable costs, profit and loss, cash flow, quotes, purchase orders, invoices, receipts, taxes, and return on investment (ROI)
- Contracts: negotiation, typical industry clauses, cancellation and liability issues

3. Project Management

- Key stages of project management: strategy, planning, executing, monitoring and controlling, and closing
- Identifying objectives, audience, stakeholders, deliverables, and evaluation methods
- Feasibility studies, SWOT analysis, strategic decision making, problem solving, and contingency planning

- Project plans, budget management, critical paths, time management and reporting systems, resources, and procurement
- Monitoring, change control, and evaluation

4. Event Management

- Client account management, pitches and proposals
- Venue hire, site inspections, spatial design, layout, flow, floor plans, and ancillary services: power, sanitation, waste/recycling, heating/cooling, tents, and telecoms/internet
- Managing group travel, accommodation, and destination management services
- Vendor/supplier sourcing and management
- Food and beverage planning
- Design and production: audio, video/projection, lighting, staging, rigging, scenery, décor, furniture/equipment rentals
- Entertainment/speaker/artist management, technical requirements, and riders
- Staff selection, management, delegation, and briefing
- Logistics, transportation, shipping, load-in, build and de-rig management
- Managing onsite check-in, parking, transport, security, and first aid/emergency services

5. Legal, Health and Safety

- Event safety
- Risk assessment and method statements
- Emergency response plans
- Types of insurance; personal injury, property, cancellation, supplier etc.
- Licensing, permits, use of public highway, and noise pollution
- Confidentiality, copyright and trademark considerations

6. Marketing and Technology

- Event marketing, promotion, communication materials, invitations, pre-event registration, and databases
- Integrating digital, social media and mobile apps
- Applying new technologies
- Photography, video, and usage issues

Unfortunately, most of the event-planning courses I have seen advertised tend to focus only on the topics listed in the Event Management section above—and even then many of these are either absent or not broken down into sufficient detail. If you're going to invest time and money studying, you really need to ensure that not only are all of the topics listed under Event Management covered, but that the course also includes those listed under Business and Finance, Project Management, and Legal, Health and Safety, and at least some from the Marketing and Technology section. Employers will be looking for you to demonstrate an awareness of these topics. Don't be tempted to take a course because the topics look more fun to study. If you wanted to train as a chef, you wouldn't take a course that only taught you how to bake and decorate pretty cupcakes, would you?

• Depth of Study

One thing that concerns me about event-planning courses is the depth to which topics are covered. I would suggest you contact any course provider and ask for a breakdown of how long is devoted to each topic. That way you can compare how much time is devoted to soft topics versus the more important ones. You should also get them to define the depth of each topic too; are they intended as 'An Introduction to…..' If so, ask them to explain exactly what you'll be able to do by then end of the module. For example, if there is a module on health and safety, will they simply introduce the various components or will you be able to conduct your own risk assessment paperwork by the end of the module? Personally, I would recommend you grill them for detailed information on each topic in the program, before you part with your money.

- ## Starting Your Own Event-Planning Business

The other red flag to be wary of is when a course provider implies that taking their course will enable you to start up your own event-planning business. It's simply inconceivable that someone can take a quick event-planning course then start up their own business, without having first worked in the industry for several years. Chances are you'll just end up with a nice website and some business cards, but no clients. If a course dedicates entire modules to starting your own event-planning business, I would really question how well they understand the industry. You will not need this type of information for at least 3-5 years, by which point what you've be taught might be out of date. In all likelihood, you'll probably learn all you need to know by working for other event companies throughout your career. When schools try to sell this type of information to beginners, it makes me question the credibility of the course-provider and whether they are just out to make a quick buck.

- ## Work Placements/Internships

One of the most important elements any event-planning course should offer is some form of work placement or internship with reputable companies in the industry. So much about training to become an event planner comes down to experience, so it's vital that there are opportunities to put the classroom theory into practice in the real world. If you are paying for an event-planning course, you really ought to expect them to provide some of these opportunities. A good school will recognize the importance of this and it will form part of the course anyway. It will also be a testament to the reputation of the school if they have good links with the industry. If they don't offer work placement opportunities, you have to ask yourself, why not? Do employers in the industry not consider their training credible? Or are they just interested in selling you a course, with no real concern for whether you get work afterwards?

"If you're going to do an event management degree, I would strongly recommend that you pick a four-year course that includes a one year work placement, rather than a standard three-year course. This industry is all about experience and if you come out of college after three years having organized virtually no events, then you're not going to be that much better off than someone who did a marketing or business degree. Often, those placements are quite good jobs, so that experience means you come out of college with a massive advantage."

Liz Sinclair, Managing Director, ESP Recruitment

- ## Caliber of Teaching Staff/Author of Course

The caliber of the teaching staff should also be considered. Research their credentials and biography; where, when, and in what capacity they have worked in the industry. Have they achieved a significant level of experience/success in their own career, prior to teaching? Crucially, is the tutor still working in the industry or do they teach full-time? This is quite a key point. Because of new technologies, coupled with the rise of experiential marketing, the event industry has been constantly evolving and procedures and practices continue to change at a rapid pace. If a tutor hasn't worked in the industry recently, how well placed are they going to be to teach about it? Of course, in the case of unaccredited courses, the credentials of the person who authored the course are even more important.

"You often find that the people who teach those courses just don't have the vast industry experience and knowledge. They're not the people

who are actually out there and working in the business at the moment. So is that really who you want to be taught by?"

Martin Turner, former Global Head of Events for Credit Suisse

• The School's Teaching Environment/Premises

This factor is relevant if it is a for-profit school. The size and type of premises can give you a good clue as to how established, credible, and professional a school is. Many for-profit schools operate out of office suites, which, for me, re-enforces the fact that they are actually a business whose primary motivating factor is to make money. That's not to say that every for-profit school operating out of an office suite is untrustworthy. However, for me, it's a red flag and a warning to evaluate all the other factors mentioned in this section before parting with any money. Nowadays, anyone can set up a business, call it a school or academy, and start offering courses. You need to research further to ensure that the quality of education being provided by that business is of a high standard.

Similarly, you need to scrutinize a for-profit school's website, read it objectively, and learn how to distinguish between facts and 'sales speak' to ensure you don't misinterpret their credentials. For example, a school may hire rooms from a well-known college or university in order to provide their courses in a classroom environment—perhaps at evenings/weekends. That doesn't necessarily mean that the course is endorsed by or affiliated with that college or university—it could just be a venue for hire.

• Endorsements

Look to see whether a course has any significant endorsements; these might be from leading figures in the industry or professional associations. For example, if a course were endorsed by ILEA (International Live Event Association) then that would certainly add to their credibility.

Similarly, look for any testimonials on their website from reputable employers that might have taken students on work placements. I remember being impressed by one course that had a testimonial from a leading experiential agency claiming that eight out of 10 work placement students from the course went on to paid employment with them—which is a great testament to their training.

The other thing to look for is testimonials from former students—but make sure you scrutinize these. Look for testimonials that talk about what they went on to do, rather than ones that just say how much they enjoyed the course or how nice the tutors were. However, be wary of testimonials that don't list the person's full name as these can often be fake; for example, it might say it's from 'Mary S, Brooklyn.' The whole point of someone providing a testimonial is to put his or her name to something as an endorsement. I would even go so far as to say that even if full names are mentioned, you should still type a few of the names into LinkedIn or Google to check they are genuine and see what they are up to now.

For more information on courses, see this book's companion website at: www.eventplanningcourses.org

My Route into the Industry

Starting in Travel

From working in a hardware store, to running global meetings and incentive travel programs

Martin Turner, former Global Head of Events, Credit Suisse

Martin got his first opportunity, which would eventually lead to a very successful career in events, while working in a hardware store in Sydney, Australia. Having taken night-classes to study for a diploma in Travel and Tourism, he was talking to a customer in the hardware store one day and discovered that he was the owner of one of the most important travel companies in Sydney. *"I said to him, I hope you don't might be asking but I've just completed my Travel and Tourism diploma and I wondered if you would allow me to work in one of your travel agencies on Saturdays for free."* Appreciating the fact that Martin was prepared to work for free in order to gain experience, the man gave Martin his card and told him to call.

"You always have to look for opportunity. Don't ever be afraid to ask, because the answer is either yes or no—and it might very well be yes—so give it a shot."

As Martin's job in the hardware store was only from Monday to Friday, he ended up working every Saturday at the travel agency for a month. Perhaps somewhat cheekily, Martin had specifically asked if he could work in their premier location in a shopping center within the MLC Center, a large skyscraper surrounded by designer shops and business customers. He knew that location would attract all the high-end customers so that was where he wanted to be. Loving the work, at the end of the first month Martin decided to take a week's holiday from the hardware store and use this to work full-time at the travel agency, for free. While working there Martin made sure he was proactive and tried to learn as much as he could, to the point where the staff at the agency commented that he behaved as if he'd worked in the industry for years.

"I then started applying for jobs. I always knew I wouldn't be able to get a job without experience, so I got experience doing it for free on weekends and using holiday time—while still earning a living from my job at the hardware store."

This is a great example of how, if you want it badly enough, you'll find a way to get experience while still holding down a regular job to pay your living expenses. I've often heard people complain that they can't afford to work for free because they still have to pay the bills. But, like Martin, if you're driven enough to succeed you'll be prepared to sacrifice your weekends and holidays to get the necessary experience to move forward.

Martin then landed his first job as an international travel consultant at a travel agency specializing in group bookings. At the time, the incentive travel sector of the events industry wasn't even defined as such. These type of events and programs were just handled by travel agencies that specialized in group bookings.

"You might say it was sheer chance that I went to work for a travel agency that specialized in groups, but I don't really believe in luck. For me, luck is talent meets opportunity."

Martin remembers getting that first paying job because his employer had been impressed that he had studied for his diploma in the evenings, while holding down a day job, and that he'd gone out and found unpaid work in order to get experience.

Being able to demonstrate commitment is key to impressing employers when you're in the early stages of your career and have little experience.

The very first task Martin was given in his new job was to make all the arrangements for a group of 15 doctors who were travelling to a brain institute in Sweden. This involved organizing all their travel, accommodation, and transport.

"15 people might not sound very much but you can imagine if it's your first job, it's still quite daunting; you're thinking 'what am I going to do? Am I doing this right?' But I think that's one of the key tests about whether you're the right type of person to work in events; is it instinctively part of your nature to figure out what you've got to do and get on with it? Or are you the kind of person who has to be told?"

During his three years with the company, Martin was able to get involved with organizing all the tour programs; putting together their brochures, writing the copy, arranging flights, accommodation and ground transport, and even private-chartering a jumbo jet. From there he progressed to escorting tours, where he would actually go with the group to various destinations throughout Asia, the United States, and Europe to manage the entire program onsite.

"Escorting tours was a great introduction to working onsite at events because I had to manage several coach-loads of people. I'd make sure they all got from the airport to the hotel and checked in, and then I'd make sure they all got their ski hire or whatever else the leisure activities involved. The great thing about this business is that no matter what job you do onsite you're always learning another skill. All these things add up to a vast knowledge bank of what it means to charter a coach, organize ski equipment for 50 people, make sure everybody has a hotel room, or is insured. You're constantly learning to plan, manage, and learn how to deal with different things."

After three years, Martin moved on to a corporate travel agency, which introduced him to business and first class travel. Realizing that he had experience with groups, his new employer assigned him to conferences and incentive programs. At the time, these were not taxed and so were often very lavish and over the top, involving the creation of dream travel experiences for large groups of people. For example, it might involve taking 120 car dealers to Hawaii for a week and creating a phenomenal program of events, activities, and excursions—where there is something extraordinary happening every day and night for the entire week. During this time, he built up his knowledge and contacts by dealing with different hotels, airline reps, and transportation companies.

From there, he decided he wanted more experience working for a large corporate and so took a job with American Express as a senior international travel consultant in one of their corporate travel branches responsible for business travel, groups, incentives, and conferences. The branch he worked at was in the same building as Australia's St George Bank, and within a year, Martin and his team had succeeded in winning all of the bank's incentive travel and conference business. After several years organizing events and programs for St George, the bank approached Martin to come and work for it directly, and so at the age of 28 he became Director of Travel for St George Bank with a staff of 55 and five offices to manage.

"This was another example of talent meets opportunity. When I went to work for American Express, they put me in the branch that they were intending to close; they said to me 'we just want you to prop it up for a while.' Well I did far more than just prop it up; I went out and won that branch a huge amount of corporate business from St George, and by working so closely with them I ended up creating my next career opportunity."

Following St George, Martin spent the next four-and-a-half years as Director of Incentives and Conferences for The International Travel Group; the number three company for incentive travel in Australia. This gave him the opportunity to work on car launches, for clients such as Toyota, Suzuki, and Citroen, and to create programs based around sporting events, such as rugby tours, the America's Cup yacht race, and the 1996 Olympic Games in Atlanta.

From there, Martin decided to move back to the United Kingdom, where he was born, and turned up without a job to go to.

"I came to the United Kingdom with the vast amount of experience, but I went from being a big fish in a little pond to basically being a gnat in a lake. I knew a few people, but professionally nobody knew me here. I was very aware that I was booting myself back to base one again. I had no idea what was going to happen to me; I didn't even know what agencies to contact. So I literally picked up a copy of Campaign magazine, the marketing journal, and landed my first job with the number one incentive travel company in the United Kingdom. But I went from being Director of Incentives and Conference in a large organization in Australia, to suddenly being just one of the account managers; which was a real lesson in humility. But if an opportunity comes your way you've got to know when to just shut your mouth and take it."

This is a great example of how, in events, you have to be prepared to do anything. Even if an opportunity might seem more junior a position than you'd like, or the role is not quite what you were looking for, just take it to get your foot in the door. Once you're in you can always work your way up—which is so much easier to do from the inside.

Over the next year, Martin worked on as many programs and events as he could in order to build up a huge network of contacts, before deciding that he really wanted to be living and working more centrally in London. Once again, he picked up a copy of Campaign magazine and came across a listing for a recruitment consultant who shared his last name, and decided to turn up at her office without an appointment.

"You have to be proactive, and sometimes you've just got to have the balls to do something. I knocked on her office door and said 'I know this is very rude of me to just turn up without an appointment, but I wondered if there might be any possibility that

I could see Moira Wilson-Turner?' Fortunately for me she very kindly gave me some of her time, looked at my resume and started to go through various positions that were available. I just told her 'I really don't care what it is, I just need a job.'"

Through Moira, Martin went to interview for a six-week freelance position as logistics support on the *Vauxhall* car account at *Jack Morton*; who were initially concerned that he was far too overqualified for the freelance role.

"I said to the lady who would be my boss 'I will get your coffee, I will pick up your dry cleaning, I don't mind what I have to do, I'll do it and I'll do it really well—I just need somebody to give me a break.' And she did."

Fortunately for Martin, he was able to make a big first impression on his very first day.

"I'm sitting at my desk and the phone rings, and I'm really nervous because I'm not quite sure what I'm doing and I don't even know how to transfer a call. I pick up the phone and the person says 'is that Martin? Can you come along to the meeting room'? So off I went to this meeting room and I walked in and thought 'what the hell is going on here?' It was full of very important people, and a couple of people who I assumed were directors of the company, and they said 'oh Martin welcome, I know it's just your first day but we wanted you in here on this. We're pitching for Cadillac's business and I know there's been no time to brief you but feel free to join in.' I assumed they'd asked me in because they knew I'd worked on car accounts in the past, for brands like Toyota. I sat there and listened, and then they started asking me what I thought, so I talked about what I knew and contributed some ideas. The meeting went really well and everyone seemed to like what I'd said, then later that afternoon I got another call asking me who I was. I said, 'I'm Martin Turner; I'm a freelancer, I just started today.' It turned out there was a new event producer called Martin that had also started that day, and that was who they thought they had called into the meeting. But by then I'd already made an impression with lots of senior people, so my six-week contract

kept getting extended and I ended up working with all different types of clients."

Again, Martin's story is testament to the fact that once you get your foot in the door, that's your opportunity to go all out and demonstrate what you can do. Admittedly, the opportunity Martin had was sheer chance. But knowing him personally, I've no doubt that he would have found other ways to show them what he could contribute during his initial six-week contract—and that's the key take-home message I want to underline; as soon as you get an opportunity, even if it's only unpaid work experience, make sure you over-deliver and exceed expectations.

After a while, Martin was offered the position of European Head of Logistics at Jack Morton, which he decided to turn down.

"I think it's really important to be aware of your limitations. Whilst I had years of experience back in Australia, I'd only been in the United Kingdom for a year and three months. And while I had amassed lots of contacts in the industry here, I didn't feel I had the depth of experience in this particular sector of events yet. I just thought to myself 'I could set myself up to fail if I take this. I'm just not sure I'm ready yet.' So I said to them 'I think at this stage I'd make a much better number two, so if you're going to hire someone for this position, I'd love to be their deputy. I think they really respected that."

One of the clients Martin got to work with while at Jack Morton was the investment bank Credit Suisse, who at the time outsourced all their events. When their account director at Jack Morton left, Credit Suisse specifically requested that Martin take over the running of their account. Within two months of working on the account, the Global Head of Events for Credit Suisse, who was based in New York, invited him to lunch. At their lunch, they got on extremely well and she confided in Martin that it was proving very stressful for her to oversee all the events in Europe from her office in New York, which involved flying members of her team over because there were only three people in the UK events team. By the end of the lunch, she asked if he'd be prepared to come and work for them in-house to run the London office.

"I said to her 'you do realize I've never worked in investment banking?' At that time, I'd never even looked at the Financial Times; I didn't know an equity from a bond or anything. But she said 'you know what? We just really love working with you, and that's more important."

Often, if you're good at what you do and you get on well with people, they'll be quite happy to overlook the fact that you might not have the exact experience they're looking for—as long as they know you have the core skills to do the job. I can't stress enough how important personality is in the event industry. People hire people they think they'll get on well with, and this can very often tip the balance in your favor.

Martin was initially hired as Head of Events UK, but two weeks in, he decided to prepare a report to present to his boss, the Global Head of Events and her boss, the Head of Corporate Services.

"I realized that it was impossible to run their events business professionally the way it was currently being done. So I went in with a report that said 'this is what's wrong with your business. I've been here for two weeks; I've met with these managing directors, the three existing events staff, and all the people in advertising. I've done my due diligence; this is what's wrong with your business, this is what you need to do to fix it, and this is the minimum amount of staff you need to hire to do this properly.' I also made it clear that if they weren't going to hire enough staff, I wouldn't be staying. Fortunately they signed off on the extra head count right there."

Shortly afterwards Martin was promoted to Head of Events for Europe, Middle East and Asia and then to Global Head, to include Americas and Asia Pacific. Since then, Martin has worked for other banks such as UBS, Lehman Brothers, and Barclays Capital.

14

The Attitude You Need and the Approach You Must Take

At the beginning of your career, when you don't have a vast amount of experience to draw upon, the level of success you'll have will largely be dependent on your attitude and approach.

Show Me Why I Need You

I'll admit that, as an employer who regularly receives emails and calls asking for work, I slightly resent the passive 'please give me a job' approach I'm typically presented with. Most people that send in their resume on spec are not offering me anything that I don't already have. For the most part, they're under-qualified and seeking an opportunity to better themselves. Which is fine, I understand that. I've been in their place. However, what 99.9 percent of people approaching me for a job fail to do is to show me why *I* need *them*. If you're looking for a job in events, you really need to view from the employer's perspective and show them what you can bring to the table. What can you add to their business that will help them deliver their events?

The first thing you should do is to approach your job search assuming that employer's don't want or need you. If that's your starting point, what are you now going to do to prove that an employer does need you or should want you? How are you going to show them that you can add some value to their current set-up? Can you bring a useful skill to their events—such as languages, design/drawing skills, or first aid? Do you have strong customer-service skills and are you presentable, confident, and well-spoken enough to work in a client-facing role onsite? Do you have useful knowledge and/or insights into a particular demographic, client, sector, geographical location, or technology that is relevant to their clients and events? Can you demonstrate examples of where you've excelled at thinking on your feet and finding solutions to unexpected problems while working onsite? Or are you simply volunteering your time for free to give them an extra set of hands in the run up to a big event? Most event companies are small businesses, so committing to a salary and hiring someone is quite a big deal. When there is a genuine need to hire someone, there are often plenty of candidates to choose from. So what are you going to offer them that will make you stand out?

When I went for the fundraising jobs early in my career, I spent a long time planning and brainstorming beforehand so that I could go in armed with a long list of ideas to pitch to them. Ideas that would, potentially, make them money. So, rather than just going in and asking them to give me a job, I went in and showed them what I could do for them. Adopting this type of mind-set is particularly important at the beginning of your career, when you probably won't have sufficient experience to sell yourself based on experience alone. Fortunately, in the events industry, you can apply this attitude very easily when working onsite. Do something that will benefit a potential employer onsite at one of their events; it's a great way to get noticed and will help you to get your foot in the door. From there, you'll be perfectly placed to network for more opportunities. I'll look at this approach in more detail in Chapter 19 "How to Get Onsite Experience."

Be Proactive

Unfortunately, most jobseekers are stuck on autopilot; sitting behind a computer and blindly sending out resumes hoping to find work. Nowadays, it's hard enough securing a job this way even when you're applying for an advertised vacancy and you're super-qualified, because there's just so much competition.

Therefore, you can imagine how unlikely it is that you'll find a job—or even unpaid work experience—this way if you're just applying on spec and with little experience. In fact, it's highly unlikely this approach will result in any opportunities—paid or unpaid. Why? Because it's just too passive.

You have to be proactive. And that means doing more than just applying for advertised jobs—that's just a given. Being proactive means making your own opportunities, not just waiting for someone else to hand you one. Early in my career when I decided I wanted to write for a magazine—despite having no writing experience—I just took myself off to the cinema and theatre, paying for a ticket in the normal way, to review some shows so that I had examples of my writing. I then took these to the magazine's arts editor and offered to work unpaid, reviewing all the small fringe shows on the outskirts of town that he didn't want to go to. I created an opportunity for myself by being proactive and then pitching the idea to him in a way that made his life easier, without any costs implications. I highlighted the benefits to him. I showed him what *I* could do for *him*.

Find Your Unfair Advantage

As I'll explain in more detail in Chapter 17 "Networking, Contacts, and Relationships", a great deal of hiring in the event industry is relationship-based and relies on recommendations and referrals. *"A friend of a friend knows someone who works in events at Apple, I'll introduce you."* Or, *"I worked with this girl on X event who was amazing—great fun to work with—let's see if she's available to work on Y event too."* Recently, a friend of mine who works in events for a major TV company posted a message on Facebook asking her friends if they could recommend someone for an entry-level event co-ordinator role. The position didn't even get advertised.

The reality is people want to work with people they already know, or that come recommended by someone they know. So an introduction or connection, however vague, will often give you an advantage. Therefore, it's important to get out there, meet people, and start developing relationships

Now, having contacts and networking doesn't mean you have to come from a privileged background or have friends in high places. But you do need to be incredibly strategic; sit down and examine your social circles to see who knows whom, and then ask them to introduce you. Nowadays, with LinkedIn and Facebook it's much easier to see who your friends and family know that might be useful to you. Find your unfair advantage and exploit it. That one connection or introduction you unearth is likely to be more valuable than sending out 1,000 resumes to complete strangers.

"I met a friend's niece recently. She had been speaking to her uncle and saying that she wanted to get into events. He said, 'my friend does that, why don't you speak to her?' So she sent me a text message saying, 'you know my uncle Andrew, I hope you don't think this is presumptuous but would you consider having a coffee with me as I'd love to pick your brains about getting into events?' It's often as simple as that. Just asking around to see who might know someone; people at parties, friends of your parents, friends of friends—everyone."

Charlotte Saynor, former Vice President of Brands & Events, Fremantle Media Enterprises, and Head of European Events, Apple

When I decided I wanted to work in charity events, I asked around and one of my friends knew someone who worked at a charity. My friend asked his friend if he'd meet me for a quick coffee so I could pick his brains and ask some advice. By the end of the conversation, he'd told me to send over my resume. Within a few weeks, I'd been called in for an interview and they hired me. Would I have got my foot in the door without the introduction from that friend of a friend? Probably not.

Be Humble

In the early stages of your career, you really have to be prepared to do anything to get your foot in the door. If you have the opportunity to work on an event, or for an event company, in any capacity, then take it. It doesn't matter if you're a toilet attendant, a steward, a waiter, or the office filing assistant, it will get you in the right environment to meet people and make contacts. You might be working minimum wage (or even unpaid), putting in long hours doing a job you're not particularly interested in, but the real value in that opportunity is that you'll be on the inside. You won't be sitting at home emailing resumes to anonymous names and receiving no reply. You'll be inside the event or company, meeting and working for the very people who can advance your career.

"They've just got to be willing to get stuck in, be keen and enthusiastic, and be happy to do the mundane tasks—all with a smile, even when they are exhausted! If they can do that, then they'll make a good impression."

Charlotte Saynor, former Vice President of Brands & Events,
Fremantle Media Enterprises, and Head of European Events, Apple

Once you're on the inside, in whatever capacity, you can seek out relevant contacts, introduce yourself, and put a face to a name. It's so much easier to work your way up from within than it is to break in from the outside. I took that approach by taking a job entering classified ads at a magazine. After I'd worked there a while and got to know people, I asked if I could do some writing for them. As they already knew me, it was much easier for me to approach them. Compare that to if I had approached them cold from outside the organization asking to write for them, without any writing experience. Do you think I would have even got a reply?

It's the same in events. If someone I've never met, with little or no experience, sends me a resume asking for work experience, the chances are I'm probably going to ignore that email—simply because I haven't got the time to invest in every stranger that approaches me asking for help. However, if one of the waiters, who regularly works on my events, approaches me, explains that he's keen to get into event planning, and asks to volunteer on some future events as an extra pair of hands, then I'm more likely to go out of my way to help him. Because he's not a stranger, he already works for me—albeit indirectly—and he's right there in front of me asking for help. He's being proactive, and I know he's serious and committed because he's already working in the industry on one of the bottom rungs of the ladder (and believe me, being a waiter at events is hard, physical work where you are on your feet for ten hours straight with people either ignoring you or being rude). Be humble, take any job to get your foot in the door, and then leverage the opportunity to work your way up or create further opportunities for yourself.

Over-Deliver

One of the easiest ways you can stand out to an employer is to over-deliver and exceed expectations—which is another reason to be humble and take any opportunity on offer. If you go in at a low level and over-deliver, it's much easier to shine because you'll be exceeding expectations.

When I went for the job at the first charity, which turned out to be a street-collecting position, I actually went in and pitched other fundraising ideas to them. That showed initiative, over and above what they were looking for, so I stood out from the other people applying to be street collectors, and was given more opportunities. Similarly, I've hired hostesses to work the front desk at events and, on occasion, when their shift was finished, some of them have offered to stick around and help out with the rest of the event—even though they wouldn't be paid any extra—just to be helpful. I can tell you, as an employer, I always remember those staff and will always try to book them again. Now, imagine if one of those hostesses came to me, after going beyond the call of duty at my events, and told me she was trying to get into event planning. Of course, I'm going to be much more likely to help her, or at least keep her in mind next time we're hiring, because she has gone out of her way to help me. You should always be looking to go that extra mile and do something that isn't expected of you. It will be noticed, and you will stand out. If you keep standing out you'll develop a reputation as someone hardworking and committed who shows initiative. That's the type of person employers want to hire.

Inconvenience Yourself

One of the complaints I hear a lot is that it's hard to get experience—which usually involves doing unpaid work—at the same time as holding down a regular job to pay the bills. I appreciate it can be hard to juggle the two, but the cold harsh truth is that you've just got to inconvenience yourself and do whatever it takes. If you want it badly enough you'll find a way to make it work. Whether it's holding down several jobs at once, sofa-surfing to save money on rent, or giving up your evenings and weekends for a while—it just requires a bit of effort. Many of us have been there and done it too, so it's almost expected that you'll just have to work a little harder during the early stages of your career when you're trying to break into the industry.

When I first got into charity events, I was only being paid for two days a week and, as you'd expect from a charity, the pay was very low. I was entirely self-supportive at the time, living with roommates in central London, with no financial assistance from family. So I took a part-time office admin job for a couple of days a week in addition to a bar job in the evenings and weekends. For about six months, I held down three different jobs. I'd finish work at the charity around 6pm, jump on my bike and cycle to my bar job on the other side of London where I'd work until 2am, then I'd be up and at my office admin job by 9am the next day. I was completely exhausted and had no social life, but after a while, I was hired full-time at the charity to do events. Now, that six months of hard work looks like a very small price to pay for ending up with a full-time job in events that kick-started my entire career.

To be frank, if you aren't prepared to do something like that at the beginning of your career, then events is probably not the right industry for you. A job in events involves long anti-social hours, where you're exhausted from running around for 15 hours straight, and are then expected to be up early the following day to clear up onsite. So, if you have to hold down several jobs for a few months just to get the necessary experience, consider it event-planning boot camp—you'll be really well prepared for the realities of the job when you do make it.

Finally, probably the most important thing I can tell you as an employer is:

Don't Tell Me, Show Me

It's not enough to say you're 'passionate' about events. Since shows like *X Factor* and *American Idol*, where hundreds of thousands of people beg for a chance because they're *'really passionate'* or they *'really want it'*, those phrases have lost all meaning. If you're passionate about events, you need to *show* me. What have you gone out and done that demonstrates how passionate you are about events? It's all too easy to *say* you're passionate about working in events, but often a quick glance at your resume will tell a different story.

There's a whole range of opportunities available to work in support roles in the events industry that anyone can go out and get—both paid and unpaid—that you don't need prior experience for. It might be working as a cater-waiter, host/ess, promotional staff, event steward, usher, hotel banqueting staff, crew, valet parking attendant, or charity volunteer. This type of experience should then be combined with some volunteer event-planning experience, be that on university, charity, or family and friends' events. On their own, each of these things doesn't count for very much in the way of experience. But combined, they speak volumes. If someone just starting out listed on their resume that they'd organized three university events, volunteered on two charity events, been a steward at several public events/festivals, worked as a cater-waiter at ten corporate/social events, and been a host/ess or crew on another five events, that would show me they are serious about a career in events. It would demonstrate that they are dedicated and driven. That they're not afraid of hard work, or too proud to work from the ground up. It would also show me they have a good insight into how an event actually runs behind the scenes, because they've not only seen it from the inside, but from several different perspectives. All of that counts for so much more than just telling me you're passionate about events.

"It's not the best paid industry, so it's important that you're passionate about it. Getting involved in events in a volunteer capacity or in support roles really shows an employer that you're serious about the industry."

Liz Sinclair, Managing Director, ESP Recruitment

As mentioned in previous chapters, employers are typically far more interested in the skills and personal qualities of an event planner, rather than their qualifications. While skills can generally be developed, many of the personal qualities that make a successful event planner tend to be innate—you either have them or you don't. They define how you think, operate, and respond—particularly onsite. In the next two chapters, I'll discuss the skills and qualities that employers will be looking for evidence of, both on your resume and in an interview. It's imperative you that you cite specific examples from your experience that will demonstrate these. Remember, show, don't tell.

15

The Personal Qualities That Employers Are Looking for in You

You remember the character of Monica, played by Courtney Cox, in *Friends*? She:

- Was a self-confessed control freak,
- Anally retentive,
- And an obsessive compulsive, who....
- Alphabetized her CD collection.
- Insisted on rules and order (even when playing party games).
- Loved keeping everything clean, tidy and in the correct order.
- Indexed, color-coded, and cross-referenced her recipe cards.
- Sorted her towels into 11 different categories including everyday, fancy, guest, and fancy guest.
- Had mapped out her entire wedding arrangements by age eight and documented everything in a manual. With swatches.
- Used a label maker on everything—including her coffee cups.
- Hectored party guests not to just put lids back on felt tip pens, but to push the lids on 'until you hear the little click.'
- Knew the exact position of every piece of furniture in her apartment and could instantly tell if something had been moved an inch from its usual position.
- Insisted on working in military time when planning Phoebe's wedding, while wearing a walkie-talkie headset.
- Instructed friends to hold photographs by the edges.
- Could never just let anything go.

Well, she's your archetypal event planner.

Control Freak

Most good event planners will recognize, and freely admit to being—to some degree—a control freak. Event planners never leave anything to chance and never assume something will happen just because someone said it would. They instinctively monitor, repeatedly check, and generally exhibit behavior that most people would regard as borderline obsessive compulsive— while always keeping a Plan B up their sleeves; just in case. If you recognize those qualities in yourself, then congratulations, you're a natural event planner. If that doesn't sound like you, then you're probably in the wrong job. Chances are the person employing you will share these qualities, so they'll be looking for them in you.

"I often say to people in an interview, 'if you're going away for a weekend with friends, can you tell me what happens?', and so many people are really slow to respond, or they say lame things like, 'oh well, we usually go out for dinner, or we'll be camping.' But I'm looking for the person who says, 'oh my God! I have to organize everything, which just drives everyone else nuts. I have to know what time the trains are going, I have to tell everybody what to pack, and I need to know where we are staying...' If someone says that sort of thing to me, I'm instantly like, 'ahhhhhh yes! I like you', and the reason I do is you're a member of OCD club—of which I'm the President!' I need to know that it's intrinsically part of your nature to be organized, and that you need to be because otherwise it would drive you nuts. Candidates need to find ways to demonstrate those personal qualities. It could be anything that they drop into a conversation that gives me an insight into the way they approach things. Tell me about your wardrobe if need be; that the hangers all have to face the same way and everything is color-coded. If I hear that sort of stuff, it's great. It might sound crazy, but this job is all about detail—so I need to hire people who are naturally meticulous."

Martin Turner, former Global Head of Events for Credit Suisse

Of course, an event planner must also be able to delegate; they can't run the entire event themselves—even though most would probably prefer to. Don't forget to demonstrate that skill too!

Detail-Oriented

Being detail-oriented is essential in event planning—and it's typically something you either are or aren't. Event planners have to be extremely careful and precise—most are positively anally retentive! It really has to be an intrinsic part of your nature if you're going to work in this business. We've all heard horror stories about someone preparing a budget in Excel and not noticing that—because of an error in the formula—some of the columns haven't added up every item. Only finding out later, after the budget has been signed off, that the real costs add up to a lot more than is shown in the budget. Cue awkward conversation with the client where the planner has to admit their incompetence. Which in turn prompts the client to think, *'how is this person going to organize my event when they can't even get a basic spreadsheet right?'* As an event planner, you've got to have an amazing eye for detail so that nothing gets past you. And even if it does, because you're the type of organized person that double and triple checks everything, you find out straight away before any damage is done.

What's ironic however, is the amount of candidates who cite 'attention to detail' as a relevant skill and then send in a resume littered with spelling mistakes, punctuation issues, and random capitalizations. Typos and errors on a resume are frowned upon by everyone. However, in events, where one of the essential skills is being detail-oriented, it's inexcusable. A simple typo or error in an event budget or contract can cost your employer a lot of money. Almost every contributor I spoke to for this book said that if a resume has typos in it, it goes straight in the bin. Which might sound harsh, but really, how can we take you seriously for a role that requires you to be organized and detail-oriented if you can't even send in a resume without errors? And this is when you're trying to impress us. How sloppy are you going to be when no one is looking?

In an interview, highlight specific examples of when disaster was avoided as a result of your innate attention to detail.

Leadership Qualities

"In events, you're not selling a tangible product so you have to be able to develop rapport with a client, establish credibility, and get them to trust your opinions and interpret their needs and desires."

Christopher Lee, CEO, ACCESS Destination Services

To be an event planner, you have to demonstrate leadership qualities. Often, it's about selling yourself. An employer or client needs to be convinced that you can take on and run their event (or a particular part of it). To do that you need to come across as confident, knowledgeable, and in control. But remember, confidence has to be backed up by knowledge or experience—otherwise it's just cockiness. If you don't have very much experience to draw upon, then you absolutely must make up for that with knowledge.

Confidence also needs to be combined with a sense of calm. In my experience, people who are genuinely confident and sure of themselves are usually *quietly* confident. There's no need for any big display of swagger. The calmer you are, the more confident and in control you appear. Which is what an employer is looking for in an event planner.

You'll also need to have a strong character and demonstrate how you can motivate and manage clients, colleagues, and suppliers a like. You can't be too sensitive either, because under time constraints you've got to be able to get things done and just give or take instructions. You also can't show your emotions if you're tired and struggling with things. At some point you're going to have someone shouting at you because something isn't right, so you've got to be able to cope with that and not go to pieces or take offence. Events tend to be quite emotional; clients sometimes get very highly-strung, overwhelmed, or panicked. As the event planner, everyone will be looking to you to solve problems. You also might have to tell someone off—a supplier or member of staff—so you need to have the strength of character to be able to do that without just shouting at them.

Team Player

"At George P. Johnson, the really important thing is the fit. Obviously, we want to make sure a candidate can do the job, but the key thing is whether they are going to fit in—with the team and the culture at GPJ— because it is a very team-orientated place. It's very collaborative and we all work very well together, so we're always careful about bringing people in to ensure they fit in with the company."

Nicola Mosley, HR Manager, George P. Johnson

Don't underestimate how much hiring is done based on someone's personality and attitude. It can sound like a cliché to talk about the need to be a team player, but it's particularly relevant for the events industry. You need a team to make an event work, whether it's an internal team of planners, designers, and logistics staff, or an external team made up of suppliers, support staff, and crew. Therefore, an event planner not only has to demonstrate leadership qualities, but also work well with others and function as part of a team. A team player is dependable and reliable, actively participates, listens to others, and shares. They're the type of person who co-operates, pitches in, and finds solutions. They are committed, enthusiastic, positive, and perhaps most importantly, respectful and supportive of others.

Employers will want to see evidence of those characteristics. So, when you're interviewing, go out of your way to show how you worked effectively as part of a team. How did you share the responsibilities and support others? In particular, show examples of where you 'mucked in' and took on tasks that weren't your responsibility, just to help others and get the job done.

"When they talk about their experience, I want to hear what they've done both on their own, and also as part of a team—because so much of our job is about what we create together, so I want to see how they work with others. I definitely listen out for examples of that."

Chad Hudson, President, Chad Hudson Events

Humility and Flexibility

"You really must have a 'can-do' attitude. It's long hours, it's knackering, your feet are hurting from running around all day, and suddenly you're being asked to run to the shops in the rain to buy something pretty mundane. You've got to be able to smile, do it willingly, and not get grumpy or pouty. You need to put your game-face on and show that you're happy to be there and that you'll turn your hand to anything. It may be that I need you to go around the room, pick up all the conference materials, and put them in a confidentiality bag—because someone has to do that. I might need you to clear all the dirty coffee cups away because the caterers haven't done it and we've got senior managers about to arrive. You've got to be flexible, willing, and able—and do it all with a smile on your face."

Sharyn Scott, Global Head of Events, Linklaters

One of the biggest problems for employers is that candidates who are new to the industry typically don't want to do the rubbish jobs. Especially if they've been to college or university, they typically want to dive straight into planning events themselves. So it's usually a bit of a shock for them when they're assigned lesser support roles, and they typically make their disappointment known. I remember having a work experience candidate once, and we took her to work onsite at Elton John's *White Tie & Tiara Ball*—which is a high-profile event for a candidate to put on their resume. Onsite, the set-build encountered some problems and was running behind. Guests were starting to arrive, but in the dining tent, there was still a huge pile of sawdust, chippings, and rubble on the floor where the crew had been working. My team was busy checking in guests at the main entrance so one of them asked the work experience girl to sweep the floor. She literally rolled her eyes and reluctantly sulked off in search of a broom, moving at a glacial pace, and spent the next 10 minutes half-heartedly pushing the broom around and making sulky faces to let it be known that she didn't really want to do be doing that. What was frustrating was that, at that moment in time, sweeping the floor was an incredibly important job that just needed to be done—and done quickly—yet she acted like a princess. There wasn't time for her to make a statement about how menial she thought the task was. Events are about team work and getting the job done, even when you have to do something you don't really fancy doing; something that might typically be done by someone lower down the chain. In that brief moment, I knew that she wasn't right to work for my company. As an employer, I just don't need that kind of attitude, so she ruined any chance she might have had about being offered any paid employment in the future.

Part of being a team player is recognizing that even the menial jobs contribute to the overall success of the event. You must be flexible, muck in, and just do whatever needs doing. Things change in event planning all the time, both onsite and in the planning stage, so you've got to be the type of person who can adapt and just get on with it—without any fuss. You might have been assigned a particular role, but then you get pulled off that to do something more menial. Be flexible and roll with it.

This job will require you to do menial jobs at times, and you need to get used to that right at the beginning—because you'll still be expected to do menial things 10, 20 or 30 years into your career. It's by doing these jobs when you're new, and doing them well, with enthusiasm and a smile on your face, that will get you noticed. Once you get noticed and get a reputation for being 'up for anything', I guarantee you will be given more and more responsibility and you'll start to work your way up. But if you have an attitude about certain jobs, as employers, we'll just write you off as difficult and won't bother inviting you back. We're just too busy to deal with divas.

"One of things I expect from every candidate is a passion, attitude, and willingness to do anything that it takes to get the work done."

Dori Rodriguez, Sr. HR Associate, Jack Morton Worldwide

Resourcefulness

"I've had interns where I've given them something to do and they don't really apply any initiative; I have to spell it out to them, and by the time you finish explaining it all you might as well have done it yourself. They've really got to employ some intelligence and remember that events are not rocket science; it's mainly just common sense. So you just need to employ that common sense and get on with finding out the information."

Martin Turner, former Global Head of Events for Credit Suisse

Often with event planning, you'll find yourself having to do things you've never done before. Whether it's logistical problems, such as getting heavy equipment into a venue in Venice, Italy, with no access by road, or creative challenges such as how to create a canal using real water inside a tent—and then get all the water back out the next day. Event planning is all about problem solving. And as no two jobs are the same, that means you'll often find yourself out of your comfort zone and having to learn new things. When you're confronted with those situations, you need to be the type of person who can just dive straight in, grab the bull by the horns, and figure out how to make it happen. Demonstrate that 'can do' attitude.

When an employer gives you something to do, we're expecting you to think on your feet and take the initiate to find a solution. Hit the web to do some research or pick up the phone to a supplier and ask them for help. It doesn't matter if you don't know what the solution is, what matters is that you take on the responsibility of finding a solution. Your employer may not know how to do it themselves, and the reason they're asking you is because they need someone to go out and research how to do it. Either way, an employer or client is looking to delegate certain things to an event planner, so you've got to be the type of person that can just pick things up and run with them.

I remember the first time my company worked in the South of France for the Cannes Film Festival, and I asked one of my team to look into affordable hotels for our crew. During the festival, getting around can be difficult; roads are closed, parking is non-existent and all the nearby hotels are fully booked. When this member of my team realized we wouldn't be able to get a hotel nearby, instead of just coming back and telling me this, she researched alternative options with military-like precision. She found a couple of hotels outside of Cannes and worked out an entire plan for how we would travel back and forth each day. Not knowing my budget, she researched options for mini-bus hire, taxis, and bus routes, listed all departure times, estimated journey times, found somewhere to park our lorry, and even enquired about passes with the local town hall so that we could get access through some of the road closures in order to load-in. She laid out all the options clearly in a spreadsheet for me, along with her recommendations, and then brought it to me to review. It took me just a couple of minutes to scan her research and decide which option to go with. Needless to say, I was extremely impressed.

It's similar when working onsite. Employers are looking for planners who can think on their feet, react to problems, and use their initiative or creative thinking to find solutions—especially when under pressure. Be sure to highlight specific examples that demonstrate these qualities, both onsite and during the planning.

Accountability

Accountability goes hand in hand with resourcefulness. Not only do we want you to show initiative and find solutions to problems, we also want you to take ownership of them. That means being 100 percent responsible for a task, seeing it through from beginning to end, and making provisions for a 'Plan B' in case something were to go wrong.

Onsite at most events, the lead planner will be supported by a sub-team of other co-ordinators, assistants, and support staff. Usually each member of the sub-team will be assigned a specific area of the event to run, such as food and beverage, transport, or registration. The lead planner is expecting members of the sub-team to take ownership of their area of the event. This means making all the necessary decisions on their behalf in order for it to run autonomously, with little or no involvement from them. It's essential that the lead planner can rely on their team to oversee their respective areas of the event.

It's the same during the office-based planning stages of the event. If something is delegated to an assistant planner, they need to take full ownership of it and not be bothering the lead planner for their constant input—otherwise they might as well do it themselves. Being accountable means understanding that the buck stops with you and being prepared with a back-up plan. If something goes wrong with that area of the event, it's your problem to sort. Or, at the very least, to come with a list of possible solutions for the lead planner to make a final call on.

Drive and Ambition

"We definitely look for someone that shows drive and ambition—people that are hungry to achieve. You'll see someone's drive, passion, and enthusiasm from his or her resume, where they've taken the initiative and used their spare time to get as much experience as they can within the industry. They haven't just sat back and done a course, they're doing whatever they can to maximize their experience. That shows someone who's got passion. That experience could be onsite experience as crew, organizing college and charity events, or even leading a team up Kilimanjaro; it doesn't even have to be related to experiential, just evidence that someone's gone that extra mile and organized a group or the logistics surrounding a trip. It still demonstrates the core skills and shows drive and ambition."

Fiona Lawlor, HR Director, Jack Morton London and Dubai

The hiring process is not just about talent and ability. Personality, drive, ambition, and hard work play a big part too. The effort you have—or haven't—made prior to getting into the interview room will speak volumes to an employer. If I think back to my route into the industry, I made my own opportunities first by doing volunteer fundraising, and then by creating my own charity events at London Lighthouse. The success of one of those events, which I put together myself from scratch, led to an interview with Elton John's people to produce an event for his charity. Now, was I the most talented or best-qualified event planner available to Elton John at that time? Absolutely not, I was still leaning. However, I impressed them by being proactive, showing initiative and drive, making things happen, and being tenacious. That's very different from saying 'please give me a job because I'm passionate about events.' I *showed* them what I could do by getting on and doing it.

Street-Smart

"The good thing about going to university is that it demonstrates independence. Whereas, if you're still living at home with your parents, you might be less worldly-wise and, to do this job well, you do need to be a bit street-wise and savvy. If you've never lived away from home and you're suddenly being sent on a plane to a foreign country to run an event for 500 executives, you're going to be like a rabbit in the headlights—you're not going to cope."

Sharyn Scott, Global Head of Events, Linklaters

It's pretty much a given that employers want smart, intelligent people working for them. However, in a job like event planning, it's often not about academic intelligence. To work onsite at events, let alone run them, you need to demonstrate that you are street-smart and savvy; that you can handle yourself in all situations. It's an intangible quality, a mix of being confident, independent, informed, instinctive, astute, and having strength of character. If you're young, it might be assumed that you are naïve. So be mindful of how your personal circumstances could work against you—especially if you haven't lived away from home before. If need be, go out of your way to demonstrate how you've handled yourself in demanding situations, demonstrated independence, or taken control of a situation.

16

The Skills That Employers Are Looking for You to Demonstrate

"It's very much a people business, so communication and personality are very important, but time management and organization are equally important. I always say it takes a unique person to be successful in the events industry, because often people are very strong on communication and personality, but may lack organization skills. Alternatively, they may be strong in organization, but lack personality and communication skills. In my experience, people that are successful in events have a unique blend of both."

Christopher Lee, CEO, ACCESS Destination Services

In this chapter, I'll discuss the core skills that are essential for anybody intending to work as an event planner. Many of these skills can be taught in books, courses, classes, and online video tutorials, or developed through practice while learning 'on the job'. If you're lacking in any of these skills, show some initiative and take a few classes. Then practice on your own until you are fluent. For a list of courses, classes, and online video tutorials available, visit this book's other companion website at www.eventplanningcourses.org

The other thing to bear in mind is that, while employers are looking for you to demonstrate these core skills, it doesn't mean you have to cite experience from events. Many of these skills are transferable from other professions. What's important is that you demonstrate evidence of them—regardless of the situation.

Organizational Skills

"You've got to be super-organized. Time management and project management skills are really important and you've got to be really organized in your own life too. You might have 10 events running at any one time and you've got to be able to juggle all of those. You should be able to demonstrate that you've committed to several simultaneous projects and found a way to juggle them and make sure they all work."

Charlotte Saynor, former Vice President of Brands & Events, Fremantle Media Enterprises, and Head of European Events, Apple

Obviously, it's a given that an event planner has to be organized. If this doesn't come naturally to you, you can develop these skills by utilizing tools and following procedures. Many people coming into the industry often underestimate the sheer amount of paperwork that's involved in planning: timelines, critical paths, schedules, itineraries, spreadsheets, lists, reports, presentations, databases, and briefing documents. These are the tools you need to use in order to show potential employers that you are organized. They're looking for you to demonstrate how you work in a methodical way; that you have a system, follow a series of steps, and document everything.

However, being organized is about more than just paperwork. It's about your mind-set; being able to strategically think and plan ahead of yourself. It's about having an understanding of how everything fits together in a project plan or timeline. It's realizing that 'X' needs to happen before 'Y' can happen, or that if 'A' doesn't happen then it's going to have a knock-on effect with 'B.' When you're interviewing with an employer, you must be able to demonstrate an awareness of that 'domino effect' and discuss the steps you take, and the tools you use, to manage that process.

"If you say you're really organized, tell me how you can prove that. We ask that of all candidates."

Nathan Homan, Co-founder, Rouge Events

Communication Skills

One of the most important qualities employers are looking for are good communication skills. How you present yourself, in terms of both your appearance and manner, is key. Speaking to the various contributors to this book, the words that came up again and again to describe what they were looking for in a candidate were: confident, articulate, eloquent, calm, coherent, succinct, well turned out, professional, the ability to engage, and a good communicator. So much of an event planner's success depends on how effectively and efficiently they can communicate their thoughts, ideas and instructions; whether that's when presenting to clients, or briefing staff and suppliers.

"I want to see that you look professional and that you're confident— because if I'm buying you, then I know someone else will buy you. In events, it's often about selling yourself, because you're selling an idea to a client and you're selling your ability to run that event. I need to have confidence that you're going to be able to deliver."

Sharyn Scott, Global Head of Events, Linklaters

If you're not naturally a confident and articulate person who can speak and present well, then the best advice I can give you is to go on a short presentation skills course. It's a relatively small investment in yourself, in terms of time and money, but it will help you enormously, not only in your job search, but also once in work.

People Skills

"It's essential to demonstrate your people skills. Those front-of-house skills are so important when dealing with the CEO, celebrity presenters, or even guests. But you've also got to be able to build relationships and work well with your crew and suppliers; to persuade the person doing the rigging on your exhibition stand to work late to help you get finished on time, or to motivate your team to go the extra mile to make an event

a success. Good people skills are what set people apart in this industry."

Charlotte Saynor, former Vice President of Brands & Events, Fremantle Media Enterprises, and Head of European Events, Apple

In the previous chapter, I touched upon the role that a candidate's personality and attitude plays in the hiring process, in terms of being a team player. People skills are really an extension of that; it's the ability to communicate effectively with people at all levels.

Employers will be looking to see how well you speak to, and treat, people. If you're bossy, aggressive, arrogant, or rude, or your management style involves shouting orders, then people just won't want to work with you. It's perhaps easier to grasp the idea that you have to be polite and courteous to people above you in the food chain, but often people forget to do that to the people below. If you look down on the sweaty, burly, manual laborer installing your temporary toilets, he will pick up on that. You'll be communicating it non-verbally without even realizing. But what would happen to your event if he decided not to install the toilets 30 minutes before it starts because he thinks you've been rude to him?

Events are about teamwork and everyone has a part to play, no matter how small. When people are new to the industry and start managing suppliers, they can sometimes get caught up in thinking that, because they are paying the suppliers, they get to tell them what to do. But remember, as an event planner you need your suppliers in order to do your job, so it's important that you treat them as an extension of your team and speak to them as an equal. More often than not it will be you having to ask them for help and favors onsite at an event; something you didn't plan for and now need urgently, or something you want changed at the last minute. Do you think they're going to go out of their way to help you if you've been bossy, unfriendly, or short with them?

"If I'm going to hire event support staff, I don't necessary even look for them to have event experience. It's more about having great customer-service skills. It might be that they worked at a retail store for a few years

while in college. That experience can give you an understanding of whether they are personable. Are they ready to speak to people and attend to their needs? They're the people I want. It's about being presentable, well spoken, looking people in the eye, and smiling. If you have those skills, regardless of the industry, highlight them."

Bill Jones, Vice President, Managing Director, Events, The Channel Company, formerly UBM Tech Channel

Similarly, it's equally important to have highly developed 'front-of-house' people skills with the guests at your event. Being able to turn on a smile, proactively greet people, make eye contact or polite small talk, and generally be welcoming and enthusiastic, is also a skill you need—one that employers will most definitely be looking for. We've all been greeted at restaurants or airport check-in desks by disinterested staff; the ones who don't smile, don't make eye contact, sigh, and roll their eyes when you ask for something. The ones who are perhaps chatting to their colleagues in between serving you, or just seem bored by the whole encounter. It just leaves you feeling annoyed and frustrated. A lot of junior event planners and support staff forget that events are a form of hospitality. They spend so much time behind the scenes planning an event, that when they get onsite they forget to switch into front-of-house mode. Onsite, there will be many times when you'll find yourself in a customer-service role. Just like a good waiter in a restaurant or friendly shop assistant, you'll be the face of the event as far as the guests are concerned, so it's important to develop these skills.

Project Management

"There are lots of ways to demonstrate project management; it doesn't necessarily have to be event management. It doesn't even have to be events—it could be amateur dramatics or sports tours."

Nathan Homan, Co-founder, Rouge Events

Project management is the essence of event planning. Whether you're planning a wedding, a corporate meeting, or an experiential roadshow, they all involve the same processes that come under the five stages of project management:

Initiating

This involves determining the nature and scope of the project, identifying objectives, audience, stakeholders, deliverables, evaluation methods, and a cost-benefit analysis. In event planning, much of this stage is developed in conjunction with the client/host in order to create the initial brief that both parties will work from.

Strategy and Planning

This stage is typically the processes an event planner will go through in order to respond to the brief with a proposal. This involves research and a feasibility study, strategic planning, creating a project plan detailing time, cost and resources, time management systems; schedules and critical paths, budget management, reporting systems, risk analysis, contingency planning, and problem solving.

Execution

The next phase is the execution/production stage; when the project plan has been approved by the client/host and the planner begins to execute the tasks contained in it. This involves co-ordinating people and resources, procurement, the production of deliverables, the distribution of information, and managing stakeholder expectations.

Monitoring and Control

Often this phase takes place simultaneously with the execution stage, and involves observing the execution in order to correct any problems, measuring the on-going activities (i.e. 'where we are'), monitoring the variables (cost, effort, scope) against the project plan ('where we should be'), and identifying corrective actions to address issues and risks ('how can get on track again').

Closing

Post-event, this stage would include administrative activities, such as archiving files, reviewing and documenting lessons learned, budget reconciliation, completing and settling contracts, project review and evaluation: target/actual, return on investment, and reporting to stakeholders

Note: Don't be intimidated by some of these terms if they're not familiar to you—they are just formal ways to describe the procedures that most event planner naturally employ. Research these terms and make sure you understand what they are and how they relate to the event-planning experience you have. Ensure that you understand the processes in each stage sufficiently so you can speak about them in a fluent and coherent manner when describing your experience in an interview situation.

Employers will be looking for you to demonstrate how you've applied this process to a project. Remember that project management skills are transferable, so you don't have to demonstrate them through event-planning experience. One of the contributors to this book, Sharyn Scott, is the Global Head of Events for the international law firm Linklaters. However, she got into the events industry from a background in project management. In her 'My Route into the Industry' case study, page 167, she explains how her first job at *Christian Dior* was supply chain management, which was followed by a job with a corporate relocations company. Sharyn used the skills she obtained in project management, planning, and logistics in both of those jobs to get her first job in the events industry—without any previous event-planning experience. It was the core skills that were important; that's what employers are looking for.

If you don't have very much event-planning experience, think about how you can demonstrate project management skills from the experience you do have in other fields.

Time Management

"I want to see evidence of organizational skills and time management, because we're sometimes working on 10 or 12 events at a time, so you've got to be able to juggle those and be able to switch from a Super Bowl party to a 40th birthday party or a wedding. You need to show me you can switch gears and jump from one project to another and be able to focus on multiple jobs at the same time."

Chad Hudson, President, Chad Hudson Events

Time management is really just one element of project management. However, along with budget management, it is one of the most important skills required for event planning. Employers will be looking for evidence that you can plan and manage your time effectively and efficiently. This means not only explaining the processes you go through and the tools you adopt—such as timelines, schedules and critical paths—but also that you can effectively handle a number of different projects at the same time. Multi-tasking is key in event planning so you need to show evidence of that.

"I want to see evidence of how you manage your time, I don't really mind how. Tell me how you had to train for a particular sporting event while sitting your A levels or finals at university, or how you would commute into central London to temp at an insurance firm while volunteering for a charity event in the evenings. Maybe you'd get in from work at 7pm then work on the charity event at night, or maybe you used your time on the train to send emails for the charity event. That's the great thing about events; there are so many transferable skills involved. It's down to you to communicate how those transfer from your own experience. It doesn't matter how unrelated or basic the examples might seem, just spell it out to me."

Charlotte Saynor, former Vice President of Brands & Events, Fremantle Media Enterprises, and Head of European Events, Apple

Budget Management

Budget management is about more than just putting numbers into a spreadsheet. In order to put together a meaningful budget you often have to walk through the entire event in your mind, visualizing it from start to finish, and considering every possibility. Adding a cost in the budget for item X might actually have a knock on effect resulting in another related cost for item Y. For example:

- If you've budgeted for staff, how are you feeding them? How are they getting home? What are they wearing? Is there a changing room onsite—does it lock? Do we need to hire rails and hangers or mirrors for the changing room?

- How are your trucks going to unload at the venue? Do you have to pay the council to suspend the parking bays outside? What happens to the trucks after they load in? Do you need to pay to put them in a car park for the duration of the event?

- If there is leftover alcohol after the event, is there a lockable room onsite to store it overnight? Have you allowed money in the budget for someone to collect it the next day? If there are lots of cases leftover, is the delivery driver prepared to lift them all or do you need to budget for crew to be onsite to help load everything into the van?

Certain costs will need to be estimated, for example, drinks are often based on actual consumption on the night. Therefore, have you estimated allowances accurately so that your budget is likely to reflect the actual bill post-event? Then you have to budget for contingencies: how much will we have to pay if a tray of glasses gets dropped? Or there are cigarette burns or stains to table linen? Often a caterer will provide a menu price based on a minimum number of guests, say $70 per head x 500 guests. However, if your numbers drop to 400, it's a very possible that the price of your menu will actually increase, to say, $75 per head.

Finally, there's monitoring. The event budget prepared at the beginning of the project is likely to be very different from the actual final budget post-event. Every time a change is made to an aspect of the event, it's going to have a knock-on effect with costs. Have you allowed enough wiggle room in your initial costs for minor changes? When a more significant change happens, say to the design of the set, have you obtained a new written quote from the supplier, updated the budget, and had the new costs signed off by the client in writing?

You need to demonstrate to a potential employer that you fully understand the potential issues surrounding budgets, and that you can manage the entire process from start to finish. That means when discussing budget management in an interview, you need to be specific and explain how the budget changed over the course of the project, and what you did to manage those changes.

Negotiation Skills

The job of an event planner is filled with day-to-day negotiations, from agreeing permission with venues and city officials over the use of space, access, and timings, to dealing with staff and suppliers regarding deadlines and responsibilities. Success in these areas will largely depend on the strength of your people skills, as mentioned previously. However, the ability to negotiate contracts is also an important skill for an event planner to master.

First, you need to be able to negotiate the best prices from your suppliers. That might include trade discounts, commissions, off-peak prices, or group rates. A lot of the time you have to be proactive and ask for these; a supplier may not offer them of their own accord. You have to be the type of person who is confident enough to haggle, in order to get the best possible deal for your employer and/or client.

You also need to show that you understand the importance of having all negotiations, and their outcomes, documented in writing. If you only get a verbal quote or agreement from a supplier, then later they forget the price they gave you and try to charge you more, you'll probably have no recourse. Having a paper trail for everything is essential.

Then there are terms and conditions, which might need re-negotiating. Any supplier you work with is going to provide you with a quote for its services. These quotes will come with a list of terms and conditions which are often pages long, hidden at the back of the proposal, and usually in a tiny font—hence the proverbial small print; probably to discourage you from reading them. Unfortunately for an event planner, it's your job to read and understand all these clauses, for each and every supplier, every time you do a job—because sometimes they will change without anyone drawing your attention to the changes. It's essential, before accepting a quote, that you understand exactly what you are committing to, and, where necessary, can negotiate terms. There are many contract-related issues you have to consider, such as:

- How long are the prices valid for?
- What are the payment terms?
- What deadlines need to be met?
- What are the supplier's responsibilities and are these clearly defined?
- Is there an exact description of the product or service being provided that mentions all the specifications you are expecting? Or is the description open to interpretation?
- What are the cancellation terms?
- What happens if there is a natural disaster preventing the contract being fulfilled?
- Who is liable for what if something goes wrong?
- What is their level of insurance cover? Have you see proof of this?
- Under which country's jurisdiction would legal action be taken? (Particularly relevant for overseas events).

Don't feel intimidated by this if it's all new to you. Just take some time to familiarize yourself with the issues surrounding contracts if you really want to stand out and impress an employer. They won't necessarily be expecting you to be proficient, but if you can show a basic understanding, with examples of where you've negotiated on price and/or terms, you'll be streets ahead of the competition.

Numerical, Written and Visualization Skills

"You have to be good with numbers, not just math, but being able to look at a room and judge how many people will fit in it, seated or standing. Or being able to judge measurements and distances; so if the stage is going to be 20ft deep, how much is that going to encroach on the available floor space? How tall is the ceiling? Is there enough room for the planned décor? It's the fundamentals of numbers, math, and geometry that all come into play regularly."

Christopher Lee, CEO, ACCESS Destination Services

Much of event planning involves being able to visualize how things are going to look, fit, and operate on the day. You need to be able to look at an empty room (or sometimes just a plot of land) and visualize how best to use that space—from both the guests' and supplier's perspectives. You've got to be able to visualize the entire experience; in terms of access, load in, front and back of house space, layout, flow, convenience, safety, sightlines, décor, hanging space, power, set build, staging, and technical requirements. It's quite a skill to be able to look at an empty plot and imagine the exact layout of a tent that needs to accommodate 1,000 people for a seated dinner, complete with space for a reception, stage, and elaborate set design.

Good numerical skills are also essential in event planning, not only for budgets, but also to judge quantities and space. Having an understanding of fractions is important; if you're allowing two-thirds of a bottle of wine per person, how many cases do you need for 350 people? Or if there's approximately six glasses of champagne in one bottle, how many cases do you need to order to cater for 500 guests over a three-hour reception? Percentages come into play all the time too. If you're holding 674 hotel rooms, and the contract stipulates that you can only cancel up to 5 percent by a certain date and all unused rooms will be charged at 80 percent of revenue, would you be able to work out where you stand? Can you read a scale drawing of a set design, where the scale is 1:200 at A1, and understand what the measurements are in reality? Can you work out what size dancefloor is needed for 350 people? Can you look at a room and know whether there's enough space to hold all your guests?

Good numerical skills are imperative, and you need to demonstrate how you can apply these right across the board—whether it's budget calculations, judging quantities, or the use of space. Cite examples and be specific.

"Once, an intern we took on had her own blog. She's really into food and baking so she writes about that on a blog and keeps it updated regularly. That shows commitment, resourcefulness, and drive. OK, so it's not completely relevant to event planning, but we happened to be doing events for Jamie Oliver at the time so it chimed quite well with that. Also, just the fact that she did that off her own back demonstrates effort and ownership of a project, which I liked. It also showed me she had good writing skills and could present information well, which you always need for pitches. She actually became my go-to person when we were putting together pitch documents and I needed her to source images or write copy, because she just got it from a visual and presentation point of view. Little things like that can all help demonstrate your skill set."

Nathan Homan, Co-founder, Rouge Events

Written and presentation skills are equally as important as numerical ones. A great deal of the job involves presenting, briefing, and reporting—both internally, to colleagues or management, and externally, to clients. How clear, succinct, and creative you are at communicating your ideas or instructions in writing will have a huge impact on your success—not only with an event, but also in your relationships with clients, suppliers, and colleagues. In terms of pitches, how well you communicate your ideas can be the difference between winning a job or not. This, of course, is similar to the interview process. Which is why employers are going to scrutinize the way you communicate your experience and skills—starting with your resume. You really need to use every point on your resume as an opportunity to highlight a relevant skill and communicate as much as possible about yourself in a clear and succinct way. If you don't, you're already failing at one of the core skills an employer is looking for.

Problem Solving/Lateral Thinking

"Being able to demonstrate that you can think laterally in order to problem solve, is probably the number one thing I look for in a candidate. If you freeze when something goes wrong then you're not going to get on in events. You need to be the type of person who thinks 'OK, something's gone wrong, I need to think my way out of this—how am I going to take control and resolve whatever's gone wrong?"

Sharyn Scott, Global Head of Events, Linklaters

Being able to problem solve is perhaps one of the most important skills an event planner can have. This applies to every stage of the event-planning process, whether that's deciding how to stage the event when responding to the initial brief, or dealing with something that's unexpectedly gone wrong onsite. Often, when staging an event, solutions are found by approaching the problem from a different perspective. Sometimes it's about taking an indirect or creative approach involving a less obvious, traditional, or logical thought process. For example:

- When I organized the launch of the TV show *My Babysitter's a Vampire* at MIPCOM in Cannes, the client wanted the event to have a high-school prom theme. The traditional approach would have been to hire a venue and dress it to look like a prom, but the event didn't have a very big budget to allow for theming. So instead, we scouted a real high-school gymnasium in the center of Cannes and managed to negotiate a deal to hold the event there. This made our budget go much further and gave the event a far more authentic look and feel.

- When organizing Elvis Costello and Diana Krall's wedding in a tent, the dining room was to be revealed after the ceremony by pushing on a section of wall to reveal a secret door. As it was in a tent and we were working from floorplans only, it wasn't obvious to suppliers that the secret door couldn't be used until after the reveal. This meant that no one realized until a few hours before that there was no direct route from the kitchens to the reception room, for staff to serve pre-dinner hors d'oeuvre, without revealing the secret door. So, thinking quickly, the area intended for use as the cloakroom was quickly re-purposed as a satellite kitchen—complete with a mini oven, grill and fryer—and the caterers managed to prepare a mix of hot and cold hors d'oeuvre from a tiny cupboard.

- For one of Elton John's *White Tie & Tiara Balls* we were giving away a brand new Audi car as a raffle prize. To do this, we needed to distribute a small envelope to every guest mid-way through the dinner. However, to create a buzz we wanted to ensure everybody would open their envelope at the same time, so we couldn't just have the envelopes sitting on the table throughout dinner. Instead, we stuck each guest's envelope under their seat before they arrived, then at a specific point during dinner the host instructed guests to look under their seats to find out if they'd won the car. It was a simple creative solution to a logistical problem.

Problem solving and lateral thinking are skills employed throughout the event-planning process. Be sure to demonstrate these with specific examples from your experience. In particular, highlight occasions where you've had to respond to something or improvise onsite, so that an employer can see how you are able to think on your feet under pressure.

"As with most jobs the applicant will need to be able to multi-task but in events this is especially important, as is the ability to think on your feet

and problem-solve quickly when the need arises. Invariably, no matter how meticulous you have been at ensuring everything has been checked, double checked and triple-checked, something unexpected will come up on the day of the event, it's how you deal with it that's important."

Farida Haqiqi, former Events Manager, The British Red Cross

Creativity

"As a company we are very ideas-led, and we deliberately target creative individuals because we believe that everyone in the company should have an input into the creative process. At the end of the day, it's the big idea that sells and that's what makes us successful. Whether you end up in technical, logistics or production you need to have a creative way of thinking. If you're in logistics, you need to be able to think about unique venues, or if you're in technical you need to be interested in keeping ahead of trends and new technology, so that when the creative director comes to you with an amazing idea you can deliver it and be creative from a technical point of view. Of course you still have to have the organizational skills, attention to detail and all those other core skills, but now we want people who are bright and creative in addition to that."

Fiona Lawlor, HR Director, Jack Morton London and Dubai

Creativity is, without doubt, an important skill for an event planner. However, there's a reason I've left it until last. That's because without all the other basic core skills, it's useless. Most employers are looking for strong event planners—who are also creative. Meaning that first and foremost they want you to have project management skills, be organized and detail-oriented, resourceful and accountable, a problem solver, and a good negotiator. They want you to have excellent people skills, be able to communicate well, and demonstrate good presentation, numerical, visualization, and written skills. Then on top of that, they also want you to be creative. It's the cherry on top of the cake, but you've got to offer them the cake first.

Many young, enthusiastic candidates get blindsided by the creative side of events. However, creativity in events is about more than just being able to decorate a room, style a table, or design an invitation. It's about finding creative ways to communicate a very specific brand/corporate message in order to achieve certain objectives; be it media coverage, increased sales, or an improved customer experience. All of which has to be measured to demonstrate both tangible and intangible results. Therefore, all the creative aspects of an event must serve a purpose.

When a candidate goes into an interview, firstly it's important that they don't just lead with how creative they are. If you come in talking about how you love the creative side of events, an employer is likely to roll their eyes and think you have no idea what the job actually involves. Most employers will be quite happy to hire someone who can demonstrate the core project management skills but who isn't perhaps that creative. However, no employer is going to hire someone as an event planner who's really creative, but doesn't have the necessary project management skills. So, demonstrate those first, then go on to show your creative skills.

Secondly, when you do talk about your creative skills, don't just talk about the surface level aspects—the styling and décor, the food and the entertainment. Instead, relate everything back to the business objectives. Show how the creative choices you made were strategic and what they achieved. For example, you might have worked on a long-running annual charity event that had become a little tired, and so attendance numbers were in decline. You could then explain how you decided to replace the traditional printed invitations with digital ones sent by email, which incorporated animation and sound, and how that resulted in a 30 percent increase in ticket sales. It's the way you use the creative aspects that an employer wants to hear about; show that you can think strategically and find creative solutions to meet specific objectives.

My Route into the Industry

Starting in Project Management

From sales promotions at Christian Dior, to Global Head of Events for an international law firm

Sharyn Scott, Global Head of Events, Linklaters

Sharyn got into the events industry by using her background in project management, which is a great example of how certain core skills that might have been learned in other jobs are transferable to event planning.

Her first job, age 21, was as part of the promotions team at Christian Dior where she was responsible for co-ordinating in-store sales promotions with various department stores. When a customer purchased a certain amount of Christian Dior products, they would receive a gift with the purchase, such as a make-up bag filled with that season's products. Although there was a small element of event organizing, where they might get all the sales staff for one particular chain of department stores together over champagne to give out the gift bags and set the sales targets, the majority of her work was supply chain management.

"It was quite a complex diary to plan; co-ordinating which company is making the gift, which other company then has to stick the Christian Dior logo badge on, and all the logistics of getting that gift into the right store on the right date—and you're dealing with thousands of items. That's where my grounding in logistical planning came in; being very detailed and focused on the minutia. I had to source the right suppliers to provide the gifts, but the company material inside 'might come from Paris, whereas the gift is being manufactured in the United Kingdom. Then the people who made the bag didn't necessarily make the logo badge to add to it. Then another company has to stuff the bags, before another company would distribute them. It was a project management

role really, and that's what I do now as an event planner; we're taking a group, working out the best way to deliver a brief, and looking at all the elements we need to get from A to B and on to Z."

After two years at Christian Dior, Sharyn took a project management job at a company called Move Plan, which involved co-ordinating large corporate relocations for clients such as the French bank Société Général and the UK Government's Department of Environment. These were often very complex logistical exercises moving up to 2,000 employees and all their furniture into new offices over six consecutive weekends, and involved liaising with building contractors, architects, office premises, space planners, and IT specialists—sometimes for up to one year in advance. It might seem like a jump to go from organizing sales promotions at Christian Dior to large corporate relocations, but actually, what's involved in the two jobs is really quite similar, and being able to demonstrate those project management skills using examples from her time at Christian Dior helped Sharyn get the job at Move Plan.

"I think it comes back to the core skills you need to demonstrate to do this job. When I think back about how I got that job; I was 23—quite young—and I didn't have a huge amount of experience. But it was very much about being able to think laterally and showing that I understood the domino effect; that is, if something happens, what's the knock on effect? It was about showing I was really organized by citing specific examples from my time at Dior, being super-aware of everything you're doing and the impact of that, and being able to speak to lots of different types of people with confidence—because a lot of the time you're selling yourself. They're buying your ability to deliver for them. Confidence was really important too. I had to stand in front of clients at Move Plan and give presentations to explain how the move was going to happen, so that had to come across in my original interview."

I can't emphasize enough the importance of confidence. Time after time, everyone I interviewed for this book brought up the issue of confidence and how, in the event industry, you really are selling yourself. An employer needs to feel comfortable knowing that you can take on the running of an event. To do that you have to come across as confident, calm, and in control. This all comes down to the strength of your communication, presentation, and people skills—which employers will be assessing you on based on how you conduct yourself in an interview. If need be, record yourself doing a presentation for a mock-interview then watch it back to see how you came across.

After four years at Move Plan, Sharyn moved on to what would be her first event-planning role, although interestingly, it wasn't advertised as such. It was another project management position, this time for a large travel company called Going Places, to co-ordinate their annual global conference for 1,200 people.

The previous year, the company had tried to organize the conference themselves internally. The event was held in Tenerife, in the Spanish Canary Islands, and they'd used their own admin staff and secretaries to handle all the cruise ship arrangements. Needless to say, things didn't go that smoothly and so it was decided that a project manager was needed for the following year.

"It was big numbers, big logistics, and lots of project management involved. I had to liaise with various destinations that were bidding to host the event, charter aircrafts, negotiate flight slots—there was lots of contracting and liaising with different suppliers."

Again, to get the job Sharyn had to demonstrate her skills in planning and logistics. It didn't matter that she didn't have event experience. She was able to show how the principals involved in corporate relocations, all the meticulous planning and organization, could easily be applied to event planning. That is what reassured Going Places that she was able to project manage a conference. Those core skills are what's important; that's what employers in the events industry are looking for. If you don't have much event experience, think about how you can demonstrate planning, organization, and logistical skills from the experience you do have.

Following the successful event, the company asked her to organize a party for 5,000 people with three months' notice, to celebrate their fifth anniversary. This involved setting up a satellite office where she had a team of people to manage different aspects of the event, such as delegate management, logistics, transport, AV, and production. *"I was very much learning on the job, I'd never booked a band before, didn't know what a green room was, or a rider."* Fortunately, she hired a fantastic production company to handle the technical elements and throughout the process became great friends with the owner. *"I learned an awful lot from him; spending time in the edit suite learning about PowerPoint, show production and all those elements. He taught me all about the technical production side of events and really helped me through all of that."*

Following the anniversary party, Going Places offered Sharyn a permanent position as their Event Manager, with a team of staff. What was interesting was that, at Going Places, there were opportunities for staff from other areas of the business to get involved in the event planning. Staff from the call centers and retail sites volunteered to come and work on the conference or party on secondment. *"Those volunteers gained some amazing experience. They got to travel overseas and help manage this massive beast of an event, which was hugely complex involving five or six hotels, a conference center, coaches, and flights. None of us were event professionals so it was a great learning experience."*

This is a great reminder not to overlook opportunities that might already be on your doorstep. You may work for a company that holds some events of its own. They might be organized internally at the head office, or they may hire an external person or agency to do it for them. Either way, it's much easier to volunteer and get experience via 'warm leads' than it is to go cold-calling. Consider what opportunities might be close to you; if not in the company you work for, then maybe at one that family and close friends work for. Use any and every contact you have.

After four years in her role as Event Manager at Going Places, Sharyn moved on to an agency that specialized in corporate conferences. After six months, she realized the role was too sales-based, whereas she enjoyed the logistics side of event planning, and so she moved on to work for the investment bank Credit Suisse as a freelance event planner. This marked the beginning of a six-year freelance career working for corporates such as Citibank, Barclays Capital, BNP Paribas and various agencies including one that specialized in pharmaceutical conferences, before finally taking up her current position as Global Head of Events for Linklaters.

"I was very keen to straddle both the corporate and agency sides of the industry. I realized early on that to work for an agency you need to have a very different mind-set to that of a corporate. Having gained most of my experience in corporate, I actually had a better offering for the agency side, because certain things that we did on an agency side weren't always as professional as the way you have to do things on a corporate level. I think that stood me in good stead and made me very sought after in the freelance market."

Having worked as an event planner in both a corporate environment and on the agency side, I whole-heartedly agree with Sharyn that it definitely pays to try both. Surprisingly, they are quite different experiences and so it will give you a well-rounded approach to the job. Both sides have things to learn from each other, so having experience in both can only make you more valuable to prospective employers.

Many event planners work freelance because the pay is often very good; you charge the client a day rate but you can sometimes end up working at the same place for anything from one to three months—or even up to a year sometimes. For Sharyn, the shorter contracts were a great test of her skills and gave her even more confidence. *"Those three-month contracts where you hit the ground running taught me that I could go in at any stage, pick up an event, and run with it. Although I was in and out of the office with luggage so much that I became known as the wheelie-bag girl; because I wasn't around long enough for people to learn my name!"*

17

Networking, Contacts and Relationships

"When you get even just your big toe in the door, forget about going out and socializing for at least a year. Instead, go to every single industry event that you come across. When I first went to industry events, I didn't know a soul and it was the hardest thing ever, but that's what you've got to do. It's all about networking. When you start getting to know people and seeing them regularly, next time they've got a six-week contract and they're looking for a freelancer to help, they'll look to their friends and acquaintances first. You've got to go out and do the legwork and meet people. Get out there, meet people, and get your face known."

Martin Turner, former Global Head of Events for Credit Suisse

Before you start seeking work experience, it's important that you understand how the events industry works in terms of hiring. I can't stress enough how much of the process comes down to networking, contacts, and personal relationships.

In so many cases, job opportunities—particularly work experience opportunities—don't even get advertised. Instead, positions are filled through introductions, recommendations, and referrals. This is because there are usually plenty of people with suitable experience to do the job. Therefore, the employer is looking for someone who can do the job *and* is going to fit in—someone who they 'click' with and want to work alongside, someone who they can trust.

To find someone on the same wavelength, the first thing an employer is going to do is think about who they already know, or ask around among their existing colleagues, friends, and contacts to see if anyone can recommend someone. Therefore, to put yourself in the running for the best opportunities, it's imperative that you develop a network of contacts from day one of your career.

What typically happens is that you'll work with someone onsite at an event, perhaps you're there as freelance support staff, or even work experience. You're pleasant, friendly, fun to work with, and get on with everyone. You stand out because you do your job well; you go beyond the call of duty, pull together as part of a team, and do whatever needs to be done to make the event a success. You bond over the long hours, the stress of the job, and support each other. You generally make an impression—for the right reasons—and so your colleagues, employer, or the client remembers you. You exchange contact details with everyone, follow up after the event, swap any photos, and keep in touch—perhaps via LinkedIn.

Then weeks, or months, later one of the other freelancers you worked with has been hired for an event and they need some more staff. She remembers you were good at your job and fun to work with. She has you on her LinkedIn network so she recommends you to her employers to work on the same event. Or maybe the client from the original event remembers the front desk staff being very smiley and chatting to delegates as they checked in, and so they ask the event organizers to see if they can book the same support staff as last time. Alternatively, the event planner you worked with on that original event has now landed the job of Head of Events at X company. She has a couple of permanent positions to fill and she remembers that you were such a team player, always doing more than was asked of you, so she drops you a line to see if you're interested. That's how hiring in the event industry works 90 percent of the time.

"Networking is important because there's so much competition in this business. If you've met someone in person and they're in a position to give you a job—even if it's further down the line—that's definitely going to give you a one-up on the next person who's also looking for a job.

This industry is all about who you know, so you've got to get out there and strike up relationships and make acquaintances."

Chad Hudson, President, Chad Hudson Events

Networking Online

"A lot of networking can be done by social media these days. LinkedIn is definitely a good start. There are lots of experiential and brand experience groups on LinkedIn, so people should join as many of those as possible and contribute to them. That will keep you abreast of what's going on in the industry, and you'll also be alerted to any jobs that come up."

Fiona Lawlor, HR Director, Jack Morton London and Dubai

You can also do some networking via social media—if you're clever about it. Don't just join online groups and straight away start approaching people asking them for opportunities. Instead, slow down and remember that it's all about relationship building. Get involved in online discussions, comment, reply, share, post questions, and build an online presence for yourself by interacting with others. Don't just charge in and start asking for jobs or work experience—people can spot the 'take, take, take' approach a mile away. As in real life, potential employers will want to know you a bit first, before they'll go out of their way to help you. So show them that you take an active interest, that you post and respond to questions in an intelligent way, and that you contribute rather than just take.

That said, online networking should only be done in addition to, not instead of, face-to-face networking. There's nothing better than meeting and working alongside someone to start building relationships. When I worked in events at the investment bank Credit Suisse, there were a couple of freelance support staff/ hostesses, Lisa and Julia, who stood out because they were always so friendly and attentive when dealing with guests. Then, behind the scenes, they were great fun to work with and always chipped in and offered to help with other areas of the event. I then left

Credit Suisse and went on to start my own event production company. When I needed some front desk staff for high-profile VIP events for celebrities such as Elton John and Kevin Spacey, the first people I thought of hiring were Lisa and Julia. I'd worked with them before so I knew they were hard working and professional, we all got on well, and they had the perfect manner when it came to dealing with clients and guests. So, instead of hiring staff from an agency in the usual way, I simply contacted them directly and booked them to work on some of my events.

Similarly, in the early days of setting up my own company, I continued to work freelance for Credit Suisse, and all the other freelance staff I worked with would often discuss and share contacts, or suggest other event companies, corporate clients, and staffing agencies that recruited freelancers. I was constantly being told that X company was looking for staff and that I should send Y person my resume. Often these were companies I'd never heard of, nor would I have come across if it weren't for one of the other freelancers introducing me to them. I remember freelancing on one event with a guy, and then several months later, he emailed me to say he was freelancing on the US Open; they were looking for some more staff and was I interested?

"Networking is really important. Join ILEA as a student member so you'll get notified of all the talks and industry events, then go to the trade shows and get chatting to people. We run an event called The Eventice, where event management students compete for a job. The final stages are held at International Confex and last year, in addition to the two candidates who won jobs, another two landed jobs as a result of the networking they did at Confex."

Liz Sinclair, Managing Director, ESP Recruitment

This is why it's imperative that you get out there and get work experience—however basic or 'bottom of the career ladder' it may seem. In doing so, you'll put yourself in an environment where you're going to meet people, make contacts, and let them see first-hand what you can do. There really is no point in sitting at home sending out impersonal resumes to people you've never met (most of which won't even be read) looking for jobs or work experience. Instead, take any event-related work you can get just to get yourself in the right environment to network and work your way up. These are opportunities of your own making. You don't need to have any existing contacts to get started, you just need to jump straight in at the bottom, take any event support role, do the job well—over and above what's expected—and start making contacts. It's those contacts you can then use to find your next opportunity. That's why it's so important that you treat every job or work experience opportunity as if it's the best opportunity in the world. Because every job, however basic, is an opportunity to show people what you can do; what your attitude is, what your manner is like, your work ethic, how well you work with other people. This is what people are going to remember when they're recruiting or recommending in the future.

Everything you do today affects the job opportunities that will come your way tomorrow.

"The alumni career network here in the United States is a great tool. Graduates give their names and information about what they're doing many years after graduation and offer to give advice to people who are interested in following in that field. So that's a great way to start building your network and hear about possible opportunities or get introductions. I get a lot of people from where I graduated approaching me in that way. People who enroll in the network are genuinely willing to help so it's a great networking tool."

Dori Rodriguez, Senior HR Associate, Jack Morton Worldwide

18

The Experience Employers Will Be Looking for on Your Resume

"I'm looking for someone who's demonstrated a commitment to learn about our industry; they've either done a certificate program, got relevant work experience, or they've volunteered. Don't just turn up from college or from a different profession saying you want to work in events. What have you done to prepare yourself to work in the events industry? If you haven't put the work in, then you're really asking me, as the employer, to take all the risk with our service and reputation on the line."

Christopher Lee, CEO, ACCESS Destination Services

When you're first starting out in the industry and looking for work experience or entry-level positions, an employer will want to see evidence of consistency, commitment, and drive on your resume. It's simply not good enough for a candidate to fall back on the excuse of *'I'm just getting into the industry so I don't have any experience yet.'* For an employer to give your resume even a second glance, you need to demonstrate to them that you are resourceful and proactive; that you've gone out and got a significant amount of experience—however basic—of your own accord. Don't *tell* them you want to get into events, *show* them— by the effort you've put it. You can demonstrate consistency, commitment, and drive on your resume with a combination of:

- Extra-curricular activities
- Onsite experience
- Office-based work experience

In this chapter, we'll look at extra-curricular activities.

"I would like to see that they've demonstrated a desire to do events at whatever level; at school, college, university, outside of work, or even within the company they're currently employed by. They might be in a job now that isn't event-specific, but they've volunteered to do the Christmas party, a board meeting, or perhaps delegate registration at the company's sales conference. I want to see they've been tenacious and demonstrated a desire to get as much experience as possible and have a willingness to learn."

Charlotte Saynor, former Vice President of Brands & Events, Fremantle Media Enterprises, and Head of European Events, Apple

Extra-Curricular Activities

"Candidates need to show what effort they've made via their extra-curricular activities. Alternatively, perhaps they've already had six months working in the industry, which would show that they have a real passion for continuing their career in it. It's all about demonstrating passion and enthusiasm."

Fiona Lawlor, HR Director, Jack Morton London and Dubai

How you use your free time outside of work or college is one of the key things an employer is going to scrutinize, because it speaks volumes about your level of commitment and drive. Employers aren't looking to hire people who've only done exactly what's expected of them and no more. We want to hire the people who've gone the extra mile, taken charge of their career, been proactive, and made things happen. For an employer, the clues to how driven and committed a candidate *really* is are often found by looking at what they do *in addition* to work or college.

"I like it when people are involved in a lot of different things; it could be things they do in their personal life, or if they're juggling multiple jobs and going to school, or that they still make time for community programs or charity work. If someone can manage their time, and is busy and involved in many different things, then that tells me a lot about them."

Chad Hudson, President, Chad Hudson Events

Student Events

"I want to see that they've made a lot of effort to get them to the point where they're even in the room with me. What effort have they made to prove to me that they want to get into events, by the experience they've already got? Unfortunately, it's no excuse to say I haven't got any. I spent three years working evenings, weekends, and holidays for £6.50 per hour while I was at university to get relevant event experience, so I expect others to make the effort too. I once hired an intern because her resume showed me that she'd been involved in so many different events while still at university. She hadn't just done one or two student events, she'd been involved with charity balls, student fashion shows, sat on various committees—all sorts of things. It was really obvious that she wasn't just sitting on the sidelines; she was out there driving lots of big student events. I could see that she'd taken every opportunity she could to organize events."

Nathan Homan, Co-founder, Rouge Events

If you're at college, take every opportunity to get involved with events—whether its student balls, sporting events, fashion shows, debates, or field trips. Even though these might seem small and insignificant in comparison to professional event experience, they serve two purposes. Firstly, they *show* an employer that you are genuinely interested in event organizing; that you are committed and proactive. Secondly, they provide an opportunity for you to demonstrate the core skills that employers are looking for. It may have only been a college field trip, but if you can use that on your resume to demonstrate project management skills, or experience in travel and logistics, then it counts as relevant experience. It may have only been a college debate event or visiting guest lecture, but if you can use that to demonstrate experience of speaker management, then it is relevant experience. It might only have been a student fashion show but if you can use it to demonstrate experience in technical production, staging, and show calling, then it's relevant experience. Remember, it's not so much the type of event an employer is going to be looking at, it's the skills you demonstrated during the event planning.

181

"A candidate might have led a team up Kilimanjaro; it doesn't matter that it's not event experience, they're demonstrating that they are someone who's gone that extra mile and organized a group. Those are the skills and drive we're looking for."

Fiona Lawlor, HR Director, Jack Morton London and Dubai

Family Events

"People often leave out stuff that they don't think is professional enough to put on their resume. But if you're just starting out you should definitely put everything that's relevant on there. It's still an event, so it will be a talking point and an opportunity to show what you did."

Martin Turner, former Global Head of Events for Credit Suisse

Like student events, family events such as weddings and other celebrations might seem insignificant, but if used correctly on a resume they can also demonstrate core skills. What's important when citing family events as experience is to look past the surface elements, such as the decoration and styling, and use them to show all the things you did behind the scenes. Did you compile a budget in Excel to keep track of costs? Did you get competitive quotes in from several different suppliers? Did you negotiate with suppliers on price? What did you do to confirm orders with suppliers and provide them with the necessary delivery details and times? What sort of schedules did you draw up? Did you make sure you had a list of mobile numbers so you could reach everyone on the day—especially if it was a Saturday when many supplier's offices are closed?

If you can use your sister's wedding as a way to demonstrate your project management skills and show an employer how you think and operate, then it doesn't matter that the event itself is only a family wedding. It is however, important that you go into sufficient detail about the behind-the-scenes processes that you followed. Believe me, an employer isn't going to care about the rustic flowers, the quirky photo-booth, or the vintage theme and decor. Instead, talk about how you obtained several different quotes for the rustic flowers then negotiated on the price to get candles thrown in for free. Or how you decided where best to position the quirky photo-booth in order to manage traffic flow at the party. Or what provisions you made for the delivery, installation and de-rig of the vintage decorations; did you make separate arrangements to have ladders, tools, and fixings onsite, and did you think about how they were going to be removed post-event?

"Defining your role is the important part. If it was just helping out or doing the meet and greet at the local swim club Christmas party, that's not going to be enough. If a candidate can show they organized it or specifically did X, Y and Z, for example I managed the catering or I handled the venue hire contract, that's going to get my attention."

Sharyn Scott, Global Head of Events, Linklaters

Volunteering

"If you have the opportunity to volunteer, or do an internship with a charity, you should make this your priority in order to build up as much experience as possible. Not all charities will ask for experience, but in general, it helps if you can show that you know something about the planning stages of an event, be it office-based or onsite. In addition, volunteering means you already have a foot in the door, if you build up a good working relationship with the events team and show plenty of initiative, you'll be first in line to hear about any vacancies that come up and should be in a strong position to secure the job."

Farida Haqiqi, former Events Manager, The British Red Cross

Whether you're at college or in work, volunteering in the evenings and at weekends is something everybody can do to get experience. It might be local community events, charity events or large scale public events that need lots of onsite staff. Incidentally, many community and charity events are run by volunteer committees, so joining a committee can be a great way to get involved in the pre-event-planning stages—rather than just working onsite. If you're already in work, there might be opportunities to volunteer within your company, by organizing their charity days or the office holiday party.

"I've just taken on someone in my team who used to run the meeting facilities here. He was our front-of-house catering guy, trained at the Four Seasons, who managed all the client-entertaining spaces in the building. He'd worked as a waiter and on reception, so he had the customer-service skills, but he really wanted to get into events. He kept approaching me over the course of about two years. He helped out at our children's Christmas party every year because he wanted to show me 'look, I'm really good at this and I really want to get into it.' Then, an opportunity arose to bring someone into the events department at a junior level, so I hired him. I think it's important to give people an opportunity, so I did with him because I trusted that he genuinely wanted to get into events. He was very professional; he dresses in the right way, is always well turned out and I know people respect him in the building, so that all helped me make the decision. He's coming along in leaps and bounds, I'm really happy with him."

Sharyn Scott, Global Head of Events, Linklaters

Be strategic though; make sure you get a wide variety of volunteer experience. Being a steward at a festival or public event demonstrates enthusiasm, commitment and humility, so it's great to have on your resume, but it's not developing very many of the core skills. Therefore, volunteer a couple of times as a steward then, once you get your face known and have a contact on the inside, explain that you're trying to get more event-planning experience and see if you can volunteer in a different capacity next time—perhaps in the organizers office or backstage. Network, be proactive, and try to take on more responsibility in order to get the most you can out of volunteering—don't just stand there handing out flyers. Remember that the reason you're getting volunteer experience is so you can talk about it in an interview as a way to demonstrate knowledge and skills—so you need to put yourself forward for as much responsibility as possible.

"The more things you've turned your hand to onsite at events, the more interesting you're going to be to me as a candidate."

Sharyn Scott, Global Head of Events, Linklaters

When you do begin volunteering and you are 'just an usher', perhaps handing out maps at a festival, be as proactive in that role as you can. At a job interview you could explain that, although you were 'just an usher', you took it upon yourself to find out: where all the emergency exits were, where the fire assembly point was, how far the nearest first aid tent was, where the nearest toilets were, the procedure for reporting an incident, and what the fire code word was. Then explain how all of that gave you a good understanding of some of the health and safety aspects required in event planning. That shows an employer that you were more than 'just an usher'; you were showing initiative, taking responsibility, and thinking like an event professional.

There really is no excuse not to have some volunteer event experience on your resume. How can you expect to sit in front of an employer and tell them you want a job in events when you haven't even made the effort to go out and volunteer? The lack of any significant volunteer experience on a resume, certainly at the beginning of your career, is a major red flag to an employer. It's very easy for you to *say* one thing in an interview, but employers will be looking at your resume to see what you actually *did*—or perhaps more importantly—didn't do.

"I do use a lot of internal staff from other departments on events. For The X Factor live final sponsorship events, I needed so many chaperones to manage the flow of people that I had to borrow staff from various departments and from the sponsor companies as well to help out. If someone's already working full-time, they should definitely investigate whether there are any volunteer opportunities within their own company at events they do."

Charlotte Saynor, former Vice President of Brands & Events, Fremantle Media Enterprises, and Head of European Events, Apple

Use of Holidays

"If they've had holiday jobs, what were they? Because that shows they've got initiative and they're not just living off their parents. I want to see what they've done with their holiday time; have they worked in the industry during their holidays? Have they been a waiter/ess on any big events? Have they gone to work for a tent company? Or have they just spent it in the South of France with family and friends? Using their holiday time to get some relevant industry experience shows that they're serious, that they're willing to work, and they're not scared of long hours."

Charlotte Wolseley Brinton, former Head of Events,
Rhubarb Food Design

If you're in college, where you're likely to have quite a few weeks of holiday each year, it's imperative that you use a good chunk of that holiday time to get some experience. Employers like it when candidates have inconvenienced themselves in order to get experience. It's a two way street; show us you're committed and driven by what you've already done, and we'll hire you so you can develop those skills even further. But if you haven't done the groundwork, don't expect us just to give you a paying job.

Often college students find themselves working during holidays anyway, but so many of them take the obvious route of working in restaurants and bars. If you're going to work in the holidays, be strategic about it and make sure you're getting relevant event industry experience at the same time. Go to work for an event-staffing agency as a waiter or crew on big events, or as promotional staff on a product launch or experiential campaign, or as a waiter in the banqueting department of a large hotel that does conferences and events. There are plenty of accessible job opportunities working in support roles in the event industry, which will enable you to get experience while still paying the bills.

"What they've done in their gap year or summer holiday is definitely of interest. There are those that go surfing and there are those that go to

Malawi to work in a school. Obviously, working in Malawi sounds quite challenging so it would give me something to go on in terms of their personality. I'm sure it goes without saying that if you're going to do a gap year, try to so something that you can use to talk about in interviews rather than just have a holiday."

Nathan Homan, Co-founder, Rouge Events

If you're already in full-time work, it may not be as easy to devote a lot of your holiday time to getting experience, but don't rule it out—just be strategic. Let's say you get three weeks paid holiday a year, giving up at least one week to get some good experience is probably a realistic sacrifice and will look impressive to prospective employers. However, make sure you use that one week wisely in order to make it worthwhile. If you can identify an event, in the field of event planning that you're interested in, you could try approaching the organizers to offer your time for free for a week leading up to the event. This way you'll likely get a mix of office-based and onsite experience at a critical time in the event-planning process. You'll be able to see the event through from the final stages of planning, through the build, event and de-rig—which will count for a lot more, in terms of experience, on your resume and will therefore justify sacrificing a week of holiday time.

"I don't want to just see a resume telling me what fabulous school you went to or what grades you got. I want to see that you've taken some initiative to get event experience. They've got to have some experience on there, because if they don't, that tells me that they've made no effort whatsoever and expect to go straight into an event job; but I'm sorry you haven't actually tried to get any kind of experience. Have you sacrificed any of your personal time to try and get some experience?"

Martin Turner, former Global Head of Events for Credit Suisse

19

How to Get Onsite Experience

"Master the position you are in before you set your sights on a promotion. Think of martial arts, you spend months learning the absolute basics of how to move your hands in a certain way before you do anything else. Until you master the details and build a strong foundation, you won't be any good at the advanced stuff. It's like a building, the stronger the foundation, the more stories you can securely add on top of it."

Christopher Lee, CEO, ACCESS Destination Services

Once you've amassed a range of experience from extra-curricular activities, you then need to get more professional onsite experience. The good news is that most of this work is paid. The bad news is that it's hard, physical work with long hours.

Fortunately, the event industry offers quite a few different points of entry for those just starting out, in the form of support roles. These include:

- Wait staff
- Crew
- Promotional staff
- Registration/front desk staff, also known as host/esses
- Hotel banqueting staff
- Steward/marshal/usher
- Valet parking attendant/taxi marshal/traffic marshal
- Charity volunteer

This type of on-the-ground experience is invaluable, yet most people over-look it because they want to start higher up the career ladder and therefore think that these support roles are beneath them. Instead, they just identify the main event-planning companies in their area and approach them directly for work experience or jobs—then wonder why they don't hear anything back. Whereas in reality, you're going to meet more potential employers—and be of more interest to them—if you work on the ground at events and use that front-line experience to develop skills, gain insights, and—crucially—make contacts.

"Starting at the bottom is absolutely the way to go. What that says to a potential employer is that the candidate has a real hunger and enthusiasm for the industry and that they're prepared to do whatever it takes to get some on-the-ground experience. It speaks volumes."

Fiona Lawlor, HR Director, Jack Morton London and Dubai

This type of work, although seemingly basic, will give you a great insight into how an event runs from the inside. You can observe: what's involved in the set-up, how rooms are laid out, the technical equipment involved, and how the day/evening is structured. You'll learn about flow; how guests are greeted, checked in and moved around, how food service works, what health and safety procedures are in place, what needs to be done for the de-rig and load out, and—perhaps most importantly—how to behave in front of clients and guests. It's knowledge you can go out and get yourself—you don't need to pay for a college course to learn this—and by doing so, you'll demonstrate the drive and initiative that employers are looking for.

"I like to see some sort of relevant skills experience; where they've taken the initiative to get some sort of background in the industry they're applying for. If I see on a resume, that someone's been working in a bookstore, that's not of interest to me. But if they've been working as a cater-waiter, I know they understand how to take care of guests and that's more important to me; that they've at least worked somewhere that will give them a skill to help them in the event industry. I like it when they've gotten involved in the industry, even at a basic level."

Chad Hudson, President, Chad Hudson Events

Just remember though, you need to take a strategic approach when gaining experience through support roles; use them to develop skills, acquire knowledge, and make contacts. You can teach yourself how events really operate on the ground, from a number of different perspectives. For example, as crew, you'll experience set up and de-rig. As a host/ess you'll understand check-in, delegate registration, and customer service. As wait staff, you'll experience back-of-house, room layout, flow, and timings. As a steward or usher you'll experience crowd management, venue/site layout, and health and safety procedures. As promotional staff, you'll experience consumer interaction, sponsorship, brand positioning, marketing objectives, and how these integrate within an event or experiential activity.

Therefore, when you take this kind of shift work, don't just turn up and do the job they are paying you for. Instead, use it as an opportunity to observe, question, and learn. Arrive early or stay late so you have time to scrutinize the way the event has been designed, structured, and laid out. Chat to the suppliers and crew, ask them questions, and generally look around and soak up as much as you can about the way the event has been planned. Maximize the opportunity.

"The key thing to being successful in the events business is to spend a little bit of time within each area of the business—which will really enable you to understand the entire process of how the event comes to life."

Bill Jones, Vice President, Managing Director, Events,
The Channel Company, formerly UBM Tech Channel

The Benefits of On-the-Ground Experience

In addition to understanding how events operate, on-the-ground experience serves two other, often overlooked, purposes.

Demonstrating Attractive Qualities

First, it gives you the opportunity to demonstrate qualities such as humility, dedication, commitment, passion, and initiative—all of which are very attractive to an employer. As I've mentioned before, one of the biggest problems for employers is that candidates who are just starting out often don't want to do the menial parts of the job—especially if they are college graduates. It's as if they expect to go straight into planning events, and therefore look down on tasks they consider the 'grunt work.' Whereas, if you deliberately go out and seek a range of on-the-ground experience to better your understanding, you are demonstrating humility and genuine commitment to an employer. It shows us that you're serious about getting into events, that you've been proactive, and are not afraid to work hard and start at the bottom. I would say this approach is even more important if you have been to college, particularly if you've studied event management, because if an employer is concerned that you think you know it all (and they will be!), demonstrating humility by working on the ground will go a long way towards countering that perception.

Networking

The second purpose of getting on-the-ground experience is that it gets you in the right environments to network for office-based work experience. When you're working in a support role, you have the potential to meet the event organizers—your future employers—and to start building up a network of contacts by introducing yourself to suppliers, crew and your co-workers. Meeting someone in person, working alongside them on an event, doing your job well and going beyond the call of duty so that you get you noticed, is a far more effective way to get on a potential employer's radar than just sending out resumes to someone who's never met you. So, make sure you go out of your way to introduce yourself to everyone you come into contact with onsite (at an appropriate moment when things are quiet!). Get your face known, be polite and friendly, engage with people, offer to help before or after your shift, and get their business card—or at least their full name so you can look them up on LinkedIn.

Remember though, you must be respectful to whoever has employed you to work onsite, which means first and foremost making sure you do the job you've been hired for. Don't neglect your duties because you're off trying to network or get noticed by the event organizer. Do your networking whenever there's a quiet moment, so that it won't affect your work—or better still, do it before/after your shift, or during your break.

Using On-the-Ground Experience on Your Resume

This type of experience will also give you some real—possibly high profile—events to put on your resume. Admittedly, your role within those events will be fairly limited as support staff. However, listed on a resume they'll catch an employer's eye and you can then use them to demonstrate how you turned them into an opportunity to learn. They'll act as a talking point for you to show that you can think strategically; that you took those jobs not just to be a waiter, but also to learn about things like service, room layout, flow, and production design—from the inside. You'll also be able to use each piece of experience to demonstrate a relevant skill. For example, as a waiter, you can demonstrate customer-service skills by explaining how you dealt with complaints, or as a host/ess, you can demonstrate delegate registration and database skills. Of course, the mere fact that you've gone out and worked on the ground will also look good on your resume. Employers know that being a waiter or crew at events is hard work with long hours—so it will demonstrate that you know what's involved and that you can do it.

"I do think that getting a variety of experience is beneficial. If someone comes to us as a DMC (Destination Management Company), and he or she has some experience with transportation, some experience with event production and some experience with catering, that's going to

look like a more well-rounded candidate than someone who has only spent time in one of those disciplines."

Christopher Lee, CEO, ACCESS Destination Services

When working in support roles, make a point of trying to collect as much information about each event as possible—so that you can study it later and 'reverse engineer' it to understand what decisions were made during the planning stages. Chat to some of the suppliers onsite to see if you can get copies of (or photograph with your phone) the production schedule, load-in/out schedule, stage plan, or set designs. Get a copy of the service schedule and floor plans from the catering company. See if there are any spare itineraries, agendas, or delegate packs you can get hold of to see what materials were used to communicate the event-planning arrangements to the attendees. On larger events, there might be a staff-briefing document or folder; this probably won't be available to support staff but if you get chatting to one of the event co-ordinators or supervisors after your shift, you might be able to get hold of a copy.

Take photos of as much of the set-up and layout as possible, so that you can cross-reference this against floor plans later to better-understand everything. Often it's helpful to do a visual walk-through of the event by taking pictures of the route the guests take. Make sure to find the load-in/out areas too, and walk these through taking photos of the route so you understand any access restrictions for the build/de-rig. Finally, get some pictures of the event in action if appropriate. Just keep in mind when taking photos you might have to get permission first, as some events will have confidentiality issues. However, if you explain that you are just taking them to learn about event planning, and that they are for study only and won't be published anywhere, then you might be able to negotiate permission. In Chapter 23 "Preparation You Must Do for an Interview", I'll explain how you can also use this information to build yourself a portfolio.

Now that we understand the benefits, let's look at some of the different entry points for getting onsite event experience.

1. Wait Staff

"Direct front-line service experience is really useful. In banquets for example, where you're actually serving someone. We all know the pressure of a live situation—where the food is running late, it arrives cold, or doesn't taste good—and you have to be able to deal with that right there on the spot. That's comparable to what we do with clients in event planning, just on a smaller scale. Someone coming from a service profession is going to have transferable skills."

Christopher Lee, CEO, ACCESS Destination Services

Many wannabe event planners look down on the idea of being 'just' a waiter/ess at events, when actually it's one of the easiest ways to get your foot in the door. While I'm not advocating that you spend months doing this sort of work, signing up with a staffing agency and doing 10-20 shifts as a cater-waiter could put you on the inside of a range of different events, from product launches to awards ceremonies and corporate meetings. Also, because it's mostly evening and weekend work, it's the type of thing that can easily be combined with study or a day job.

a. What You'll Learn

There's a lot that you can learn in a short space of time from simply doing a few shifts as a waiter—especially if you're strategic about it and go in prepared to observe, analyze and learn.

• Event formats/room layouts

You'll experience first-hand the different event formats—receptions, seated dinners, buffets, dinner-dances, etc.—and how these affects the staging and use of space, along with the different types of room layouts used: classroom, theatre, dinner, etc. This will help develop your spatial design skills and ability to visualize, for when you're planning your own events later.

• Flow

You'll get an understanding of the importance of managing flow, both from the guest's perspective; through arrivals, cloakroom, registration, reception, dinner, and departures, and from the staff's perspective; in terms of how front and back-of-house are linked, the flow of meal service and how the room is split into sections and served in 'waves.' Again, this is all something you will need to develop a feel for when planning your own events—so seeing different set-ups in action is a great way to learn what does and doesn't work.

- ## Set-up/de-rig

You'll experience set-up and de-rig for both front and back-of-house, and witness how everything works in terms of delivery, load-in, storage, prep, plating and service, bars and dispense, equipment, clearing, load-out and collection. Pay attention to the caterer's timings and schedule so that you understand how long it takes to set up a room for a seated dinner for 500, or why the kitchens are laid out in a certain way. Believe me, when you're an event planner working with a catering company they'll always be asking you for more space or set up time, so the more you understand about their needs, the better your planning will be.

- ## Space requirements

You'll start to develop a feel for how much space is needed for 500 people standing or how best to layout 50 dinner tables so everyone has sightlines to the stage and enough space between tables for service. The more you can visualize space requirements and measurements, the better.

- ## Customer service

You'll get 'front-of-house' customer-service experience and learn how to speak to and interact with guests in the proper way— including knowing when to address them, when to be invisible, and how to deal with tricky requests, demands and complaints. All of which is good training for dealing with clients, sponsors, delegates and VIP's when you're an event planner. If you're working as a waiter and a guest complains about something (which they will), learn to have a few lines prepared. Look them in the eye, apologize, and say something like *'I'm so sorry Sir/Madam, I'll look into that straight away and get it sorted for you, please bear with me and I'll be right back.'* Then, follow through and deal with it yourself if you can, or refer it to your manager. Either way, it's how you speak to and make the guests feel, at the first point of contact, that is an important skill to learn. There's really no better place to learn this than as a waiter onsite where, in all likelihood, you'll have to deal with some very tricky—and at times rude—guests.

• Timings/schedules/running orders

You'll also get an understanding of timings, schedules and running orders. Many events are structured around the food service, so it's important to understand how much time to allow for each course, and how to plan entertainment, presentations, speeches, awards, and auctions around them. Try to get hold of/photograph the schedule from the caterer's operations manager at the end of the shift so that you can study it later. By working as a waiter and observing different formats and running orders, you'll learn a great deal about time management and what works and what doesn't from other event planner's successes and failures.

• Production and staging

You'll also have the opportunity to study the technical, production, and staging requirements employed for different types of events; how an awards ceremony differs from a wedding for example. Turn up early for your shift and watch this being set-up. Chat to the crew and suppliers; ask them questions about the production, design, and staging decisions that were made during the planning stages. Why did they choose to fly the speakers overhead? Did the location of the power-supply dictate the position of the stage? Why did they choose projection screens over LED's—was it a budget issue? Why did they front-project onto the screens instead of rear-project? See if you can get a copy of (or photograph) any stage plans/set designs to study them later. You can teach yourself what a 10ft wall height looks like in relation to an average height person—does that leave any space to hang anything overhead? What does a 12ft stage on a floor plan look like in reality when it's surrounded by dining tables? How many tables would you have to take out to have a 20ft x 20ft dance floor in front of the stage? This is all really useful knowledge that you can educate yourself with just by being onsite, observing, poking around, and asking questions. If you explain to crew and suppliers that you're trying to learn, they'll probably respect that and try to help you out—assuming you've chosen the right moment to ask.

- Suppliers

You'll also be exposed to different types of entertainment, technology, creative theming, décor, and set build ideas. Soak all this up, make a note of the supplier so you can look them up online later, and start to build up your own little black book of suppliers and ideas.

Seeing first-hand all the different factors that go into service, timings, layout, flow, set-up, de-rig, staging and production—and experiencing them yourself—will be invaluable when you're the event planner deciding how best to stage the event.

"Experience in people and crowd management is useful. Just knowing that you can take care of guests; that you know how to speak to them properly and help them find the way to a VIP seating area, or from their table out to their town car. Those kinds of people and service skills are very important to have, so any experience that demonstrates how they've looked after or interacted with guests onsite is useful."

Chad Hudson, President, Chad Hudson Events

b. Networking as a Waiter/ess

In addition to everything you can learn just from being onsite, one of the best opportunities you can get from being a waiter/ess is the chance to meet the event planner. Find out who they are early on in your shift, then keep an eye on them throughout the event. If they're standing around not looking too busy at any point—and you have a spare moment—check in on them; ask them if you can get them a drink or a seat. Believe me; they'll love that sort of attention. Most event planners are running around so much that they often forget to stop and re-hydrate or grab anything to eat.

Once you've made an impression on the event planner, go and find them when your shift is over. Explain that you're trying to get into events and offer to help them with the rest of the event or the de-rig; there's always clearing up to be done at the end. It won't be very glamorous work, and you'll already be tired from having worked your shift, but it will be appreciated by the event planner and you'll definitely make an impression. After the event, wait a week, and then drop the event planner an email or a message on LinkedIn. Remind them who you are and ask them if they've got any other events you could work on <u>unpaid</u> (make that very clear) to get experience—or better still, any office-based work experience. The fact that you looked after them onsite and helped out—unpaid—after your shift will make them much more receptive to the idea of helping you.

Don't forget, there's likely to be more than just one event planner/co-ordinator onsite. Sometimes, the event co-ordinators will be freelancers who will be working on other events for other clients. Get friendly with them too and see if they know of any other events you could volunteer on. Remember to make it clear you're just looking for unpaid work experience at the moment. If you're working as wait staff and you're asking for paid work, you probably won't get much help, as they'll know you don't have enough experience yet. Just remember, when you're networking onsite, make sure you give something back *before* you start asking for favors. Help them before you ask them to help you.

Finally, don't forget to network with the catering company that is employing you. Develop relationships with the onsite managers and/or head waiter/ess and use that to ask for office-based work experience with them. Catering companies have their own in-house event planners and assistants who work directly with all the event-planning companies that you'll eventually be seeking jobs with. Getting office-based work experience with a catering company is a great stepping-stone to work your way up to, and make contacts for, event-planning positions.

c. Action Points

- Find out who the main event staffing agencies are in your area and sign up with them for shift work

- If you're unsure who the agencies are, call a couple of local catering companies and ask them who they use. Remember, there might more than one staffing agency to sign up with.

- Some catering companies may hire their staff directly, rather than using an agency, so reach out to them too. This can give you the opportunity to develop a more personal relationship with a catering company.

2. Hotel Banqueting Staff

Most large hotels with ballrooms hire casual banqueting staff to work as waiters when they have events. In fact, one of the contributors to this book Nathan Homan, co-founder of Rouge Events, got his start in the industry by working his way up from casual banqueting staff at London's prestigious Dorchester Hotel.

"I often recommend to people who are trying to get into the industry to take a catering or hotel route, because you can get paid while you're learning—as opposed to interning where you probably won't. Then,

when you get to the point of applying for event-planning jobs, and you've got on your resume that you've worked on lots of big events at the Natural History Museum, or you worked in The Dorchester ballroom for three years during university, you can bet your going to stand out more than someone whose just organized a couple of student balls or a small charity event."

Nathan Homan, Co-founder, Rouge Events

a. What You'll Learn

Although most of the opportunities to learn and network will be similar to those you'll get working as a waiter for a staffing agency, it's definitely worth getting experience of both, for a number of reasons:

• Access to meetings and corporate events

One of main advantages of being a banqueting waiter is that, by targeting the right type of hotel, you will be able to obtain experience and contacts in different areas of event planning. For example, a luxury hotel is likely to attract weddings, award ceremonies, and charity/gala dinners. Whereas a conference hotel is likely to attract meetings, conventions and other corporate events. I would encourage you to get first-hand experience at as many different types of events as possible. However, you may find that by working as a waiter for a staffing agency you don't get to work on many meetings and conferences—just because the majority of these are usually held in hotels. Therefore, you can seek out experience and network with corporate event/meeting planners by working in banqueting at a conference hotel.

• Training

Nowadays, most catering service at events is relatively informal. However, prestigious hotels often provide formal service training, which includes the way you speak to and interact with guests. Highly developed customer-service skills are very attractive to employers; being able to demonstrate that you know how to treat business clients, guests, and VIPs will definitely make you stand out.

- ## Prestige

Whether you're seeking paid work or work experience opportunities, you should always target the most prominent companies in their particular sector. Experience from well-regarded, prestigious employers will count for so much more on your resume. If an employer sees on your resume that you've worked in banqueting at a 5 Star hotel, it tells them that you've been well trained, taught high standards, understand the importance of customer service, and know how to conduct yourself in a professional manner when dealing with affluent guests, business customers, and VIPs. So, if you're going to get experience in banqueting at hotels to round out your experience—and I recommend that you do—there's no point working in a 3 Star provincial hotel. Approach the best 5 Star hotels that you can, in either the luxury or business sectors, to add some prestige to your resume.

b. Networking as Banqueting Staff

The same advice applies here as it does with networking as a waiter. Find out who the event planner is onsite and make contact by doing something for them. In addition to coming into contact with meeting planners, you'll also have the opportunity to meet registration/front desk staff—also known as host/esses (see next section for more information). These are great people to know and network with as they often have greater responsibilities and more involvement with the event planner. Therefore, it's much easier to work your way up to office-based event planning from host/ess work. Introduce yourself to the host/esses at an event, maybe bring them refreshments or offer to help them before or after your shift, then you can ask them to introduce you to the specialist staffing agencies that recruited them. Better still; many host/esses end up working directly for event-planning companies, so they often have great in-roads to future event jobs.

c. Action Points

- Research all the 5 Star hotels in your area, and then divide them into two groups: luxury and business/conference.

- Contact the HR or banqueting departments and ask them how to apply for casual work.

- If you've already got some experience as a waiter for staffing agencies, focus on targeting business hotels so that you'll get experience of corporate events and come into contact with meeting planners.

3. Registration/Front Desk Staff aka Host/esses

"If you've got little or no experience, I would suggest you sign up with staffing agencies or host/ess companies, because all the corporates have to hire host/ess teams to work on events—it's a phenomenal way to get experience. The other thing is, if you are really good at what you do as a host/ess you can often be promoted to supervisor and I know people that have gone on to work as corporate event planners via that route. You just need to get in that environment, do the job well, and network like crazy.

Martin Turner, former Global Head of Events for Credit Suisse

When an event planner needs support staff onsite, they will often use 'host/esses.' (This is an informal term often given to registration or front-of-house staff). These are freelance staff, often recruited via an agency, that are used for client-facing roles onsite. Generally, this means greeting guests and managing the check-in or delegate registration process. As a result, host/esses have to be well presented, well spoken and understand the importance of customer service. Although host/esses are still support staff, they are generally considered one level up from waiters, crew, or stewards. This is because they act as the face of the event, representing the client/host. As such, they often have more direct involvement with the event planner than wait staff.

Host/esses are used frequently for meetings, conferences, and conventions/exhibitions, so this type of work is often a great route into corporate event planning. One of the contributors to this book, Lisa Simmons, started her event career working as a hostess. From the contacts she made as a hostess, and later as a supervisor, she went on to work as a freelance event manager for clients such as Microsoft and Credit Suisse before working her way up to senior event-planning positions at Barclays Capital, Linklaters, and Goldman Sachs.

a. What You'll Learn

Working as a host/ess means you'll see the event from the client facing front-end. This is an opportunity to learn:

- **Front desk set-up**

This might include registration desks, signage and displays, laptops/pads for check-in, AV screens, telecoms and Internet access, name badges, guest lists (including reconciling them post-registration), delegate information packs, and gift bags. Obviously, the front-end of the event is one of the most important in terms of creating a professional first impression, so having an understanding of what goes into this is a valuable learning opportunity. I've seen so many events where the front end is really badly designed or managed: the flow just doesn't work so bottlenecks are created, there's a long line for the cloakroom, staff don't where the toilets are, signage is obscured, or front-desk staff speak to guests in a rude manner or hold personal conversations in front of them. By working as a host/ess you'll experience the good and bad first-hand, which will be great training for when you're the event planner. Remember to get a copy of the floor plan and take pictures if you're allowed to, so that you can talk through the set-up and flow to demonstrate your understanding later.

• Operations

Host/esses are typically fully briefed on all operational information affecting the front end, such as timings, running orders, one-on-one meeting facilities, breakout rooms, fire and evacuation procedures, where all the necessary facilities are, i.e. toilets and cloakrooms, and all meal, break and transport arrangements that affect the guests. This will give you a great insight into all the details the event planner has had to think about and will teach you what you'll need to brief your support teams in future, when you're the planner. Also, by working on the frontline you'll find that guests ask you all sorts of questions about the event, so this type of work will certainly keep you on your toes and train you to be fully informed about everything.

• Customer service

Host/esses are hired because they know how to behave, speak to, and deal with guests in a professional manner. Often, it's these skills that will get you noticed by an event planner. That event planner will then remember you and hire you again. The more that happens, the closer the relationship you will develop with them, and the easier it will be to take on more responsibility and work your way up.

• Managing suppliers

As an extension of the event planner's team, a host/ess will often find themselves dealing with smaller issues and problems that arise onsite. This might mean dealing with the venue manager to arrange for some furniture to be delivered to the reception area, checking with the banqueting manager that the breakout refreshments are ready on time, or liaising with security and valet parking. This is a great opportunity to demonstrate initiative and show that you are resourceful. The best host/esses are the ones who just get on and deal with any small issues themselves, without bothering the event planner. It's also an opportunity to develop relationship with suppliers, so make sure you get their contact details. The more people you've worked with—the ones that have actually seen you in action—that you can follow up or network with for future opportunities, the better.

- Databases

Conference and meeting planning typically involves registering guests on a database when they arrive and issuing badges; which is often the job of the host/ess. A familiarity with this process— how the databases are set up and operate—is a really useful skill to have. During her time as a hostess, Lisa Simmons recalls being hired directly by Credit Suisse to work as an assistant planner in their offices for several months in the run up to a large event. Because she had demonstrated proficiency with their database onsite as a hostess, they thought she'd be a good person to input all the pre-event registration data for another big conference they were organizing. This gave her an opportunity to make the switch from onsite support staff, to office-based assistant event planner.

- Production

Like wait/banqueting staff, working, as a host/ess will give you the opportunity to get behind the scenes and study the room layout, staging, and production. However, with host/ess work you're more likely to be working on corporate events and meetings, so there will be different things to observe and learn, such as technical production, AV, presentations, speaker facilities, exhibition stands, stage sets, and breakout rooms.

- Advanced duties/supervisor role

The more experienced you become, the more competent you are, and the stronger your relationship is with the client, the more advanced your duties are likely to become. Whereas you might start off just checking delegates in on arrival, if you push to take on more responsibility, you could end up performing duties traditionally performed by the internal event-planning team, such as transport co-ordination or speaker management. That's exactly what happened with Lisa Simmons when she was a hostess for Credit Suisse; because she was competent and eager to do more, they trusted her with more responsibility.

b. Networking as a Host/ess

As you'll be working directly for the event planners onsite, networking is more about demonstrating what you can do. Host/ess work gives you the opportunity to show initiative, offer to take on more responsibility and excel at customer service. Use it to *show* that you can do more than just what's required of you; go the extra mile, exceed expectations and see it as an opportunity to audition for an onsite co-ordinator role. It's all about impressing the event planners by what you *do* and how you *behave*. *Show* them why they need you onsite and why they should book you again in future; stand out.

"As a hostess, I really pushed myself and was always trying to take on more responsibility on whatever job I did for them [Microsoft]. I was super proactive, always volunteering to do other things. I actually went to the woman who ran the agency while I was on hostess duties and said, 'I'd really like to take on more and be a supervisor.' Because I was always doing more than I was supposed to be doing when I was onsite at events, the team at Microsoft really started to recognize that and they eventually offered me an assistant event management position."

**Lisa Simmons, Project Manager EAME Events,
Goldman Sachs**

Don't forget to network and make friends with the other host/esses too. Working well as part of a team, doing your job well, and getting on with everyone is likely to lead to you being referred for other work. So make sure you get in with the host/ess mafia!

"I was running an event at the Tate Gallery and there was a young girl who I thought was part of the Tate event-planning team, but it turned out she was just freelance support staff; a hostess that they'd hired to help with the flow of guests. This girl was amazing! I stood and watched her; as people arrived she walked up to guests, smiled, took their name, and got them a name badge—even though she wasn't part of my team who were supposed to do that. She took the arriving guests' coats and told them where to go, showed them where the toilets were, the whole routine. Well, I'd never experienced anything like it because I hadn't asked her to do any of that. She just took the initiative, got stuck in, and was really professional about it. It transpired she was an actress, but she wanted to get into events, so she did this on the side. I was so impressed by her; her attitude, her initiative, and her ability to talk to people and make them feel comfortable and welcome. It might just sound like small little things she was doing, but it was impeccable customer service and spoke volumes about her attitude and initiative. Just based on that I hired her to come and work onsite at one of our events—a big partners meeting. She was very proactive, very professional, and very welcoming—to the point that she made some of my own team seem quite inefficient by comparison!"

Sharyn Scott, Global Head of Events, Linklaters

c. Action Points

- Find out which staffing agencies provide host/esses for events in your area and sign up with them. Explain that you've been working as wait/banqueting staff, that you're getting as much experience as possible to become an event planner, and you now want to make the shift from food service to host/ess.

- If you're having problems finding these agencies, or they're reluctant to take you on without experience, approach them from the inside. Take a few shifts in banqueting at a business hotel and make contact with the host/esses that way. Befriend them and ask them to introduce you to their agency—they'll be more likely to meet with you if one of their own has put you forward.

- If an agency asks you to come in for an interview, take a portfolio with you (more on this in Chapter 23 "Preparation You Must Do for an Interview") that shows them all the photos, schedules, and other onsite information that you've been gathering from each event you've worked on. This will show them you're serious about getting into event planning and keen to learn, so they'll probably be more likely to give you a shot.

- Remember that as a host/ess you need to be well presented and well spoken, so from the moment you pick up the phone to contact an agency, you need to present yourself as an articulate business professional.

4. Promotional Staff

Promotional staff are similar in some ways to host/esses; however, they tend to be used more for brand marketing, experiential, and sponsored events; to promote a product onsite. For example, a drinks brand might sponsor a music festival and hire promotional staff, sometimes referred to as brand ambassadors, to work at the event and engage with consumers. This might include demonstrating/sampling products, distributing information to create awareness, collecting personal data for direct marketing, or managing the interactive elements of an experiential activity.

One of the unfortunate things about promotional work is that it's very much biased towards looks and appearance. Whereas host/ess work requires you to be well presented and well spoken, promotional staffing agencies expect all of that AND place a great deal of emphasis on looks. Which is why a lot of this work is done by actor/model types. Nearly all agencies, such as Aesthetics in the United Kingdom, will require you to send in a photograph with your application; but don't let that put you off applying. Remember, these agencies put the most glamorous model types on their website. However, on a busy day, they might have to provide 100+ promotional staff to clients, and the reality is there just aren't enough model types wanting to do event work. So while half of those staff might have model looks, the remainder will just be presentable normal people who've scrubbed up well! Believe me, I've had plenty of average-looking promotional staff at my events; but they were well-groomed, well-dressed, smiley, articulate and enthusiastic—and that's often more important to a client than having a pouty model type who doesn't want to ruin her manicure.

a. What You'll Learn

- ### Events as a communications tool

One of the best things about working as promotional staff is that you'll start to get an understanding of the purpose of the event; the business objectives—be it marking, PR, sales or fundraising—behind why the event is being staged/sponsored. Being able to demonstrate that level of understanding early on in your career is going to set you apart in the eyes of potential employers. Many job candidates show their enthusiasm for all the wrong areas of event planning: the creative, the VIP guests, the design, etc. Whereas what an employer really wants to hear is that you get the business, marketing and communication objectives, how those are met by staging an event, and how the results are measured. When you're working as promotional staff, you really need to listen to how you're briefed by the brand manager or event planner. Listen, observe, analyze, and read between the lines about what they're telling you to do and question why? Why are you being asked to enter people into a prize draw? Is it to get their email addresses? Why is the brand providing interactive experiences at the event? Is it to demonstrate features of the product, or so that people will share their experience via social media and provide free advertising? What are the brand values and how have those been communicated via the design and content of the event?

• Engagement

Experiential events are all about finding ways to engage with consumers through live event activity, and post-event via both social and traditional media. Seeing first-hand the creative ways that these event planners and experiential agencies use events to achieve business objectives will give you a lot of great insights and ideas for your own career. These ideas can often be adapted for different sectors of the event industry. So by working as promotional staff on an experiential event, you might be exposed to a clever creative idea or new piece of technology that you could then mention in a future interview for a meeting-planning job—to demonstrate how it could be adapted for a business conference. That's the kind of forward-thinking approach an employer is going to love; you're not just referring to something you saw, you're showing that you've thought about how it could be applied to a prospective employer's event.

• Working on location

Events that use promotional staff are often held in many varied locations and venues, from outdoor spaces, high streets, and shopping malls, to music festivals, sporting events and exhibitions. All these different locations come with different logistical challenges that affect the event format, design, and production. When you're working onsite, pay attention to the way the event has been designed and you'll learn a lot. For example, if it's a promotional event on a busy train station concourse, how has the set been designed to ensure people stop and take part? How did the organizers get power to the set without trailing cables across the concourse? How have they addressed issues around sound levels and interruptions from announcements? How was the build and de-rig planned so as not to interrupt with the normal day-to-day running of the train station? What health and safety precautions were taken in terms of public liability, trip and slip hazards, or fire evacuation procedures? If you're handing out food samples, have allergies been considered? What if you give out something with nuts in and someone goes into anaphylactic shock, and then they try to sue the organizers? These are all things that will have (hopefully) been considered by the event planner in the design stages, but you can educate yourself onsite by analyzing the production and questioning how and why everything was done the way it was. If you're lucky, you might even be able to quiz the event planner and ask them about the choices they made during the planning.

- Confidence and communication skills

Promotional work is not for wallflowers. Being able to approach strangers at events, engage with them, and communicate information or get them involved, is no easy thing. It takes a certain type of person to be able to do it well. You have to be driven, confident, personable, polite, friendly, articulate, and able to deal with rejection. Having this type of work on your resume tells an employer a lot about your character—and it's the type of skills and qualities they're looking for.

b. Networking as Promotional Staff

Promotional work is a great way to network in the brand marketing and experiential sector of the events industry. Not only will you have the potential to network among the other promotional staff and the event-planning company that has staged the live activity, but you might also be fortunate enough to come into contact with the representatives from the host brand/end client. All of which are potential sources of future work/work experience. So, as before, be strategic; go out of your way to make an impression, exceed expectations, get noticed, make contacts, and follow up afterwards.

Sometimes, an experiential agency might need some casual promotional staff that they can call on for smaller pieces of work here and there. It may not be worth them going through an agency to book just one or two promotional staff. On other occasions, budgets will be tight so they'll be looking to hire people as cheaply as possible—by going direct rather than paying an agency commission. Therefore, it's definitely worth cultivating relationships with these agencies while you're onsite and they can see how good you are in action. Make it clear to them that you're keen to do more work for them because you're trying to get into event planning. If they know you're good at your job, enthusiastic, and hungry to learn they'll keep you in mind. But it's important to maintain the relationship; not to the point of pestering them, but the odd email or LinkedIn message every month or two is enough to remind them you're around and available.

"The fact is, if you do a couple of seasons at a hotel or with an event staffing agency, and keep your eyes and ears open to learn as much as you can, when you come to go for event jobs you'll already know how these big events run on the day. That will be a huge advantage over someone who might have been to university, but hasn't really worked on many events. That, as a minimum, is great. At least you know how the end product works. Now we can teach you how to get to that point. That shows resourcefulness."

Nathan Homan, Co-founder, Rouge Events

c. Action Points

- Get some good photos taken where you look your best: well groomed, presentable, and smiling!

- Sign up with the promotional staffing agencies in your local area. Make it clear in your application that you're training to work in event planning and so are hungry to get experience 'on the ground'—it might just set you apart from the out of work actors and models who are just doing it for the money.

5. Crew

"If you're a big strong guy, get yourself off to the crewing agencies because you'll see so many different types of events—and that type of access will provide incredible experience. Doing something like that is great from an employer's perspective too, because a lot of young people would think that's too much like hard work—because it's too physical and they're not interested in doing the physical stuff—but events are really physical work. If someone came to me and they'd spent all summer working for a crewing company putting up structures I'd be really impressed because it's heavy work, it's dangerous, and it's hard."

Nathan Homan, Co-founder, Rouge Events

Onsite at events there are often two types of crew members; specialist crew, such as electricians, carpenters, riggers, sound and lighting technicians, and general crew. General crew are there to lift and unload things, to help install staging, sets, and furniture and to generally help set-up and de-rig the event. These guys (and they are predominantly guys) are essential to any event because there will always be jobs that need doing onsite that fall between the cracks of the event planner's responsibilities and the suppliers' responsibilities. That or some of the jobs that fall under the event planner's remit are just too physically demanding for them to do themselves. Unfortunately, because most of it is physically demanding manual labor, this type of work is often only an option for men. That's not meant to be sexist in any way; it's just how it is in reality. It's rare that a crewing agency provides females for this type of work.

Working as crew, hard as it is, can provide a great opportunity for men trying to get into event planning. If you have the strength and stamina to work as crew AND you're capable of learning event planning, you're going to be a pretty attractive package to potential employers. Men are typically under-represented as event planners anyway, so when one comes along who has the ability to be a planner and is also willing and able to do practical jobs/physical work onsite if things are in a jam—that's a pretty valuable asset to any events team. It's the unfair advantage that a strong fit man has if they want to be an event planner; so use it.

a. What You'll Learn

• Construction

As an event planner, you'll often be designing events to be held in tents where you won't have the luxury of being able to see what the venue is going to look like in advance. Everything will be built up from scratch; walls, doors, windows, roof linings, floor, carpets, power, heating, water supply, lighting, toilets, sound, furniture, cloakrooms, kitchens, fire exits, trackway (temporary road), waste removal facilities—and that's before you start to think about all the decorative elements. This means you'll be working from drawings and floor plans. Often, you will have visualized the interiors a particular way—perhaps with the use of drawings or 3D modelling. Then you get onsite and start the build, and it won't be exactly as you'd imagined it. There are always unforeseen factors when working in temporary structures. Measurements might not be exact, or there may be an unexpected crossbeam or support brace on the tent wall that didn't show on the plans, and now your set doesn't quite fit.

Being able to work onsite during the construction stage of an event, before you become an event planner, will give you a huge advantage. There are many restrictions when working with temporary structures, which are easy to overlook until you have a solid understanding of how they are constructed. You'll learn about site access and temporary road surfaces, how tents are erected; in what order and how long it takes. How power and heating are fed through the space, the difference between freestanding heating/cooling units and the in-roof tube-sock variety—plus the pros and cons of each. You will also learn about the practicalities of a site and it's terrain; how to plan for soft, wet or uneven ground, how the fabric linings are attached to the walls/roof using baton frames, and weight load restrictions that affect what you can hang and where. You'll learn about different internal wall and apex heights, how the lighting truss and rigging points are dictated by the position of the tent's frame, how you need to insert wooden frames and batons behind the wall linings if the planner wants to hang something on the walls, and how the location of support braces can interrupt the theming and décor. You will learn so many useful things that will deepen your knowledge and understanding of how to design and build an event from the ground up.

b. Networking as Crew

Most crew working onsite are just there as crew. If you're an event planner in training, going back to the floor to work as crew, it will be relatively easy for you to stand out and shine. Most crew work shifts during the build and set-up of the event, then they disappear during the event, and come back for the de-rig (or another shift takes over). If you're working onsite as crew, make a point of getting noticed by the event planner by asking them if there is anything else you can do. Make sure you're clean-shaven and bring a change of clothes; some smart black trousers, shirt, shoes and whatever you need to freshen yourself up come the end of your shift (because you're likely to be a sweaty mess by then!). Find the event planner and offer to stay on and help them with anything that might need doing during the event—for free. Explain that you're trying to get into events and are happy to do anything just to learn; even if it's just general grunt work. Remember, you're really there to network with the event planner so it doesn't matter what jobs you end up doing. Believe me they'll be impressed—and I'd be very surprised if they didn't take you up on your offer. An extra pair of hands onsite will never go a miss, especially if the person is enthusiastic and capable. Remember to bring a packed meal for the evening. The event planner might be able to include you in their crew meals if they have spares, but they'll be even more impressed if you've come prepared.

c. Action Points

- Find out who the crewing companies are in your area and sign up with them.

- If you're having problems finding crewing companies, call up some tent hire companies in your area and see if they can recommend any agencies to you.

- If you want to be sure to get some experience working on events in tents (which I would recommend), you can also contact your local tent hire companies to see about working for them directly. Remember, a lot of tent events happen during the summer months, so if you're at college, it's the perfect work to do in the holidays.

6. Steward

"Festival volunteering or stewarding is relevant onsite experience because we do live outdoor events, so being familiar with that kind of event by working at it is helpful."

Nathan Homan, Co-founder, Rouge Events

Stewarding is a great way to get experience on large outdoor events such as festivals, sporting events and challenges—such as marathons and bike rides, and other public events. Often, event security and staffing agencies will advertise causal stewarding positions in the run up to a large festival or event, and full training will be given. Events such as these, held over large sites, pose a whole different set of challenges to, say, a conference or special event held in one or two rooms—so there can be a lot to observe and learn.

A couple of things you have to be careful about when seeking this type of experience is, a) that you are using the opportunity to learn something while onsite; you're not just standing around taking tickets, handing out flyers, or pointing people in the right direction and b) that it doesn't look on your resume like you were just there to have fun. If you've only worked as a steward on a well-known music festival, an employer is probably going to suspect you just did that so you could go to the festival for free. Whereas, if you've been strategic about it and obtained stewarding experience on a festival, a marathon, and a public event—such as a Remembrance Day parade—AND you use it on your resume to demonstrate skills and knowledge, that's going to impress an employer.

"Increasingly we're seeing more people coming in with experience of stewarding at festivals. Things like that are definitely useful because it's building their knowledge of the different types of events. But if you've been a steward at a festival, talk to me about that experience in a more formal, corporate way to show you understand the business side of it."

Nicola Mosley, HR Manager, George P. Johnson

a. What You'll Learn

• Health and safety

Large public events are a great place to learn about health and safety, because there will be a higher expectation from the organizers to have this all thought-out and documented. As a steward, you're likely to be well briefed on things like evacuation procedures, first aid facilities, fire safety, site layout, security, people flow, crowd management, and trip hazards. You'll pick up little gems of knowledge by performing these roles onsite; like knowing that every event should have designated fire assembly points in case it has to be evacuated, or that if you discover a fire there is usually a code word to discretely alert other staff of the location without causing panic. On most events, this will all be documented so you should be able to get access to some form of staff briefing manual so that you can study it later at home.

• Site layout

Working onsite at large events gives you an opportunity to study and understand the layout of the site, before you need to plan your own events. Just being able to visualize all the different elements that go into the construction of the site can be really useful. For example, knowing that if you're planning an event in a muddy field you're going to have to lay trackway (temporary road) so that the supplier's lorries can load in equipment without getting stuck in the mud. Alternatively, understanding how to maintain public right of way when closing off roads and sidewalks by channeling people with temporary fencing, crash barriers, and signage. It's also about seeing and understanding the different equipment used for large outdoor events; single pod toilets versus trailers, tower lights, generators, skips, catering trucks, fencing, security and crash barriers, stages, tents, public address systems, and signage. So if you're holding a music festival and an entire field is being turned into a temporary car park—what equipment are you going to need to do that? How will you mark out bays and lanes? How will it be lit at night? How will you get power to the lights? How are you going to plan the entrance and exits so that it functions properly without bottlenecks? Will you have traffic marshals? What happens if it rains and cars get stuck in the mud; have you budgeted for an onsite tow truck?

By studying each event you work on, you can teach yourself so much about event-planning process from the decisions other planners have made. Gather as much information as you can onsite and take pictures of all production elements; lighting, staging, fencing, trackway—all the boring behind the scenes construction elements that no one else will be looking at. Then, after the event, study the site map and cross-reference it against pictures you've taken so that you can teach yourself what was used to make each area of the event function successfully.

Unfortunately, most of the jobs you will be given to do onsite as a steward will probably be quite basic. Therefore, it's down to you to get as much as you can out of the opportunity by using the time onsite to learn. You might have to do a six-hour shift just ushering people in the right direction, but it will be worth it if you can use the time before and after your shift to observe, poke around, and scrutinize the event-planning arrangements, or to meet the organizers, make contacts, and ask questions.

b. Networking as a Steward

On larger events such as these, it might be harder for you to get noticed by the actual event planners—not that you shouldn't still try. However, there will always be volunteer supervisors or team leaders to network with, not to mention other stewards who may also work on other events. Every person you meet onsite has the potential to be a useful contact. Chat to the volunteer supervisors about future opportunities, or after your shift go and find the organizers office and see if there is anything else you can do to help. Always explain that you're trying to get into event planning, and that you're working on events like this to get experience. If people can see you're being proactive and trying to learn, they will often be more sympathetic and go out of their way to help if they can.

There will usually be some sort of health and safety supervisor onsite at these events too, so try and find them after your shift so you can pick their brains. Ask them questions about the way the site was laid out and what precautions were taken, to better your understanding—or ask to shadow them for the remainder of the event/future events. Explain that you are trying to learn and see if they'll let you see a copy of the site safety plan. This will include risk assessments and method statements that document the potential risks that were identified during the planning stages, and the precautions taken to address them. The earlier you can start familiarizing yourself with these, the better your understanding will be of all the things you have to consider as an event planner.

c. Action Points

- Locate the organizers of festivals, public and sporting events in your area and enquire about stewarding. Large events will be actively looking to recruit staff and volunteers so it shouldn't be too hard to find something.

- Research public and community events organized by the local council and community groups in your area too. Some councils will have their own public events teams, so you might be able to shadow them onsite at the events that they supervise.

- Always explain that you're an event planner in training so you'd like to take on as much responsibility as possible. If you make this clear, they might assign you a less basic role.

7. Valet Parking/Taxi/Traffic Marshall

Transport co-ordination plays a significant role in most large events, especially meetings/corporate events and VIP/special events. Typically, this involves onsite staff co-ordinating any number of cars, taxis, mini-buses, or coaches to provide:

- airport transfers for guests to/from their hotel
- transport between different venues/off-site activities
- drop-off and pick-up points at each venue, including coach parking facilities
- valet parking facilities
- marshalling services to direct vehicles and keep traffic flowing
- transport home for guests at the end of an event

In fact, transport co-ordination is typically one of the management roles assigned to fully-fledged event planners/onsite co-ordinators. Therefore, employers are likely to be impressed if a junior candidate has some experience in this area, and that will make you more attractive to them.

That said, unlike the relative ease of obtaining work in other support roles, it might be harder to find opportunities with transportation companies without having previous experience. Probably the best way to make an in-road is to look for work as a valet parking attendant, although even this has some barriers to entry. You will certainly need a full and clean driving license, many employers will insist you pass a criminal background check, and some will impose age restrictions (21/25+ only, although some will accept 18+) to reduce risk/insurance premiums. Once you get some experience as a valet parking attendant, you can then enquire about opportunities in other transport co-ordination roles with the same company, such as taxi/traffic marshalling, as many provide their own training for this. It's also the kind of evening/shift work you can do while studying.

Remember that customer service is a key part of transport co-ordination roles, especially valet parking. How you present yourself and how professional you are in dealing with people can often make up for a lack of previous experience—especially if you can demonstrate experience in other areas of hospitality and crowd control. Therefore, I would suggest you approach transportation companies after you already have some experience as an event steward, waiter/ess, and host/ess.

a. What You'll Learn

• Logistics

Until you've experienced the logistics that go into moving large numbers of people around—safely and on time—it can be easy to underestimate the skill involved. It might include directing vehicles, liaising with vehicle drivers, managing drop-off/pick-up points, arranging parking facilities, complying with health and safety requirements or public highway rules and restrictions, negotiating with police and council officials, ensuring effective traffic management and flow, time management, and crowd control—not to mention customer service. Often it's not just a question of a coach/car pulling up at the venue and dropping off/picking up. At airports, there are many parking restrictions so you might find yourself having to use radios/phones to liaise with individual drivers to arrange a continuous relay of cars, parked elsewhere, to drive up to the pick-up area without keeping impatient guests waiting. When using coaches to transfer large numbers of guests between different venues, there may be little or no space to stop outside the venue without brining traffic to a standstill. Or maybe 300 people are going to exit a conference at the same time and you need to get them to cross a busy road safely in order to get them onto coaches, while police or council officials watch you closely to ensure your group doesn't create an obstruction to public right of way. Or maybe the guests are taking different coaches to different locations, so you've got to ensure that the right people get on the right coaches and the process flows smoothly and without delay. In fact, just getting 300 people onto coaches, when they're all dawdling, chatting to each other, or stopping to ask you a myriad of questions, can itself be a challenge. Again, this work might not sound very demanding, but when dealing with large numbers and many moving parts, it requires a lot of strategic planning to ensure it all runs smoothly onsite. Working for a transportation company, even if initially only as a valet parking attendant, you'll be able to observe the solutions that have been put in place to manage this process, which will give you a good understanding of how to do this when you're planning the event yourself.

- **Customer Service**

Transport co-ordination roles are also a great opportunity to demonstrate customer-service skills to potential employers. As a valet parking attendant, you'll often be the first point of contact for guests, so your appearance and manner will be important—you may even be given some training for this. Similarly, as a taxi marshal, you'll often be faced with drunk, impatient, and even abusive guests at the end of the night, which is a great way to demonstrate how you can manage these types of situations.

b. Networking in Transport Roles

One of the great networking opportunities working for a transport company is getting to work alongside the onsite event planners/co-ordinators. The main event planner will assign one or more experienced event co-ordinators to supervise all transportation at the event. Often these event co-ordinators are freelance staff, so they will work for a number of different event planners. Alternatively, they may be full-time event planners who work for the same company as the main event planner, and are helping out on the day. Either way, if you start as a valet parking attendant and are then able to move up into a more significant transport supervisor/co-ordinator role at that company, you'll have the opportunity to impress the onsite event co-ordinators with how well you perform your duties. This can help you make the jump from working for a transport company, to working directly for an event-planning company as one of their onsite co-ordinators responsible for supervising transport.

c. Action Points

- Obtain experience in hospitality/crowd-control/marshalling roles before applying for work with a transport company. This will help with a lack of previous transport experience.

- Research event transportation companies in your area rather than applying for valet parking jobs with hotels. This way you will have the potential to move into taxi/traffic marshaling or general transport co-ordination roles—plus you'll be working on large events, rather than just parking hotel guest's cars.

- Ideally, enquire with transport companies that you come into contact with while working onsite in other support roles. This way, they can see that you are confident, articulate, and presentable.

8. Charity Volunteer

"When it comes to volunteers, I'm always looking for ones with initiative and a willingness to work beyond what is expected of them. The best volunteers I've worked with have been those that have read the briefing notes sent to them prior to the event, listened carefully to the volunteer briefing on the day, made sure they were on-hand throughout, and those who were still around at 3 am to help with the packing up. These were the volunteers I knew I could rely on to do whatever was asked of them—and they were the ones I would consider employing if a position came up. The last thing you need is someone moaning that they don't want to lug things around because they're too tired. At the end of the event everyone is exhausted, but you have to work together as a team and just get on with what needs to get done."

Farida Haqiqi, former Events Manager, The British Red Cross

Charities always need volunteers to work at their events, and these can be quite diverse, including gala dinners, auctions, movie premieres, and challenge events like fun runs and bike rides. Obviously, unlike most other support roles, these are unpaid. However, the good news for you is that a lot of charity volunteers aren't all that good. They often need a lot of hand-holding, many don't show very much initiative, they're generally not very confident, aren't used to jumping into an unfamiliar situation and just getting on with things, and they're the first to start whining about dinner breaks and finish times. So, if you can go in with a confident, can-do attitude, show initiative, take on extra responsibilities, and behave like a professional, then volunteering on charity events can be a great way to shine as a junior event co-ordinator.

a. What You'll Learn

The main difference with charity events is that onsite roles are typically less rigidly defined, meaning you'll often find yourself turning your hand to a number of different things. This might include setting up the main room, arranging raffles, auctions and goody bags, or working on the front-desk. This can enable you to break out of specific roles, such as waiter or host/ess, and move closer to that of an onsite event co-ordinator—a title you can then start to use on your resume. This type of role is an important bridge between event support staff and event planner, and will be useful on your resume when seeking office-based work experience.

With charity events, if you're confident and capable, you'll have the opportunity to take on more responsibility much quicker. Charity events are often on under-resourced. There will typically only be one or two actual event planners—and even these will be fundraisers first, event planners second—the rest of the team will likely be other employees of the charity who work in non-event related positions and volunteers. It's often much more of a case of 'all hands on deck.' Typically, charity volunteers will be given at least one specific job to do, but they might not be 'active' throughout the entire event. For example, at charity dinners I've worked on, we often have a lot of volunteers to help check guests in on the front desks as they arrive. They then might not have very much to do until after dinner, when they'll be working as auction spotters. So there's often a lot of time in between assigned jobs for you get more involved and support the main event planner. If you're proactive, you could end up working alongside the event planners as their onsite assistant.

b. Networking as a Charity Volunteer

If you've got gaps in between the specific jobs you're assigned, offer to shadow the event planner. Then, if you're with them when unexpected things come up during the event (which they will) you can offer to take it on and deal with it, in order to free up the event planner's time. I used to work with a really proactive charity volunteer who would do just that. She'd stay close to me onsite, then when someone radioed me to ask for something, she'd hear it and say 'I'll deal with that, you carry on with what you're doing.' It was a real godsend at times. Just having someone capable to delegate simple things to, as and when they arose, was a big help. This kind of enthusiastic shadowing, being on-hand to help when needed and being prepared to do anything, will enable you to develop a relationship with the event planner and they'll come to regard you as someone reliable; which will bode well for future opportunities.

The other thing to remember is that most charity volunteers turn up at the event after they've finished their day job. There aren't many volunteers who are available for the entire set-up day, who are then prepared to stay on for the event in the evening. If you can get the day off work and are prepared for a long day—working the set-up and the evening event—then you're going to be much more valuable to the event planner. Also, think about offering your time to help them in the office in the last few evenings leading up to the event. This is the busiest time for planners and there will always be things you can help with, such as stuffing gift bags or checking table plans. It might not be glamorous work but it will give you an in-road to make the crossover from onsite support to office-based events assistant.

c. Action Points

- Contact the biggest charities in your area and ask to speak someone in fundraising about volunteering at events. Be aware that charities get approached by people all the time wanting to help at all the big glamorous events. Make it clear you are training as an event planner, that you understand it's not glamorous work and that you're prepared to work on any event that they need help on—not just the high-profile ones.

"I would always call applicants for a chat to get a better idea of why it was they wanted to volunteer and what they wanted to achieve from the experience. This not only helped me get an idea of how they would be useful to the team, but it also enabled me to ensure they got the most out of their experience by placing them in roles that would best suit their skills. This vetting process is crucial in my opinion, both for external and

internal volunteers. You can generally rely on internal volunteers to be a safe bet as they are representing the charity, so you know they will behave in a professional capacity. With external volunteers you have to be sure you are taking on the right person, even if it's just for the duration of the event. What you definitely don't want is a volunteer who just wants to come along and party. We've had volunteers who have come along to the event thinking they are guests rather than volunteers; they want to have fun, don't want to work, and end up having far too much to drink. This not only looks totally unprofessional but adds extra work for the events team who then have to run around after these volunteers, taking them away from their own duties."

Farida Haqiqi, former Events Manager, The British Red Cross

Be Strategic

Remember, the point of getting this on-the-ground experience is to demonstrate to employers that you are being strategic and trying to learn the business from all angles. Therefore, it's important that you get experience in all of these areas, not just one or two. If an employer sees lots of wait staff experience on your resume, they won't pay that much attention to it; they'll think you were 'just' a waiter to earn money. However, if they see that you've deliberately got experience as a waiter, host/ess, crew, promotional staff, banqueting staff, charity volunteer, steward, and a parking attendant/traffic marshal, it will be obvious to them that you have a strategy; that you took each of these jobs to learn. That shows real drive, commitment, and intelligence. Before you start seeking office-based work experience, make sure you have the following onsite experience on your resume:

- Wait/banqueting staff on a minimum of 10 events; get experience on a range of different types, such as weddings, meetings and corporate events, awards ceremonies, hospitality, sporting, and retail events.

- Steward on minimum of three different types of events; one festival, one sporting event, one public event.

- Crew on at least five different events; some must be in tents.

- Promotional staff on at least five events. Again, get a mix of experiential, conventions/exhibitions, road shows, etc.

- Host/ess on at least five events. This is your opportunity to get experience of meetings and conventions/exhibitions.

- Parking attendant/traffic marshal on at least five events.

- Volunteer on five to 10 charity/community events. Try to get a mixture of gala and mass-participation/challenge events.

Getting experience in all these areas will speak volumes to an employer, but don't be tempted to cut corners and only focus on one or two of these. The value it adds to your resume is that you have experienced a wide range of different support roles, on a wide range of different events.

"Don't just sit there waiting for the phone to ring once you've sent your resume in, get out there and educate yourself as much as possible in the meantime; research all the local venues and suppliers, take a relevant course, get more volunteer or part-time work. It's about how much effort you're putting in, either educating yourself or getting experience, when compared to the other people applying for the job."

Christopher Lee, CEO, ACCESS Destination Services

20

How to Get Office-Based Experience

'I'm a great believer that luck is actually just talent meeting opportunity'

Martin Turner, former Global Head of Events for Credit Suisse

The next stage of building up experience requires you to make the switch from onsite work to office-based event planning, in order to learn the nuts and bolts of project management. By far the best way to do this is to use the contacts you've made working onsite. It's much easier to network from within; with people that you've already met, worked alongside, gone out of your way to help, and kept in touch with, than it is to send out resumes 'cold call' style. Having a personal connection with someone is always going to open more doors.

If you seek on-the-ground experience—as detailed in the previous chapter—and approach it as I've suggested, you will undoubtedly come across *opportunities*. You then need to apply your *talent* to turn these opportunities into your 'lucky' break.

Work Experience and Internships

Keep in mind that most of the office-based opportunities you'll be offered are going to be unpaid work experience. Larger companies with on-going internship programs may offer three to six-month placements that sometimes pay a very basic wage. However, small businesses tend to offer shorter work experience opportunities ranging from a few weeks to a few months, which are likely to pay just expenses, if anything at all. Up until now, getting experience onsite has been something you could either get paid for, or do in the evenings and weekends around a day job. However, this next stage—where you need to learn about the planning stages of an event—is going to be office-based work, and therefore you'll need to be available during weekdays.

"Straight out of college, I did a 500-hour internship with a small meeting planning company who worked with a large bank. At the time, there were only four of us there, including me. Immediately after the internship they hired me and I worked with them for the next two-and-half years travelling all over the states producing meetings for its banking client."

Jennifer Miller, DMCP, Partner & President,
ACCESS Destination Services

1. Unpaid Internships

Some employers might only offer unpaid internships—which are typically three months but sometimes longer. The media has whipped up a lot of controversy in recent years about how unpaid internships are only viable if you have a rich family to support you financially. Or else they are exploitative, with candidates being expected to work long hours and just being used as slaves to fetch coffee and run errands. I don't really want to dwell too much on all the arguments about whether unpaid internships are fair or not. What I will say—from an employer's perspective—is that many event companies are small businesses, and as such, cannot afford to pay someone to learn. You wouldn't expect someone to pay you a salary to go to school or college would you? If you are taking an internship, it's probably because you don't yet have sufficient knowledge, skills, or experience for an entry-level position. Therefore, while a small business owner might be happy to teach you during an internship—so that you become more qualified for an entry-level job—as you probably won't be contributing very much to their business whilst you're still learning, it's unlikely they'll want to pay for the privilege of teaching you. Much as they might like to help, they are running a business not a school. Therefore, you need to be clear about what you are getting from an internship; a good employer will be offering you an education and professional experience that should qualify you for an entry-level job with a salary. If you find yourself in an internship where you're not getting a useful education or experience, or if you are being taken advantage of and used as a lackey, then my advice would be simply talk to your employer about taking on more responsibilities. Having the confidence to speak up for yourself, to demonstrate that you are hungry to learn while still being polite and respectful, is something any good employer should respect you for—because you're also demonstrating two of the core skills of an event planner; confidence and an ability to negotiate. If they aren't sympathetic to this, and nothing changes, then leave. There is no point sticking out an unpaid internship if you aren't learning anything; that's the whole point of an internship.

Whether unpaid internships are fair or not, that's just how the jobs market works—and I don't see the situation changing anytime soon. You just need to decide if you're going to play the game or not. The opportunities are there if you can find a way to make it work. All I can do is give you the best advice I can for how to accommodate the fact that they are unpaid. Unless you're easily able to support yourself financially, I would only recommend doing a lengthy internship if it's with one of the leading companies in a particular sector of the events industry. Weigh up how valuable the opportunity is going to be for your career. Is there a very real chance there might be a job at the end of it? If so, that's a big plus point. But you also need to weigh up the probability of getting that job; ask them how many interns go on to get a job and how many you are competing against? Or maybe the company is fairly prestigious, so even if it doesn't result in a job, a three-month stint at X company could look great on your resume and might give you sufficient office-based experience to apply for entry-level jobs—which would be another plus point.

"I get resumes sent in all the time, but someone will definitely stand out if they've interned at any type of event production company—or if they've interned with the events department one of my clients, say a movie studio."

Chad Hudson, President, Chad Hudson Events

You also need to weight up how much time you can commit to working unpaid and to what level you're prepared to inconvenience yourself. For example, if you're being offered a three month unpaid internship at a top company that you want to take, are you prepared to save on rent by couch-surfing with friends and acquaintances for a few months—which might mean moving to a different friend's couch every couple of days to spread the burden? I worked with a freelance event planner at Credit Suisse who lived quite far outside of London, so from Monday to Thursday she stayed with a different member of the team each night, sleeping on the couch. Then on Fridays, she'd take the train back to her home until Monday morning. Alternatively, are you prepared to rent a bed in a shared dorm of a hostel with a bunch of backpackers for three months? Are you prepared to take a part-time job working Thursday and Friday evenings and Saturday and Sunday daytimes, while doing the internship just so you have some money to live on? When I was working 2 days per week at a charity early on in my career—which was effectively my work experience—the pay was so low it barely covered my travel expenses, so I held down two other jobs at the same time in order to make it work. I worked in a bar during the evenings and weekends—often till 2/3am—and did data entry and admin work a few days a week elsewhere. It was horrible. I was exhausted and had no social life, but that experience at the charity launched my career in events, so it was entirely worth a few months of hardship and inconvenience. You have to ask yourself, how bad do you want it?

If you decide an unpaid internship is a valuable opportunity, then there are always ways you can make it work. It might not be fun, it might not be pretty, and it will almost certainly be hard work, but it comes down to how much you're prepared to inconvenience yourself.

"One of my employees that I hired had been an intern at Warner Bros, and while they were interning they'd also worked as a cater waiter on the side. I found that effort and commitment really impressive, but it also showed me that they had time management skills—because they were going to school, but they also had both a job and an internship. To see that someone can juggle three aspects of their life like that, and be taking an interest in the industry and thinking forward about their career development, was very impressive."

Chad Hudson, President, Chad Hudson Events

2. Unpaid Work Experience

"To get good experience, including going onsite and seeing an event from start to finish, you really need to be able to commit to two or three months' work experience. That's more useful for me as a manager so, in turn, I can use you more and train you up on some of the basics. If you're just here for two weeks you're probably just going to end up clearing-out a store cupboard or stuffing envelopes."

Sharyn Scott, Global Head of Events, Linklaters

Unpaid work experience opportunities can be a little more flexible. If an employer can see that you're trying to juggle paid work with unpaid work experience, they're likely to admire your work ethic and commitment, and be sympathetic to that by being flexible. I know, as an employer, that if someone said to me that they'd be happy to work unpaid in order to learn, but would need to leave at 4pm every day so they could work shifts in a bar or restaurant in the evening to support themselves, I'd be more than happy to accommodate that. Alternatively, if they said they could work three days a week unpaid for three to six months, but needed to take paid work elsewhere the other two days, that would be fine too. The majority of potential employers won't come from privileged backgrounds, so they'll respect you for trying to learn and gain experience while holding down a job to support yourself. We want to employ the hard workers!

"One volunteer joined The British Red Cross as an intern for six months, starting off working one day a week for a month alongside one of the corporate executives. For the next two months, she increased this to two days a week so she could join the events team for one of the days. Then, in the final three months, she was volunteering full-time to help the events assistant and myself in the build-up to our big gala ball. She was so dedicated that when the events assistant handed in her notice to move back home to Australia, I encouraged her to apply for the role. Not only did she get the job, she worked even harder to prove her abilities and within a short period of time I was able to off-load some of the more time-consuming work to her, such as the seating plan and the event brochure, both of which required a great deal of attention to detail. I felt like it was important that she develop in her role as much as possible so I encouraged her to take on small projects outside of her job remit in order to build up more project management experience. Since leaving the Red Cross she has become an event manager at another charity."

Farida Haqiqi, former Events Manager, The British Red Cross

Unfortunately, when seeking work experience you still need to make yourself available to work over a long period. If you just go in for a week or so, you're just going to end up doing filing and grunt work. In order to get involved and really learn about the event-planning process, you need to be there as close to full-time as possible, over a period of three to six months; the average length of an event-planning cycle.

"I would hope for a minimum of at least a month in order to get a feel for what the volunteer is capable of, and for them to gain at least a basic understanding of the charity and its events. Two or three months would be better still, as they would become more involved as part of the team, enabling them to play a bigger part in the planning process. When we've had short-term volunteers who have only been able to help out for a week or two, they invariably end up doing the jobs everyone else is too busy for, simply because there isn't always enough time to train them up

on anything else. Filling 600 goody bags or stuffing 3000 invitations into envelopes is immensely appreciated when the events team is working flat out on other areas, but it isn't likely to be the kind of thing that someone wanting to get hands-on experience would be looking for. If someone is able to commit for a longer period of time it ends up being more beneficial to both the events team and to the volunteer."

Farida Haqiqi, former Events Manager, The British Red Cross

If you intend to look for unpaid, office-based work experience, my advice would be to find a paying job that enables you to work shifts—ideally a mix of evenings and weekends. That way you can work a couple of evenings during the week and cram in some longer shifts at the weekend. Alternatively, commit to a longer period of unpaid work experience, say three months or more, but negotiate a three-day week. That way, you can take paid work the other two days and top up with some weekend work.

Turning Contacts into Opportunities

In the previous chapter, I discussed the importance of getting noticed onsite. You do this by:

- Doing your job well
- Being polite and enthusiastic with everyone you work with
- Exceeding expectations; doing more than is required
- Befriending and supporting your co-workers
- Seeking out the event planner and offering to help them before or after your shift
- Collecting business cards/contact details

Now that you've made a good first impression and acquired some contacts, it's time to leverage them and create opportunities to gain office-based experience.

Follow Up

Wait two days after the event, as the day after is always busy dealing with de-rig and mop-up, then establish a non-intrusive connection with everyone that you worked with or met onsite by sending them an invitation to connect on LinkedIn. Just put a very short and simple cover note on the invitation to remind them who you are in case they don't recognize your name. Something like, 'Great to meet/work [delete as applicable] *with you the other night on XXXX [insert name of event].'* Don't be tempted to write more or ask for anything from them at this stage—you don't want to come on too strong. Chances are, they're still busy closing down the event and making new connections will be the last thing on their mind.

Note: Always keep Facebook for personal contacts and LinkedIn for business. If a work-related contact, perhaps a co-worker, wants to friend you on Facebook, then it's up to you whether to accept—based on what information they'll see on your profile. (Remember, they might be a co-worker today, but in six months or a year, they might be a potential employer that you're about to interview with and those photos of you clubbing on South Beach with huge pupils might not look quite so professional). However, if you're the one reaching out to make contact, always do it via LinkedIn so that you come across as professional.

Email

Wait for a week, by which point the event planner will have probably finished wrapping up the event, then drop them an email. First, be humble and remind them who you are, if possible by recalling something you did onsite, for example *'You might remember we met onsite at the X event last week. I was the waiter who helped you pack up and load-out after my shift.'*

Then, explain that you are training as an event planner and trying to get as much experience as possible. This will show that you are being proactive and demonstrating initiative. Something like, *'I'm working my way towards becoming an event planner, so*

I've started at the bottom by getting as much onsite experience as I can in different support roles.'

If you've taken an event-planning course include that in the previous sentence too, e.g. *'After finishing my one year event management course at [name of school], I decided to start at the bottom by getting as much onsite experience as I can in different support roles.'* Potential employers love to see that sort of humility from college graduates.

Mention the quantity of experience you've built up, and the roles you've performed, e.g. *'So far I've worked onsite at over 40 different events, including conferences, festivals, sporting events, exhibitions, product launches and experiential marketing campaigns in a number of different support roles such as crew, waiter, registration staff, steward, and brand ambassador.'*

Next, tell them what you want and ask for their help, but be explicit about what you can offer in terms of time. *'I'm now looking to get some office-based work experience so I can learn more about the project management process and I wondered if there were any opportunities in your team at XXX [name of company]? I would need to continue working part-time in order to support myself, but I would be able to volunteer three days a week unpaid for three months in order to really commit to any upcoming events you might have.'*

If you're not yet ready to take up unpaid office-based work experience, it's still worth following up with contacts to see if they have any other events coming up that you could volunteer onsite at. This is a great way to get more relevant onsite experience because you'll be volunteering as part of the internal event-planning team, rather than as external support staff. To incentivize them further, offer to volunteer a day or two leading up to the event too, by scheduling your other work commitments around it or by taking vacation days. Often, there just isn't enough time to brief a volunteer who turns up on the day, so they end up doing very basic things onsite. If you offer to volunteer a day or two before, and be onsite during the set-up day as well as the event, your offer will be more attractive to employers. Write something like *'I'd really like to get more onsite work experience to see it from the event planner's perspective, and wondered whether you had any other events coming up that I might be able to volunteer on? I'm currently working full-time, but would be happy to re-schedule my shifts/take a few days' vacation in the run up to your event so I can be of more use to you before you get onsite—as well as at the event itself.'* This not only shows that you're trying to be helpful, but it also that you're willing to give up some vacation time to work for free and learn—which demonstrates genuine commitment and drive.

If you are just enquiring about onsite work, with perhaps a day or two office-based leading up to it, be sure to enquire about dates so you can plan your other work commitments accordingly, e.g. *'If you have any particular busy periods where you're likely to need extra support, please do let me know when these are and I will block out time in my calendar so I can volunteer with you.'*

Take a similar approach if they say they don't have any office-based opportunities at the moment. It's a good way to know when to get back in touch, without them feeling constantly pestered. Write something like *'Do let me know whenever your busy periods are and I'll make a note in my diary to get back in touch ahead of those times to see if you need any extra help.'* Then make sure you put it in your calendar and follow up again. Chances are they won't remember to contact you in two to three months when they start to get busy, but if you happen to get back in touch at just the right time, they might just take you up on your offer. Gentle and occasional persistence, without making a nuisance of yourself, is more likely to pay off. It's often just about timing; getting in touch just as they're starting to get busy.

Keep in mind that the goal here is for you to get three to six months of office-based work experience, which, combined with your onsite and extra-curricular experience, should give you a decent enough resume to start applying for entry-level positions with event-planning companies.

When approaching potential employers in this way, you'll also want to attach a copy of your resume. In Chapter 21, I'll go into more detail about the best way to present your experience on a resume.

"If you're struggling to get office-based experience, organize your own events for charity—that shows some real drive and enthusiasm, plus you'll get experience of every aspect from planning through to production and delivery."

Liz Sinclair, Managing Director, ESP Recruitment

3. Paid Work Experience

If you decide, for whatever reason, that gaining experience through unpaid work isn't for you there is an alternative. Instead, you can apply for paid positions with certain suppliers—with a view to working your way up to becoming an event planner. The types of suppliers most suited to this approach are:

- Catering companies
- Conference and banqueting departments in hotels
- Venues (assuming it has its own catering service)

These suppliers are involved in the two main areas that make up most events: catering and venue hire. Therefore, their role is the closest to that of the overall event planner. Whereas other suppliers, such as production, décor and transport, are really only involved in one particular, secondary, aspect of the event. At these suppliers, there will be different positions such as:

Hotels

- Conference and Banqueting Waiter/ess
- Head Waiter/Supervisor/Operations Manager
- Assistant Banqueting Manager (the Assistant Event Planner role)

- Assistant Conference Services Manager (the Assistant Event Planner role)
- Banqueting Manager (the Event Planner role)
- Conference Services Manager (the Event Planner role)

Catering

- PA to Event Planners/Team Secretary
- Office Manager
- Junior/Assistant Event Planners
- Event Planners

Venues

- Venue Hire Co-ordinator (the Assistant Event Planner role)
- Venue Hire Manager (the Event Planner role)

As with unpaid work experience, using the contacts you've acquired working onsite will give you an advantage when trying to make in-roads into these companies. If you've been working as a banqueting waiter/ess at a hotel, it's going to be much easier for you to work your way up internally from there, to supervisor and then assistant banqueting manager—which is where you really start to become an event planner. Hotels, like most other employers, like to recruit from within the organization and if you're already working for the company you're going to a) hear about promotion opportunities first, and b) have already had the opportunity to meet and impress the right people with your work. Similarly, if you're doing shifts for a catering company you'll have the opportunity to develop a relationship with them, so you can make them aware that you're looking for office-based work. Then, if an administrative role comes up—which is not going to require any event experience—you'll be able to put yourself forward with the advantage that they already know you.

"We've hired people who come from a hotel background. That type of experience means they'll have a good understanding of how to deal with hotels and venues, which is useful knowledge and information they can bring to our team. I definitely think that's a great way into the industry. We've hired people who've come from banqueting positions in hotels, venues, and even yachts. If you want to be a program manager, any type of hospitality experience is beneficial."

Jennifer Miller, DMCP, Partner & President,
ACCESS Destination Services

When it comes to taking this approach with venues, I would recommend you focus on venues that have their own in-house catering. Otherwise, the experience you'll be getting as a venue hire co-ordinator, and eventually a venue hire manager, may not be considered sufficient when applying for event-planning jobs. Venue hire management on its own doesn't really cover enough aspects, in sufficient detail, for the experience to be transferable to an event-planning role. Whereas, if the role also includes managing the catering for the venue's events, then it probably will.

"If you have the opportunity to be a PA to an event planner at a catering company, take it. I had my own PA when I was at Rhubarb but there are also team secretary positions, which are advertised as admin roles rather than events roles. If you can get in via an admin role and you're smart about it—making sure to listen and learn—and if the person you're working for is kind, they'll teach you everything."

Charlotte Wolseley Brinton, former Head of Events,
Rhubarb Food Design

Although taking this approach to becoming an event planner is more stable, in the sense that you are being paid while you learn, it's definitely going to be a much slower process. You first have to work your way up internally—from say a PA or waiter/ess—to whatever the event-planning role is. Even then, you are still only an event planner from the perspective of catering and/or venue hire. There is still another step to be made from there to becoming the overall event planner. That said, it's perfectly easy to make that step. There are many occasions when being the event planner at a catering company, or the banqueting manager at a hotel, involves planning the majority of the event. Hotels and catering companies are always looking to sell additional services to clients, such as lighting, sound, décor, and entertainment, which they will then subcontract out to the hotel's regular suppliers. In doing so, the event planner or banqueting manager ends up managing the process by acting as the liaison between the supplier and the client, effectively performing the role of the overall event planner.

It's perfectly possible, therefore, that after working as an event planner for a catering company, or as a banqueting manager at a hotel, you'll have sufficient experience to work as the overall event planner. It's exactly what two of the contributors to this book, and dozens of other event planners I know, have done. Charlotte Wolseley Brinton, who was first an Event Planner, then Head of Events, at the catering company Rhubarb Food Design, went on to start her own company Event Fusion, and Nathan Homan, who worked as Assistant Banqueting Manager for The Dorchester Hotel, went on to start his own agency Rouge Events.

There's definitely an advantage to working your way up through catering, hotels, and venues because you'll make contacts with suppliers and potential clients along the way. You'll also be able to learn everything that's required of an event planner—often witnessing what works and what doesn't—without the actual pressure of being responsible for the entire event. You can ease yourself into the industry at a slower pace, learning and networking as you go—while being paid.

My Route into the Industry

Starting as Event Support Staff

*From temping for an event staffing agency, to being a senior
corporate events manager for Goldman Sachs*

Lisa Simmons, Project Manager EAME Events,
Goldman Sachs

Lisa Simmons is a great example of someone who used onsite
opportunities and contacts to make the transition from support
staff to event planner. She initially started her career in restaurant
catering and corporate hospitality before joining The Promotions
Team, a staffing agency that provides support staff and hostesses
to work front of house at corporate events, conferences, and
exhibitions. By leveraging those opportunities, she was able to
work her way up to become a freelance event manager for
Microsoft, British Telecom, and Credit Suisse before joining
Barclays Capital full-time as Assistant Vice President in Corporate
Events. She then went on to become Events Team Leader for
Linklaters before joining Goldman Sachs as a Project Manager in
the events team.

After leaving school at 16, Lisa spent a year travelling before
applying for a restaurant management position. She was
attracted to one particular company because they were part of a
large group and, as such, offered employees a further education
training scheme to obtain catering and hospitality qualifications.

*"It was very much restaurant and hotel management type training,
but I was able to do it one day a week while I was working for the
restaurant group. Then after about three years working for them I
went on to do a diploma in hospitality supervision, which was a bit
more intense at around three days a week, but again they would
pay for me to complete the training while I was still working for
them. The fact that I was able to work and train at the same time*

really appealed to me. So I did that for five years from the age of 17–22."

From there Lisa used her catering training to make the transition into sporting and special events hospitality management, working for catering companies such as Payne & Gunter and Food Systems Plus that would manage the corporate hospitality areas at sporting and music events. This included managing the hospitality boxes at Goodwood Racecourse and Waitrose's [UK supermarket] summer concerts.

After a couple of years, she began dating someone whose mother was a freelance event manager, working predominantly for Microsoft. *"I told her I wanted to move out of hospitality and into the event management side of the industry, preferably in a corporate/professional services environment. But she said, 'I'm not going to be able to get you in as an event manager with no actual corporate event management experience, however if you go to work for The Promotions Team, the agency we use to provide hostesses and event support staff, that could be your route into working for Microsoft.'"*

Lisa started doing a lot of hostess work for Microsoft, contracted out to them via The Promotions Team, working on conferences held internally at its offices on the Microsoft campus. Hostess work involved responsibilities such as front desk registration, delegate management, dealing with the flow of people on the day and moving guests around, then reconciling the attendees lists at the end of the event. She then moved on to work on some of the larger product launches they were doing at the time, such as Office XP, supporting the events team a little further by managing the one-on-one meetings at the event. By getting a little more involved, her duties started to cross over into event management rather than just the traditional front of house event support service provided by hostesses.

"It really is about being proactive, bubbly, and having a bright personality. If people respond to you well, they're more likely to use you again. Whenever I was booked on an event, I would

always try to volunteer my time to help with the set up, so I could see how the event was run—just to get some background knowledge. Usually, when you're booked through an agency you just turn up on the day, but later, when I became a supervisor, I always used to push to go in the day before to understand the layout and work out a better plan for the team of agency staff that I'd be supervising. It's about being there on time, offering to stay late, and just making sure you're an asset to the events team. I was always very customer-service orientated, so just being happy and smiley onsite and going that extra mile makes a big difference—and people notice that. I remember in the early days as part of The Promotions Team, the clients would respond to us really well and say how friendly we were. Part of that, I think, was because I actually really enjoyed the work so there was a genuine enthusiasm that people probably picked up on."

After a while, the marketing and events team at Microsoft really started to take Lisa under their wing by teaching her more about event management. Then, after six months, they moved her over from the hostess work she was doing for them with The Promotions Team, to be their supervisor who would oversee all the staff at big events. This is when she began to work for Microsoft directly, as a freelance event manager, rather than via The Promotions Team.

"I was really lucky that I was able to make the transition so quickly, but I think having hospitality management experience also helped because I was already used to managing teams. When I was working on the corporate hospitality events I started off just working onsite at the actual event, but when I made it clear I wanted to get more involved, they started to bring me in to work on the set-up and I think that gave me a better understanding of how everything is run behind the scenes. I really pushed myself and was always trying to take on more responsibility on whatever job I did for them. I was super proactive, always volunteering to do other things. I actually went to the woman who ran The Promotions Team while I was on hostess duties and said I'd really

like to take on more and be a supervisor. So because I was always doing more than I was supposed to be doing when I was onsite at events, the team at Microsoft really started to recognize that and they eventually offered me an event management position. I still went in at a junior level though; it wasn't as if I was suddenly planning my own events. All their events were graded at different levels; you might have a level one event manager who would do all the really big product launches, then a level two event manager who might do all the conferences on campus. I was brought in as a level three event manager, which involved doing small seminars, meetings, and exhibitions. These were fairly basic events but because I'd already been working on those events for them for the past six months as a hostess, I already knew the format and how they were run. To be honest, when I was working as a supervisor I was doing most of that type of work anyway, so they were more comfortable with me taking over those events. But the bottom line is I had to be really proactive and push for the opportunity."

Even though Lisa continued to work freelance for Microsoft over a period of about three years, she carried on doing other freelance work for The Promotions Team, even though that work was more at the hostess/event support level.

"The other great thing about working freelance for hostess agencies like that is the networking opportunities. Obviously everyone you work with is also working freelance for other corporates, so because of all the friends and contacts I made I ended up doing other freelance event work for companies like Hewlett Packard and British Telecom."

Most opportunities to find work in the events industry are found by putting yourself in the right environment, inside the industry. Even if it means taking support roles, which is perhaps not where you want to be long-term, you'll be in the right places to meet people, network, and discover other opportunities.

During this time The Promotions Team won the contract to supply event support staff to the investment bank Credit Suisse, so Lisa began doing freelance hostess work for them front of house at conferences. As she had done before at Microsoft, Lisa made the most of the opportunity and took the same proactive approach.

"We were mainly working on overseas conferences in places like Barcelona, handling things like delegate registration and people flow. When I was working onsite at the bank's events, I made a point of telling its internal event planners that I had event management experience from working for Microsoft and that if they needed any extra support I could help. I'd actually only worked on maybe a handful of events for Credit Suisse over the course of a year before they started to take me on for office-based work. One of their event planners had booked a freelance event manager to come and work in the office assisting her with the online registration and data management side of conference planning. Something happened whereby the freelancer let her down, so because she knew I was already familiar with their conference database software—from registering the delegates onsite—she called me and hired me and another one of the hostesses to replace the freelance event planner in the office. We would work in the office on two-or three-month contracts leading up to a big conference, then go onsite and work at the actual event, but then we might go off and work for someone else freelance for a while until Credit Suisse had another big conference and they'd hire us again. It actually worked out really well because it meant I could juggle freelance contracts between Credit Suisse, Microsoft, and a corporate hospitality agency called Keith Prowse."

Working directly for Credit Suisse in an office-based planning role, Lisa was mainly supporting the lead event planner on each event. Initially, she started off working on areas such as delegate management but gradually started to get more involved in other areas, such as food and beverage and production. However, she was not yet running an event herself; she was still supporting the lead planner. Eventually, one of the lead event planners left Credit Suisse to work for Barclays Capital and poached Lisa to go and work with her. She began by freelancing for Barclays, in between contracts for Credit Suisse, but within six months had been offered a full-time position as Assistant Vice President in the corporate events department running seminars and conferences.

This really illustrates the importance of doing the job well and getting on with people. You never know whom you might be working with and where they are going to end up. You could be working with someone who is an equal today, who is responsible for hiring others tomorrow. Often, the way you perform in your currently position acts as the key to your next one.

"I worked at Barclays for four-and-a-half years and during that time I worked with Sharyn Scott, who was freelancing, on a couple of events. We got on well and went out socially a few times. One day I noticed on LinkedIn that she'd taken over as Head of Events at Linklaters, so I dropped her an email to ask if she was looking for any staff. She said 'absolutely!' and invited me to come in and see her. She hired me as Events Team Leader and I was there for 18 months before moving on to Goldman Sachs. When I was looking to move on from Barclays, I was very proactive about it. I looked at all my contacts to see who was doing what and then just dropped them all an email. Funnily enough, I was offered another position at the same time as the job at Linklaters, which also came from just checking in with contacts and networking."

Once again, this demonstrates the power of networking. Sharyn hadn't advertised the position at Linklaters; she filled it based on whom she knew. Lisa had done a great job when they'd worked together in the past, they got on well, and Lisa had been proactive in approaching her.

"The turning point in my career really was in being able to make that transition from doing event support work as a hostess for The Promotions Team, to working as a freelance event manager for Microsoft. That experience then enabled me to make a similar transition into office-based event planning for Credit Suisse. But it was working for The Promotions Team that enabled me to get my foot in the door. Then it was just a case of doing the job well, making myself invaluable onsite, being proactive and lobbying to take on more responsibility. To be honest, there were a lot of people who used to work for The Promotions Team who were experienced freelance event managers and they'd use it as an opportunity to get work for big corporates. A lot of the time staffing agencies use models and actors who are just looking for a bit of extra work, they're not really interested in the event side, so if you're clever about it, take an interest, and go the extra mile, you can really stand out and the client will ask for you again."

Personality also plays a big part; if you like the people you work with, you want to book them again. After I left Credit Suisse, I booked Lisa to work on some of my own high-profile celebrity events. I knew that not only could I count on her onsite, she also had great customer-service skills and I felt completely comfortable putting her in front of celebrity clients and VIP guests. She knew how to behave, how to present herself, and how to speak to people. It might sound like a really small thing, but I remember when she was working on the front desk of a conference for Credit Suisse, checking delegates in. She stood out because she made a point of looking every single delegate in the eye and smiling as she welcomed them (which is not always easy to do after you've done 500 in a row!). It sounds like such a simple thing but it can make a huge difference. When there's so much bad or indifferent service at events, planners really notice the support staff that do it well—and we book them again and again.

21

How to Present Your Experience on a Resume

In Chapter 19, I talked about the importance of gathering information and photos from events that you've worked on, in order to build a portfolio to take to interviews. However, before you can impress a potential employer with your portfolio, you've first got to get an interview—and that's where a strong resume is important.

Preparation

It's important to be strategic when seeking work experience; you have to be aware of how it's going to look on paper. In 2013, I was judging a competition called *The Eventice*, which is a take on the TV show *The Apprentice*, where candidates compete for a job in the UK events industry. As part of their entry, they had to submit a short introductory video where they talked about their background and experience, then answer a few short questions. Watching 20 to 30 of these videos, I became very aware that some candidates stood out simply because their experience included some notable events and/or employers. For example, one candidate had been an intern for the BBC on the 2012 Olympics and had also volunteered at the Hay Festival (a well-known literature and arts festival in the United Kingdom). This candidate was then followed by another whose experience was interning at a provincial hotel that I'd never heard of, and working in a restaurant and wine bar. Which of those two candidates do you think I remembered after watching 20 to 30 videos?

In reality, the candidate who interned for the BBC at the Olympics might not have gotten any event-planning experience from that internship at all. The BBC were there to broadcast the Olympics, not organize it. He may have been a glorified tea boy onsite for all I know. However, the fact is it made him stand out. Both the Olympics and the Hay Festival are prestigious events, so that got my attention—and at the resume stage, that's what you need. Something that makes you stand out.

The experience you get now is going to become your 'calling card.' You won't be able to impress an employer with your skills and knowledge in an interview, if your resume isn't strong enough to get you in the door in the first place. I'm not saying you should only focus on getting superficial or high-profile 'names' to drop on your resume, but it is important to consider what image your experience projects on paper—especially when it's compared alongside dozens of other resumes all applying for the same position. It's important to have both quality experience, in the sense that the actual role you performed was relevant and you could learn from it, and quality employers/events that will make you stand out. Banqueting experience at the 5 Star Four Seasons in London is going to count for a lot more on your resume than banqueting experience at the 3 Star Royal Station Hotel in Newcastle. Similarly, if you're going to work in hospitality to support yourself during college, don't work in a restaurant or bar, work for a staffing agency as a waiter/ess on events so that it counts for something on your resume. In short, make sure the work experience you obtain makes the best impression on paper.

Resume Format

"Don't use a resume format that starts with your education. If you have experience that should be the first thing you show off. I see so many resumes where the first page is taken up with their name in a big fancy font—sometimes with a picture—and every kind of contact detail imaginable; from their address and phone number to their twitter account, then in the middle of the page is their education, the bottom of

the page lists all their computer skills and languages, then finally their experience is all hidden towards the back on page two. If you have experience, flaunt it, that's what I'm most interested in."

Christopher Lee, CEO, ACCESS Destination Services

There are three main formats of resume:

- A chronological resume is where the employment history is listed in reverse date order.

- A skills-based/functional resume details the key skills and achievements first, giving a candidate the opportunity to highlight significant achievements regardless of chronology, followed by a separate section that lists employers and dates.

- A combination resume offers the best of both by presenting your work history in chronological order but also highlighting relevant skills and achievements under a sub-heading for each employer. This format is useful for highlighting transferable skills, incorporating unpaid experience that demonstrates relevant skills, or for when the job title/employer doesn't reflect the level of responsibility held or skills obtained.

At this early stage in your career, it's far more important to show employers that you have relevant transferable skills, gained through support roles, extra-curricular, and volunteer experience. Therefore, I would recommend using a combination resume. However, don't get too hung up on how you think a resume ought to be laid out. You need to present the information in a way that best showcases your skills and experience—as long as it still reads in a logical way. Don't let your experience get strangled by the format of your resume and it end up doing you a disservice.

Job Objective Statement

I've noticed that some American resumes open with a one-line 'job objective' statement; telling the employer exactly what you are looking for. This is not traditional in some countries, however in this situation, where you are looking for work experience/internships opportunities, I think it's a great idea.

A job objective statement should be extremely concise; definitely no more than 10 words. Don't be tempted to add unnecessary adjectives—just get straight to the point. If you're offering to work unpaid and full-time, make that clear in the statement, as it will be a big advantage. For example:

- Objective: Three Month Unpaid Internship

If you're offering to work unpaid for three months, but intend to ask if you can leave early in order to juggle it with paid evening work, save that sort of negotiation for later; if you're given an interview. Concentrate on getting your foot in the door first. However, if you're offering to work unpaid part-time, perhaps three days a week, I would suggest you be up-front about that from the start; to save wasting anyone's time, as some employers will only consider full-time work experience candidates, e.g:

- Objective: Three Days per Week Unpaid Work Experience

When looking for work experience/internships, always state specifically that you are looking for unpaid work. Money is the first, and probably most significant, barrier to entry—followed by how much time you can offer. If you remove the expectation of pay from the equation, an employer is far more likely to give you an opportunity—which is all you are seeking at this stage. The good news is that some employers do pay their interns, so you might get a nice surprise later, but in the first instance, make it clear you're prepared to work for free just to learn.

Personal Profile/Summary

I strongly believe that all resumes should include a personal profile/summary at the beginning—in this case, following the job objective statement. It's a great way to provide a quick overview about yourself and give a broad summary of your experience. A personal statement should include information such as:

- Who you are and your background
- Industry experience and transferable skills
- Personality traits
- Career aim

A personal profile is a particularly useful tool to employ early on in your career, when the experience on your resume might be a bit thin or unfocused. It will give you an opportunity to define yourself to an employer and position yourself in a certain way, rather than letting your experience (or lack of) define you.

In the United Kingdom, these tend to be written as introductory paragraphs using complete sentences. However, I would strongly advise you bullet point this and cut out all the unnecessary 'filler' that reads the same from one resume to another, such as 'looking for an opportunity to utilize my skills and experience' or 'looking for a challenging and fulfilling position....' Everyone says the same thing so it's fairly meaningless and will only make the employer roll his or her eyes—or worse, stop reading. Use the minimum amount of words to say what you need to say. At best, an employer will only skim-read your resume anyway, so make it as easy as possible for them to absorb the information quickly. For example:

Personal Profile

- Onsite event co-ordinator with experience in corporate, charity, experiential and special events

- Experience in various support roles: event co-ordinator, host, steward, crew, brand ambassador, hotel banqueting/special events waiter, and valet parking attendant.

- Skilled in delegate registration, operations, logistics, customer service, and managing speakers, suppliers, staff, and volunteers.

- A resourceful and detail-oriented team player with excellent communication, people, negotiation and problem-solving skills

- Looking to contribute my onsite knowledge, skills, and insights to add value to the event-planning process

Without a personal profile, an employer might glance at your resume and just see waiter/ess, crew, volunteer, steward, etc. But with the personal profile, it tells employers that you have good all-round experience; that you've been strategic in getting a variety of onsite experience to learn about the delivery of events, in preparation for becoming a planner. It demonstrates initiative, humility, and dedication—and that you've laid a strong foundation for your career as a planner. Finally, it tells an employer that you are bringing knowledge, skills and experience with you that could benefit their company; showing what *you* can do for *them*. As an employer, that would impress me.

Demonstrate Core Skills and Knowledge

"We get so many resumes that land on our desks, so it's important that people take the time to make it relevant to the job they are applying for. They need to highlight all the skills they know we're looking for in our job description and demonstrate these through things they've done in the past; be it events they've organized, helped organize, or from experience in other roles. It can be anything—as long as it demonstrates those key skills and draws our attention to them. If you just send an email with an attachment—sometimes we don't even get a covering note— and the resume could be applying for anything, then you're not getting that drive and passion across."

Fiona Lawlor, HR Director, Jack Morton London and Dubai

You need to think of your resume as an opportunity to demonstrate the core skills an employer is looking for, by using real-world examples. For every piece of experience you list on your resume, you need to relate it back to the core skills. Use-sub headings under each piece of experience to show how X, Y, Z role demonstrates your project management, organizational, or customer-service skills, or how you managed suppliers, guests, staff, and volunteers onsite.

I've been sent so many resumes from people starting out in the industry who just present the bare facts about their work history. They simply list the employer/event, dates, and at best a sentence describing what they did—usually in the most literal way that doesn't really tell me anything useful. For example:

Freelance and Volunteer Experience

Premiere Corporate Hospitality   August 2012
Event administration and transport co-ordination

Fusion Event Staffing   April – August 2012
Front desk host on various corporate events. Greeting guests on arrival, issuing badges.

Purple Strawberry Catering   January – April 2012
Waiter on various events

This generic description of their role is so vague that it doesn't tell me, as an employer, anything about what the candidate *really* did; what they contributed, what they learned, how much they understand—nor does it highlight any particular skills so that I know what they are capable of.

When you are just starting your career, and you don't have a huge amount of experience on your resume, it's important to make what little experience you do have count. For each piece of experience, you must elaborate, be specific, and give context to everything that you did. Really drill down into the role you performed to squeeze as many skills or achievements out of each piece of experience as possible. Use it to show what you can do and what you understand. As an employer, I want to know what you can turn your hand to onsite. Even when it's the most basic on-the-ground experience, you can still use it to demonstrate your knowledge and understanding of event production and delivery;

show an employer that you used the opportunity to teach yourself—that you were more than 'just' a water/ess or steward.

"Once, a girl came in for an interview and happened to mention that she'd spent a summer teaching at a summer camp, but she hadn't put anything about it on her resume—probably thinking it wasn't relevant. I said to her, 'that's the sort of thing when you're starting out that you could include on your resume, because it will tell me something about you.' Anything like that can be used to demonstrate team skills, communication skills or managing people, so it's always useful—even if it's not directly related to events."

Nicola Mosley, HR Manager, George P. Johnson

Start by including a short overview of your role; a general explanation of what you did and in what capacity. This is also a good way to include any notable events you worked on and the size and type of event. Next, bullet point your specific responsibilities, being sure to relate each one back to the core skills, or use it to show where you took ownership of key areas of event planning and what you achieved. For example, the experience mentioned previously could have been written as:

Premiere Corporate Hospitality   August 2012
Event Co-ordinator

Assisted in the project management of 20 corporate hospitality dates at London 2012 Olympics. 200 guests per day.

- **Database Management**: Established new input protocols to improve efficiency when co-ordinating guest list, travel, and accommodation requirements. Co-ordinated ticketing and payments, daily reports, and the preparation of welcome packs for attendees.

- **Project Management; Transport and Logistics**: Negotiated group discount and project-managed all transport requirements including budget, schedule, route planning, pick up/drop off points, parking permits, driver contact lists, contingency planning, supplier liaison, and full onsite delivery. Implemented new protocol of daily real-time checks for roadworks/traffic congestion to prevent delays and insisted suppliers provide out of office contacts for weekend events.

- **Team Management**: Managed recruitment process, created briefing documents, and supervised all onsite travel co-ordinators. Motivated outdoor staff with provision of rain ponchos/warm refreshments and covered duties to allow for breaks.

- **Customer Service/Delegate Management**: Acted as first point of contact onsite, greeted guests, and managed flow of arrivals.

Fusion Event Staffing   April – August 2012
Event Support Staff: Supervisor/Hostess

Working in client-facing roles supporting the event-planning team onsite at 20+ conventions, experiential events, and meetings, including:

- Goldman Sachs Emerging Markets Conference, 500 attendees
- The Ideal Home Show, 250,000 attendees
- Microsoft Developers Conference, 5,000 attendees
- Toyota Yaris Press Launch, 150 attendees

- **Venue/Supplier Management:** Managed set-up of arrivals area including furniture, signage, displays, AV equipment, telecoms, Internet, and stationary. Took pre-emptive measures to alleviate crowding by requesting additional ropes/stanchions from venue.

- **Delegate Registration**: Greeted guests, issued badges, prepared welcome packs, brochures, and gift bags, database management and guest-list reconciliation. Implemented channeling/lane systems to manage flow more efficiently during times of overcrowding.

- **Speaker Management**: Assisted with the co-ordination of speakers: greeting on arrival and confirming their AV, catering, and transport requirements to ensure seminar programs ran to schedule.

- **Time Management:** Supervised breakout rooms and managed flow of delegates to ensure one-on-one meeting program ran to schedule.

- **Transport/Logistics:** Co-ordinated the transfer of guests, speakers, and VIPs between venues.

- **Brand Ambassador:** Facilitated consumer engagement, conducted product sampling, demonstration and promotion, encouraged participation and data collection.

Purple Strawberry Catering   January – April 2012
Waitress

Experience at 40+ events, including:

- Elle Style Awards, 500 attendees
- Apple iPad Air press launch, 150 attendees
- Cartier VIP client in-store event , 70 attendees
- Google's Zeitgeist conference gala dinner, 1,000 attendees
- Elton John's Annual White Tie & Tiara Ball, 500 attendees

Experience in operations, logistics, and customer service for the successful delivery of 40+ events including award ceremonies, weddings, conferences, and gala dinners. I used these opportunities to gain an understanding of:

- **Spatial Planning:** observed room layouts and learned the most effective use of space, along with techniques to improve flow and ensure efficient service.

- **Operations:** Volunteered to be part of the advance set-up team in order to understand the logistics of delivery, load-in, storage, prep, plating, service, bars/dispense, equipment, cloakroom, seating plans, staff catering/uniforms, load-out, waste removal, and collection.

- **Time Management:** Responsible for room set up, equipment prep, and the implementation of schedules and running orders.

- **Customer Service:** Experience in problem solving, dealing with complaints, and communicating with clients and VIPs. Ensured I was fully informed with regard to timings, facilities, and menu knowledge.

- **Team Work:** Assisted bar staff, kitchen porters, cloakroom attendants, and other waiting staff with their duties to ensure quick and efficient set-up/de-rig of event.

A lot of this information would never been included on a traditional resume used later on in your career. However, as you are just starting out it's all about communicating your passion and drive through the effort you've made and the knowledge, skills and experience you've gained in support roles. Don't get too hung up on the fact that it's not a traditional resume; this approach speaks volumes about the type of candidate you are.

You should also use this approach for any family, student, charity, or community events you've been involved in. Although these are smaller, seemingly less significant events, they can often give you an opportunity to demonstrate more skills because you are likely to have been involved in the project management stages, rather than just onsite delivery. Drill down into each one and use it to demonstrate what you contributed or learned. Don't just literally say what you did; demonstrate transferable skills with real-world examples—even if it's not from an event.

Tailor Skills and Experience to the Employer

"You have to be smart about how you word your resume. You need to get across the key words and the key skills—and show that you know what they are. Your resume needs to speak the right language to hit all the right buzzwords."

Sharyn Scott, Global Head of Events, Linklaters

You should always tailor your resume to the employer. Broadly speaking, this would involve highlighting your logistics, problem solving, and communication skills when targeting corporate employers and by showcasing experience from business events, such as meetings and conferences. Similarly, if you're targeting brands and experiential marketing agencies, highlight your communication, creative, and digital skills by citing experience of brand marketing events. Specifically, you should also align the content of your resume to the job description. If you're applying for an entry-level position—or any position for that matter—read through the job description and pick out all the key words and phrases used to describe the duties involved, and also the qualities they are looking for in the candidate, for example:

Duties

- Venue research
- Supplier management

263

- Budget management
- Onsite delivery
- Production of presentation materials and proposals
- Post event evaluation and reporting

Qualities

- Team player
- Ability to work under your own initiative
- Self-motivated with a polite and courteous manner
- Professional in dealings with high-profile clients

You then need to mirror each one of those points back to them in your resume. You do this by finding specifics examples from your experience that demonstrate where you have performed the same duties or exhibited the personal qualities they are looking for. Remember, it's not about just writing on your resume 'I am a team player' or 'I am self-motivated with a polite and courteous manner.' It's about demonstrating this through specific examples from your experience. Show them; don't tell them. Make sure the examples stand out on your resume and re-word them accordingly to use the same key words and phrases used in the job description.

If there is no job description available, search on recruitment websites for similar jobs from similar types of employers and take your lead from them. In the case of work experience/internships, find job descriptions for the most junior/entry-level event planning roles from similar employers and mirror that language.

Separate Unrelated Experience

Recently I was sent a resume where the candidate had obviously been told that his experience should be presented in reverse chronological order, starting with the most recent and working backwards. While that is the traditional format, in this case it was working against him. Some of his best event-planning experience had been pushed onto the second page—leaving non-event related jobs listed on the first page. As a recent college graduate, his most recent jobs were as a waiter in a couple of different restaurants; jobs he was doing while seeking event-related work experience. If an employer was skimming his resume and just saw his recent restaurant work, they might not even bother reading on to the second page.

If you're just starting your career, you're likely to have some non-event experience on your resume. Separate this out under 'Other Experience' and put it towards the end, so that you can lead with the most relevant event experience. That's all an employer is going to be interested in. Don't worry about trying to make all the dates connect in chronological order without any gaps—it's not as important as the experience itself.

Education

Don't take up valuable real estate on the first page of your resume by listing your education in detail. Move this to the end. Unlike some other professions, education is not as important as experience. If you've got a relevant qualification that you want to draw the employer's attention to, bullet point it in the in the personal profile/summary, e.g. *'Recent graduate of Leeds University with a 2:1 BA (Hons) degree in Event Management.'*

Event v Employer

On a traditional resume, the headline for each piece of experience is the name of the employer. However in the event industry, sometimes the event is more significant that the employer. Don't be constrained by format, decide for yourself which is going to make more of an impression, the event or the employer.

I was recently sent a resume where the first piece of experience read:

June – August 2012	**Globe Events , 10 Apsley House, 17 Upper Richmond, London SW15 2SH**
Position:	Event Assistant in Corporate Hospitality during London 2012 Olympics
Duties:	Administration of client/guest database……..

Remember that most employers will, at best, skim-read a resume. Which is exactly what I did when I received this one and all I saw was Globe Events; a company I hadn't heard of. Imagine how differently I would have reacted had it read like this:

London 2012 Olympics   June – August 2012

Event Assistant, Corporate Hospitality

Globe Events, 10 Apsley House, 17 Upper Richmond, London SW15 2SH

Duties: Administration of client/guest database….

Clearly, the event itself is of far more significance here than the employer, so don't be afraid to swap the order around or draw attention to it with a larger bold font. The purpose is the catch the reader's attention.

Similarly, a lot of the on-the-ground experience on your resume will likely be obtained by working for a staffing agency. However, the events themselves are going to be of much more significance than the agency, so make sure you bullet point some of these up-front to grab the reader's attention. For example:

Fusion Event Staffing   April – August 2012
Event Support Staff/Hostess

Experience at 20+ events, including:

- Cisco Live, 17,000 attendees
- Goldman Sachs Emerging Markets Conference, 500 attendees
- The Ideal Home Show, 250,000 attendees
- Microsoft Developers Conference, 5,000 attendees
- Toyota Yaris Press Launch, 150 attendees

Give Context

When listing event experience on your resume, don't assume the reader is going to know the event. For example, a resume I received read:

<u>Freelance & Volunteer Work</u>

Recruitment Agency Expo   February 2013
Seminar speaker management: co-ordinating all speakers and ensuring over 50 seminars ran to schedule

Peace One Day   October 2012
Encouraging and assisting guests to bid at charity art auction at Philips de Pury

Involve   September 2012
Event administration and supplier liaison. Compiling delegate packs for international employee engagement conferences

I wasn't familiar with 'Recruitment Agency Expo', so it would have been far more beneficial for the candidate if he had given it some context. Simply adding the venue would have given me an insight into the location and scale of the event. I might not have heard of the event, but if I knew that it was a three-day expo at a major convention center, the type that has capacities in the tens of thousands—as opposed to a one day event in the banqueting room of a small regional hotel—it would have told me so much more about their experience.

Similarly, I'd never heard of 'Peace One Day.' To me it sounded like the name of the event, but actually, it turned out to be the name of a charity. If someone is skim reading, Peace One Day isn't going to mean anything. Simply renaming that heading Peace One Day Charity: Art Auction would tell me so much more.

Finally, as the reader, I didn't know whether 'Involve' was the event or the employer. In this case, it was the employer, which again, I hadn't heard of. It would have been far more beneficial to lead with the fact that they'd worked on an international employee-engagement conference, as it demonstrates experience in meetings and corporate events. Also, there was a missed opportunity to include the name of the client. A quick glance at Involve's website shows they organize conferences for many well-known brands in the United Kingdom, such as the hardware store chain *B&Q* and the supermarket *Sainsbury's*— either of which would have added some extra weight the experience gained.

A few simple amendments to the way this experience was presented would have told the reader far more. For example:

Freelance & Volunteer Work

Recruitment Agency Expo   February 2013
NEC, Birmingham 1 – 3 February

Seminar speaker management: co-ordinating all speakers and ensuring over 50 seminars ran to schedule

Peace One Day Charity: Art Auction   October 2012
Philips de Pury, London

Encouraging and assisting guests to bid at auction for the Peace One Day charity

Sainsbury's Employee Engagement Conference   September 2012
The Four Seasons Canary Wharf, London E14
Involve, Riverside House, 26 Osiers Road, London, SW18

Event administration, supplier liaison, and compiling delegate packs for international employee engagement conferences

Job Titles

Always add a job title for every piece of experience. Often, when working onsite or in a volunteer capacity, there may not be an official job title given for your role, but you should always add one for the purpose of your resume. Try to make it sound as professional as possible without exaggerating your role. For example, instead of just saying you were a volunteer at a 5km charity run, you could refer to yourself as an event steward. If you were a volunteer at a charity gala dinner, refer to yourself as an onsite event co-ordinator. These are little details but they all contribute to how you position yourself to potential employers. Your aim is to work your way up until you can start including more event assistant and event co-ordinator roles on your resume, and less support roles. A good way to bridge the gap is through volunteering, as these will often involve less rigidly defined roles that you can legitimately call assistant or co-ordinator.

Be strategic and make sure your roles escalate from basic experience, such as crew, steward, waiter/banqueting staff, to more involved roles, such as host/ess and supervisor, then onsite event co-ordinator or assistant, until finally when you're working in an office-based role as an events assistant.

Testimonials

If you're just starting out and don't yet have a lot of experience to put on your resume, you can always drop in an impressive testimonial. Technically, these are probably better suited to include in your portfolio, however that's only going to help you once you've secured an interview. Therefore, I think it is fine to include one on your resume if you have sufficient space. That said, don't include one just for the sake of it. If you can get a testimonial from a prestigious employer, or you've recently completed a three month office-based work experience placement, that's when I would make a point of including one on your resume. In fact, it's especially useful to have a good testimonial if you've completed an internship or long stretch of work experience, because a cynical employer might read your resume and wonder why you weren't offered a job at the end of it. If you have a glowing testimonial, it will help counter any negative assumptions until you have an opportunity to elaborate at the interview stage. Add any testimonial you have to the end of the piece of experience, for example:

London 2012 Olympics   June – August 2012
Event Assistant, Corporate Hospitality
Globe Events, 10 Apsley House, 17 Upper Richmond, London SW15 2SH

Duties: Administration of client/guest database
         Researching transport routes to Olympic venues
         Compiling scripts for bus hosts on route landmarks
         Liaising with suppliers and logistics
         Compiling departure packs for guests and distributing tickets
         Assisting VIP guests at Olympic events

"Ben was a fantastic addition to our team leading up to the games. His attention to detail, work ethic, and great attitude made a very hectic period more manageable. We would recommend Ben to any company looking for a committed, hard-working team player."
                   Mr A.N Example, Managing Director, Globe Events

Just remember it's meaningless without the name and job title of the person you're quoting, so don't forget to include that.

Length

Keep the length of your resume to two pages maximum, never three, and bullet point as much as possible to avoid long paragraphs of text—there's more chance someone will actually read it then. I've read that some people recommend a one-page resume for recent graduates and those with little professional experience, but I don't recommend that. A two-page resume gives you the opportunity to demonstrate on the ground and volunteer experience, along with extra-curricular activities. That shows drive. It takes a certain 'go-getter' to be able to fill a two-page resume when they're just starting out.

Spelling Mistakes and Typos

"You wouldn't believe how many sloppy emails we get with grammar and spelling mistakes. You really have to ensure you're presenting yourself in a profession manner."

Dori Rodriguez, Senior HR Associate, Jack Morton Worldwide

Every contributor that I interviewed for this book said, in one way or another, that if a resume contains spelling mistakes or typos; it goes straight in the bin. I can't stress enough the importance of this. Think about it; event planning is all about attention to detail. If you're trying to convince an employer that you'd make a good event planner, but your resume is littered with mistakes, do you really think they're going to give you a shot? Remember, an employer is judging you based on what you *show* them, not what you *tell* them. It's easy to miss mistakes when you've written the resume yourself, so get at least two other people to proof read it for you.

Hobbies and Interests

"I always look at the hobbies and interest section to see what people do in their spare time. That's where the personality comes through."

Charlotte Saynor, former Vice President of Brands & Events, Fremantle Media Enterprises, and Head of European Events, Apple

This is the type of thing I usually see in the hobbies and interests section of a resume:

'Movies, reading, travel, and music'

Well great, you've basically described the hobbies and interests of about 90 percent of the population. The point of the hobbies and interests section is to give an insight into your personality. It might also provide areas of common ground for you to make a connection with the person interviewing you. If you're going to mention general interests such as movies, theatre or dance, be specific. Saying you like art house cinema, immersive theatre, or contemporary dance is going to tell me more about your personality. You can also use this section to highlight interests that might be relevant to the position. For example, if you're sending your resume to experiential agencies highlight creative hobbies and interests that might relate to that type of event planning, such as web design, blogging, photography and film-making.

Additional Skills

"Languages and first aid skills are always brilliant. Languages are always a phenomenal skill to have because you're often working on events overseas."

Martin Turner, former Global Head of Events for Credit Suisse

Don't forget to list any additional skills that might be useful for events. Languages are probably the most significant, followed by first aid training. However, experience in drawing, design and graphics software—such as CAD, Illustrator, Sketch Up, 3ds Max or similar—is always a great bonus, as is any interior/set design skills. For jobs in experiential or with creative agencies, any skills in digital, coding, web design, social media, search engine optimization (SEO), or photography/video/editing are also worth highlighting.

Creative Presentation

Getting creative with the way you present your resume can be a great way to get yourself noticed. I recently stumbled across a website called www.employingchris.com. Note: backup copy at www.becomeaneventplanner.org/employingchris.html. A young guy, Christian Brock, had been working as crew on various events while studying event management at university and was now seeking work as an event planner. On the website, he'd presented his background and experience in the form of a comic strip—

staring himself. He'd also used an honest, non-nonsense, and humorous tone throughout, while still communicating the essential facts about his skills and experience.

I thought the website was fantastic, not just because the creative approach made him stand out, but because his personality really shone through in the tone of his writing. It wasn't just another dry resume listing facts; instead, it really brought the person behind it to life. At the time, I didn't have any work I could offer him, but because I'd been so impressed, I remembered him and passed his website onto others in the industry.

Of course, this type of approach isn't going to work for all resumes. Chris was looking for work from creative and experiential agencies, so it happened to be perfect. It probably wouldn't have been as appropriate if he were looking for jobs in meeting planning, where there are more formal expectations. In that situation, an impeccably presented traditional resume would probably be more suitable. Therefore, always remember to tailor the presentation of your resume according the employer.

Sample Resume

The following pages contain a sample resume* incorporating all the advice above. You can see how, when it's all put together, it's possible to build an impressive looking resume in the early stages of your career using fairly basic experience.

*On regular-sized paper, this would be a two-page resume—and wouldn't look so cramped.

NAME	Address Line 1	Tel:	### ### ####
	Address Line 2	Email:	example@domain.com
	Address Line 3	Date of birth:	####

OBJECTIVE: Three month unpaid internship; junior events assistant role

SUMMARY

- Event Co-ordinator with experience in corporate, charity, experiential, and special events
- Experience in various support roles: event co-ordinator, registration staff, steward, brand ambassador, valet parking attendant, special events and hotel banqueting waitress
- Skilled in operations, transport and logistics, project management, production, delegate registration, customer service, health and safety, and speaker/supplier/staff management
- 2:1 Honors Degree, Marketing & Communications, Brunel University
- Resourceful, detail-oriented, team player with excellent communication, people, negotiation, and problem-solving skills
- Fluent in English, Spanish and French
- Looking to contribute my onsite knowledge, skills, and insights to add value to the event-planning process

EVENT EXPERIENCE

August 2012   LONDON 2012 OLYMPICS

Event Co-ordinator (Intern)
WPR Corporate Hospitality, 452 Upper Richmond, London SW15 2SH

Assisted in the project management of 20 corporate hospitality dates at London 2012 Olympics. 200 guests per day.

- **Database Management:** Established new input protocols to improve efficiency when co-ordinating guest list, travel, and accommodation requirements. Co-ordinated ticketing and payments, daily reports, and the preparation of welcome packs for attendees
- **Project Management, Transport, and Logistics:** Negotiated group discount and project-managed all transport requirements including budgeting, scheduling, route planning, pick up/drop off locations, parking permits, driver contact lists, contingency planning, supplier liaison, and full onsite delivery. Implemented new protocol of daily real-time checks for roadworks /traffic congestion to prevent delays and insisted coach suppliers provide out of office contacts for weekend events.

274

- **Team Management:** Managed recruitment process, created briefing documents, and supervised all onsite travel co-ordinators. Motivated outdoor staff with provision of rain ponchos/warm refreshments and covered duties to allow for breaks
- **Customer Service/Delegate Management:** Provided first point of contact onsite, greeted guests, and managed flow of arrivals

January-July 2012 EVENT SUPPORT STAFF

Supervisor/Hostess/Brand Ambassador/Valet Parking Attendant
Fusion Event Staffing, 33-35 Old Street, London EC47 6RG

Working in client-facing roles supporting the event-planning team onsite at 20+ conventions, experiential events, and meetings, including:

- Cisco Live, 17,000 attendees
- Goldman Sachs Emerging Markets Conference, 500 attendees
- The Ideal Home Show, 250,000 attendees
- Microsoft Developers Conference, 5,000 attendees
- Toyota Yaris Press Launch, 150 attendees

- **Venue/Supplier Management:** Managed set-up of arrivals area including furniture, signage, displays, AV equipment, telecoms, Internet, and stationary. Took pre-emptive measures to alleviate overcrowding by requesting additional ropes/stanchions from venue
- **Delegate Registration:** Greeted guests, issued badges, prepared welcome packs, brochures, and gift bags, database management and guest-list reconciliation. Implemented channeling/lane systems to manage flow more efficiently during times of overcrowding
- **Speaker Management:** Assisted with the co-ordination of speakers: greeting on arrival and confirming their AV, catering, and transport requirements to ensure seminar programs ran to schedule
- **Time Management:** Supervised breakout rooms and managed flow of delegates to ensure one-on-one meeting program ran to schedule
- **Transport/Logistics:** Co-ordinated the transfer of guests and VIPs between venues, liaised with coach drivers, managed drop off/pick up points, and facilitated guest parking to ensure effective traffic management and flow
- **Brand Ambassado**r: Facilitated consumer engagement, conducted product sampling, demonstration and promotion, encouraged participation, and data collection

[END OF PAGE 1, IF PRINTED FULL SIZE]

May/July 2012 WIRELESS FESTIVAL/ST PATRICK'S DAY PARADE

Event Safety Steward: Showsec International, 16 West Walk, Leicester LE1 7NA

- **Health and Safety:** Investigated disturbances, responded to emergencies, raised alarms using coded messages, supported emergency services with evacuation procedures, and monitored for signs of overcrowding

April 2012 BRITISH RED CROSS 10K RUN

Event Safety Steward: British Red Cross, 44 Moorgate, London EC2Y 9AL

- **Crowd Control.** Managed people flow, conducted pre-event checks, liaised with security/first aid/facilities to provide public with accurate information

March 2012 INTERNATIONAL WOMEN'S DAY: PUTNEY STREET PARTY

Organizing Committee Member: Women in Business Network, South London Chapter

- **Project Management:** Responsible for budget management, supplier liaison and arranging local council permits, road closures, and parking suspensions. Used drawing software to accurately visualize/measure space requirements
- **Negotiation:** Maximized budget by inviting local cafes to donate catering, persuaded local schools to provide students as set-up crew/stewards, and negotiated free use of indoor athletics track as wet weather backup venue
- **Marketing:** Created website, social media campaign, online competitions, and stunts to promote event resulting in 30% increase in visitors from 2011

February 2012 FASHION TARGETS BREAST CANCER: FASHION SHOW

Volunteer Co-ordinator: Breakthrough Breast Cancer, 2 High Holborn, London WC1 7EX

- **Production/Time Management:** Management of back-stage area including build and de-rig, facilities, catering and equipment. Co-ordinated hair and make-up, dressers and models to ensure fashion show ran to schedule

August 2011 WEDDING

Wedding Planner: Mr & Mr Wheeler-James

- **Project Management.** Created budget, schedules, running orders, contact lists and managed all catering, production, and entertainment requirements
- **Negotiation:** Negotiated 10% discount off original quotes, additional décor items for free, and refunds post-event for poor quality items
- **Logistics:** Supervised all pre-event travel and accommodation arrangements for guests, co-ordinated delivery and load-in schedule for suppliers, and managed all onsite transportation between venues

2008 - 2011 DORCHESTER HOTEL/ADMIRABLE CRICHTON

Special Event Catering/Hotel Banqueting Waitress

While at university, gained experience in operations, logistics, and customer service on 150+ events. I used these opportunities to gain understanding of:

- **Spatial Planning:** Observed room layouts and learned most effective use of space along with techniques to improve flow and ensure efficient service.
- **Operations:** Volunteered to be part of the advance set-up team in order to understand the logistics of delivery, load-in, storage, prep, plating, service, bars/dispense, equipment, cloakroom, seating plans, staff catering, uniforms, clearing, load-out, waste removal and collection.
- **Time Management:** Responsible for room set up, equipment prep, and the implementation of schedules and running orders.
- **Customer Service:** Experience in problem solving, dealing with complaints, and communicating with clients and VIPs. Took proactive steps to ensure I was fully informed with regard to timings, facilities, and menu knowledge.
- **Team Work:** Assisted kitchen porters, cloakroom attendants, and bar/wait staff with their duties to ensure quick and efficient set-up/de-rig of event.

2008-2011 NUMEROUS CONCERTS, FASHION SHOWS, BALLS, GUEST LECTURES AND FUNDRAISERS

Student Union Events Committee: Brunel University

- **Project Management.** Created budget templates, introduced schedules/ critical paths/reporting systems/online registration for all events, and created preferred supplier list offering discounted rates for all future student union events.
- **Artist/Speaker Management:** Booked acts, negotiated contracts, co-ordinated AV, transport, and green room/rider requirements.

EDUCATION

2008 - 2011	**Brunel University**	
	2:1 Honors Degree: Marketing & Communications	
2006-2008	**Richard Taunton College, Southampton**	
	A-Levels: Spanish (B), Business Studies (B), French (C)	
2002-2006	**Bitterne Park School, Southampton**	
	10 GCSEs: Grades A-B inc. English, Maths, Spanish, Art, French	

[END OF PAGE 2, IF PRINTED FULL SIZE]

22

How to Approach Employers

"I get a lot of emails, and even though I'm passionate about giving people opportunities, I just don't get time to answer all my emails. You've got to be as creative as you can to get the opportunity, or try to use the people you know to get an in-road"

Charlotte Saynor, former Vice President of Brands & Events,
Fremantle Media Enterprises, and Head of European Events, Apple

In Chapter 20, I explained how to turn the contacts you make onsite into opportunities to gain office-based work experience, by following up via LinkedIn and email. Unfortunately, this approach is only likely to work when you've already met them in person. If you try emailing someone cold to ask for work/work experience, the chances are you won't hear anything back. Most employers simply don't have to time to reply to emails asking for help. Phone calls are similarly tricky. Even if you're able to get through to the correct person, which is unlikely, it's never going to be the right time. Instead, you have to find a way to make yourself stand out.

Introductions and Associations

"Introductions from other people are much more powerful—my whole career has progressed like that—so you've really got to work out who you know and how you can use that to network. There's no excuse not to network nowadays, you've got things like LinkedIn and there's a lot of information about people online that you can find out."

Charlotte Saynor, former Vice President of Brands & Events,
Fremantle Media Enterprises, and Head of European Events, Apple

By far the best way to get a potential employer's attention is by way of an introduction. It might be a family member, a friend, a friend of a friend, a work colleague, or just someone you got chatting to at an event. This industry is all about networking. The first thing you should do is to scrutinize your friends and contacts; trawl through their connections on LinkedIn to see who knows whom, so you can ask for an introduction.

Obviously, the stronger your connection with someone the better, as then they can go one-step further and actually recommend you when introducing. However, there is also a lot of currency in just knowing someone by association. If you can name-drop a mutual contact or association in the opening line of your email, a potential employer is going to invest a little more time in reading it. To some degree, they'll probably feel more obliged to keep on reading because it's not a random anonymous person emailing them—which is easier to ignore—it's someone connected to their professional/social circle. This simple connection, however vague, is often what opens doors and creates opportunities.

Recently, I wanted to pitch an event to an organization with which I had no relationship. I looked it up on LinkedIn and discovered that the main contact person and I had a few connections in common. These connections weren't close friends of mine—and I hadn't spoken to most of them in years—so I didn't feel comfortable contacting them out of the blue just to ask them for an introduction (although I can be a bit reserved like that, if you're just starting out you need to be a bit more bold!). Instead, I fired off an email to the contact person at the organization and in the opening line, I explained that although we'd never met, we had some friends in common, and I named them. Low and behold I got an email back later that day, and I'm convinced it was because I name dropped a few contacts we had in common. It just gives you a way in that's harder to ignore.

Therefore, if you don't have anyone who can actually recommend you, do your research and find some sort of association with that person. It might be that you went to the same college as them or they used to work at the same company as a friend of yours. Just find some association that you can use in the opening line of your email to make a connection. A friend of mine who runs her own event-planning agency recently discovered that one of the other parents at her son's school happened to be the head of marketing for a major film distributor, and so was responsible for hiring event agencies to organize their premieres. Using the fact that their sons went to school together, she was able to reach out and make contact with that person despite having never met them.

Similarly, prior to working at FremantleMedia Enterprises, one of the contributors to this book, Charlotte Saynor, worked at Disney. She shared with me how she came to hire her second in command, Anna, an event manager in her team at Fremantle.

"Anna was working for Disney and although we didn't know each other well, she knew someone there who I'd worked with closely. She called me up and said 'I work with X person, I hear you've just moved to Fremantle, I'm looking for a job, I'd love to chat to you, can we have a coffee?' Ironically, she'd asked our mutual work contact about getting in touch with me and she'd actually said 'no, Charlotte's just started her new job so don't bother her yet.' But Anna thought, 'stuff that, I'm going to drop her a line anyway.' We went out for a coffee and she was still working for me five years later. I didn't have a full-time role to offer her just then, but I suspected I would fairly soon, and so I got her in freelance and that eventually turned permanent.

Anna had done some launch events, but she didn't have trade show experience. So, interestingly, if she'd been up against other candidates then she might not have got the job, but because she came in freelance and proved she could fit in culturally and we worked really well together as a team, I was happy to teach her the trade show side of things.

Because she was bold enough to call me up, I could tell she was hungry for it. Also, because she had worked at Disney, I knew she had a similar background to me—working for a big corporate—and that she'd understand where I was coming from in trying to set up a new events department from scratch within a large organization."

In this situation, Anna used the name of a work colleague to introduce herself, even though the work colleague had advised her not to bother Charlotte just yet. I admire Anna for that. You mustn't hold yourself back because of someone else's opinion—because that's all it is; an opinion, and in this case that opinion was wrong.

Research and Timing

"Make sure you know who you should be sending your resume to. I'm the CEO of the company and I get hundreds of resumes sent to me looking for work, and frankly 99 percent of those I pass on to someone else. If you've studied a company, you might find the correct contact on their website. If not, call them up. Ask the person who answers the phone who they recommend you approach. Don't just send your resume straight to the top of the organization."

Christopher Lee, CEO, ACCESS Destination Services

If you don't have an introduction or association, and you're going to approach a potential employer cold, spend a little time doing some research first.

Have a plan and make a targeted approach—don't just take a scattergun approach and send your resume out to everyone. Decide which type of events you want to get experience in, and then identify the companies that organize those events. Look at their websites and decide why you want to work there. Really spend some time on this stage. When you're desperate for work experience, it can be tempting just to approach all the main players in each sector—because chances are, at this stage in your career, you'd be happy to work for any of them. It's important however, to really fine-tune what it is that appeals to you about each potential employer and the work they do. If you analyze this and are clear in your own mind, it will influence how you tailor your resume towards them and how you answer certain questions if you get an interview. If you're clear about what you like and what you feel you can learn from them, that passion will come across to the employer and you'll do a better job at convincing them why you're a good fit for them. Imagine for a moment that you could have a job with all of the companies on your shortlist if you wanted. Now that the need for a job has been removed from the equation, ask yourself which one you'd choose first, then second, then third, etc.—and why? Make a note of your answers and keep them in mind when making your approach.

Working your way through your shortlist, check each company out on LinkedIn and identify the key people that work there. Find out if they have a formal internship/work experience program and who the contact person is—an HR person, the office manager, or a receptionist. Find out what they do with your resume—actually ask the question—do they pass it on to someone else, or is it them that looks at it? Personalize your resume for each company by looking at what they do and aligning the existing experience on your resume to that.

"Make a good first impression, starting with the person who answers the phone. Remember that a lot of companies in the event industry are small businesses where the management team are very hands on. We've had many occasions where someone on our team has put a call through about someone scheduling a job interview, and they've said to me 'this person sounds really smart, you should definitely talk to them.' Or they might say 'you're going to get a resume emailed to you by someone I was really impressed with talking to on the phone.' Never underestimate the power of a good first impression."

Christopher Lee, CEO, ACCESS Destination Services

The other factor to consider when making an approach is timing. If a company has a formal internship program, you can probably apply throughout the year, as they will keep all applications on file until their next intake. That said, it's worth doing some research to find out when their next intake is, and then working back several months. If you can make a big impression with your application and it's timely, you might stand out from the other resumes that have been sitting in a file for the past six months.

"Often the key is timing. So if I've got interns who are finishing in June, then around the beginning of January, I'll probably start thinking about getting new interns in to replace them."

Nicola Mosley, HR Manager, George P. Johnson

If you're approaching a company that doesn't have a formal internship program, do some research to find out its busy periods. You'll stand a much better chance of success if you approach them before a busy period, when they'll be grateful for an extra pair of hands. Remember to make the approach about two months before the busy period though. Otherwise, they might already be too busy to interview you and make all the arrangements.

"Always look at the calendar of events for different sectors. In TV for example, we have two big trade shows: MIPTV in March and MIPCOM in October, both in Cannes. It's a very busy time when lots of events are happening. If someone contacted me in August and said 'I know this must be the run up to a busy period for you with MIPCOM on the horizon, I'm trying to get some office-based work experience, can I come in and help you get ready for this big show by volunteering?' To me, that would make a great first impression because it shows they've really thought about it; they've researched the industry and they're offering their services at just the right time. Nowadays with the Internet, there's no excuse for not doing the research beforehand."

Charlotte Saynor, former Vice President of Brands & Events, Fremantle Media Enterprises, and Head of European Events, Apple

Get Creative

"Whether they email or write in, applicants should take the time to put something together that will create a bit of interest and help them stand out."

Nicola Mosley, HR Manager, George P. Johnson

Considering we live in a digital age where we communicate more and more in a visual way, I'm amazed how many talented job applicants still fall back on a traditional text-based, Word document resume. Job seekers are often so preoccupied with doing everything 'the right way', that it can stifle creativity and prevent them expressing any originality or personality. Which, ironically, is exactly what employers are looking for. I'd say that, at least 99 percent of the time, a creative approach is going to be considered refreshing and is likely to be remembered. It's just a question of judging how far to take it. With any creative approach, it's important first to consider the type of employer you are approaching, and what degree of creativity is going to be appropriate. Any approach still has to be professional, so it's important to get the tone right for your audience.

"Somebody once sent me a link to a customized Google map. On it there were pin points of all their experience, so where they went to college, where they grew up, where they had interned and they told their story that way."

Rachel Vingsness, Senior HR Manager, Jack Morton Worldwide

As with Christian Brock's website, www.employingchris.com, taking a creative approach to your resume presentation can really get you noticed. One of the contributors to this book, Martin Turner, the former Global Head of Events for investment bank Credit Suisse, shared a story with me about how a friend of his, also an event planner, went about her job search at the beginning of her career when she didn't have very much experience.

"With the little bit of experience that she had working on an event for PricewaterhouseCoopers, she put together a resume in the style of a newspaper. All the headlines were things about her; '[her name] runs front desk at PWC conference' and she included all her other information and skills in the style of articles, headlines and columns. Now, some people might say that's crazy. Just like some people probably told a then unknown Madonna back in 80s that it would be crazy to just turn up to a nightclub in New York with a tape and ask the DJ to play her

demo—but look where that got her. Sometimes, you just have to try a different approach—what's the worst that can happen? So, this friend got her newspaper resumes printed—this was in the days before digital—and sent them out to about 20 event companies and she got lots of calls as a result. Most of them said, 'look we don't have anything just yet but we want to see you because this is the most original approach we've had for a job in ages."

Another option is to turn your resume into a mini-portfolio; sent as a well-designed PDF with images. Think of it more like a presentation, instead of a traditional resume, and explain that you'd like to talk them through it in more detail when you meet. You still need to make sure it contains all the relevant information that an employer would expect to see on a traditional resume—it can't be all design and no substance—but use graphics, call-outs, bullet points, styled headings/fonts, and images to tell your story in a more interesting and eye catching way.

"We've had people send a portfolio instead of a traditional resume with lots of images showing them doing things, with descriptions showing what it's all about, what skills they have, and testimonials. So they've basically done a resume but as a visual book. Those sorts of things do grab your attention and it makes the person stand out – as long as it's done well. There's no point if you've done a portfolio and there's lots of mistakes in it or the visuals are just filler that's not backed up by experience. You do need to spend some time on it and do it well. I'm really happy to receive those."

Fiona Lawlor, HR Director, Jack Morton London and Dubai

You can still make a resume look formal and professional if you're applying for corporate jobs/work experience, but by adding a layer of design, you'll make it far more enticing to the reader. Of course, if you are approaching a creative employer or one that incorporates a lot of digital into their events, you can push it even further. I've yet to see a digital resume that uses video, sound, or animation—but I think I'd be very impressed if someone sent me one!

"Being proactive goes a long way. Sometimes we don't have an opening, but a candidate has approached us in a way that makes them stand out so we think 'this is someone we definitely want to keep in touch with.'"

Rachel Vingsness, Senior HR Manager, Jack Morton Worldwide

Hand Written

"Everybody sends email in this day and age, and you can give that a shot, but I would probably be far more impressed by getting a hand-written note that was nicely packaged from somebody."

Martin Turner, former Global Head of Events for Credit Suisse

On the flip side, given that everything is digital nowadays, another way to stand out is by doing the opposite and sending a beautifully handwritten cover letter, along with your resume, by snail-mail. Handwritten letters, on high quality stationary, with elegant writing using a fountain or calligraphy pen, are so unusual nowadays that they instantly feel special. It also shows that time and care has been spent on it and that it's a very personal correspondence just for the addressee—not one of dozens of letters printed off and sent out to every company in the area.

I think for a certain type of employer, perhaps those that organize society events, gala dinners, weddings, celebrations, and events for luxury brands, this could be an appropriate approach. But it really has to be done well; the paper, the type of pen used, the handwriting—it all needs to look luxurious, professional, and elegant with absolutely no mistakes.

Keep in mind that one of the advantages of sending a package by snail-mail is that it's far more likely to end up on someone's desk, rather than being buried, or lost in their inbox. If it's well presented, and time has clearly been spent on it, I'd say it probably wouldn't go ignored.

Attention-Grabbing Mailings

A lot of creative event planners send out 3D objects as invitations in order to make sure their event stands out, which creates a big first impression and gets people talking. I myself have sent out mailings in the form of sandals, keys, chocolate bars, scratch 'n sniff cards, pill bottles and even a rubber snake. So why not apply this approach to sending out your resume?

Many years ago, I remember a friend telling me how he applied for a job as a production runner on a well-known TV breakfast show. He knew they'd be inundated with applicants, so to stand out he attached his resume to a large helium-filled balloon, packed it into an oversized box, gift-wrapped it, and hand-delivered it to their offices. By the time he got home—this was in the days before cell phones—there was a message on his answer-machine asking him to come in for an interview. Now, I should just point out, the TV show was not your typical breakfast news and current affairs show. It was a zany, celebrity-focused alternative show aimed at under 40s. So, in this case, the creative approach was entirely in keeping with their style.

"We saw a candidate once who was from a design background. He hadn't been getting anywhere sending out a traditional resume, so he designed his resume in the style of a chocolate bar wrapper and sent it out wrapped around actual bars of chocolate with a clever name and headline that got everyone's attention. If you're going for a creative job, be creative."

Liz Sinclair, Managing Director, ESP Recruitment

There's also no reason why you can't apply this technique to the digital world too—especially if you're approaching experiential agencies or the in-house events departments of brands. I remember reading about a campaign by a marketing agency called CMA Digital who wanted to demonstrate its search engine optimization skills to potential clients. To do this, they sent out bars of chocolate to key contacts, over-printing the label with the phrase 'Who Sent Me Chocolate?' and instructing the receiver to type the phrase into Google. When recipients clicked on the first search result in Google they were prompted to enter a unique code, also printed on the chocolate bar, which took them to a custom landing page with a personalized welcome message. Not only does this creative mailing have an interactive quality, but it also demonstrates their search engine optimization skills—that they were able to get their website to be the first search result on Google for a particular keyword phrase. Now, imagine if a candidate were to take a similar approach to sending out their resume—I image that would probably result in a few callbacks!

One of the contributors to this book, Liz Sinclair of ESP Recruitment, the leading recruitment consultancy for the events industry, shared with me a great story about a candidate who was applying for a job with an experiential agency.

"We'd started the interview process with her, and then the client went away on holiday for three weeks, so the hiring process started to lose momentum. She was so keen to get the job that she went to their office every day and outside the front door, she did a chalk drawing on the pavement listing all her skills. Every day was a different drawing demonstrating a relevant skill. So each one started 'The skills of a great project manager....' then there were things like 'Part 1: Motivated', 'Part 2: Lateral Thinker', 'Part 3: Networker', etc., and each one had a different drawing. So, for motivated, there was a drawing of someone in bed with a little caption and arrow that read 'where most people are at 5am on Monday morning.' For Lateral Thinker there was a picture of three full glasses of beer, and three empty glasses of beer, with a caption that read 'Moving only one glass can you arrange them so empty and full glasses alternate?' Every day all the staff at the agency, including the Managing Director, had to step over her chalk drawings to get into work, even though no one had any idea what it was all about. Then on the final day, to highlight her skills as a negotiator she drew a picture of herself with a speech bubble that said 'Enough Chalk, Let's Talk' along with her phone number. It was quite an extreme thing to do, but it certainly got her noticed and she got the job. Obviously, for an experiential agency it worked—that's exactly what it's about—but it wouldn't necessarily be appropriate for a lot of other event jobs."

Creative approaches can really make a candidate stand out, but I can't stress enough how important it is that the idea is both relevant and appropriate. Judge the tone according to the potential employer. If you're sending something in with your resume to make it stand out, make sure it's something clever. Don't send anything that could be interpreted as a gift—like a box of cupcakes. Employers' don't want to feel as though they're being bribed. Choosing something that demonstrates your skills is going to be far more impressive than sending a random object just for the sake of sending something quirky.

"You know, a creative approach might not always work, but it's the same principle as asking for help; the answer will either be yes or no, but you'll never know unless you ask. If you're too scared to take a chance and put yourself out there, then you're going to be sending out a request for a job that is as generic and boring as the other three thousand people who want the job, and as an employer I'm just not interested in that."

Martin Turner, former Global Head of Events for Credit Suisse

LinkedIn

"Some people do contact me via LinkedIn, but funnily enough not as many as I think should. I do get some very enthusiastic people that contact me on LinkedIn and they stay in touch that way. If they're not yet qualified enough for one of our entry-level roles then I just tell them to keep us updated. In six months they might contact me again and say, 'I've been working on these two festivals, or on this charity event, and here's my updated resume.' So I'm happy for people to contact me via LinkedIn when they think they might have built up enough experience to apply for a position with us."

Fiona Lawlor, HR Director, Jack Morton London and Dubai

When I gave a talk at an event industry trade show to promote this book ahead of publication, I got talking to a lot of event management students and aspiring event planners. What really surprised me was how few of them used LinkedIn. Yet they were all on Facebook and Twitter!

LinkedIn is an essential resource when seeking work and work experience. I've mentioned in previous chapters that you need to swap contact details and keep in touch with everyone you meet onsite. LinkedIn is the best way to do that. It's also the easiest way to find out who knows whom so you can ask for introductions. And, if that isn't enough, you can also use it to contact HR people, recruiters, and potential employers—it gets your resume, in this case your LinkedIn profile, right under their nose.

A word of warning though, if you reach out to someone on LinkedIn or someone looks at your profile because you've left footprints by looking at theirs, your profile is going to be the first impression you make. It doesn't matter if you then intend to follow up with a creative mailing or digital portfolio, by then they will have already made a judgement about you. Make sure your LinkedIn profile is just as detailed as your resume, regularly updated, and uses all the advanced presentation and formatting tools available to include things like company logos. Also ensure there is a picture of you, those anonymous profiles are just horrible and from the point of view of a potential employer, much easier to ignore.

The other thing I want to stress is that you shouldn't bombard people on LinkedIn. Only reach out to people when you have sufficient experience to take the next step up. For example, don't reach out to people asking for office-based work experience until they can see plenty of onsite experience on your profile. Similarly, don't reach out to enquire about an entry-level job if you don't have sufficient office-based work experience on your profile. You probably only get one shot at approaching someone on LinkedIn before it's regarded as pestering, so don't waste that one opportunity by reaching out before you're ready.

In the case of HR contacts at larger organizations, it's their job to handle recruitment and internships. Therefore, I think it's probably fine to reach out to them twice on LinkedIn. You might want to drop them a line once you've got plenty of onsite experience, just to introduce yourself and get on their radar. Then when you come back to them in six months' time, having got some office-based work experience, they'll already know you and will be able to see the progress you've made.

If you do make an initial approach just to connect, make sure you explain in your cover message that you realize you don't yet have enough experience, but that you're really interested in working for their company and are intending to get more office-based experience before applying to them. You could even ask them, based on the experience on your LinkedIn profile, what experience they would suggest you to get in the interim period.

Just remember, don't pester! They're not there to offer you free career advice. If you can reach out and make a connection, then great, but be respectful of their time and limit the amount of times you contact them to once or twice. Don't become a nuisance.

Cover Letter

"I've got letters, reams and reams of emails, and more letters from people wanting to get experience that would make you slip into a coma after reading just the first line. They just don't make an impression."

Martin Turner, former Global Head of Events for Credit Suisse

Whether you're making an approach by email, snail-mail, or using a creative mailing or digital portfolio, you still have to send some form of cover letter. In some ways, this can often be more important than your resume because it's your opening pitch—they have to read this before they even think about looking at your resume. You might have the best resume or digital portfolio in the word, but if it's a boring standard cover letter, a potential employer might not bother opening it.

Don't ever use a standard cover letter, the type of thing that is so generic and fact-based, that it could be addressed to any company. Believe me, employers can spot these a mile away and will lose interest immediately.

Your cover letter needs to create some interest. Infuse some personality into it, use it as an opportunity to tell them why you want to work for them and what you can do for them. Don't just write general statements about how you 'love the creative events they do' and that 'you're looking to further develop your event-planning skills.' If you're inspired by their work, be specific. Explain how you've been following their work and refer to a particular project that made an impression on you, and why that led to you approaching them. You also need to see it from an employer's perspective; don't just write about what you want to get out of the opportunity, tell them what's in it for them. Treat it as if you are pitching your services to them; tell them what you can do and how that's going to benefit them.

"You need to write a really good email to get my attention. Explain why you want to come into Linklaters, but don't be insincere. Don't gush on about how you love Linklaters, because we're just a law firm. I'm really not interested in someone being overly flattering, because it's not going to help them get on in events. Why do you want to work here? Why events in the first place? What do you understand about it? What skills are you going to bring to the table? How am I going to benefit from you being in my team? A lot of the time people write emails as if I'd be doing them a big favor by letting them volunteer. That's not what I want to hear. I need to hear how you can help me deliver all the events we have on."

Sharyn Scott, Global Head of Events, Linklaters

The other common mistake people make in their cover letter is just to repeat facts and information about their education, skills and experience that are already contained in the resume. Sure, you need to give them a brief idea about where you're at and what you're after, but be concise. The shorter the cover letter, the better. Don't start reeling off past achievements and experience when all of that is already in your resume. Instead, whet their appetite for the resume. Mention how you've attached a creative portfolio instead of a tradition resume—that's going to make them more curious to open it—and how you'd love the opportunity to come in and talk them through it.

"The thing is to get to the point quickly, so if you're composing an email, I'd do a great subject title like 'Recent graduate seeking volunteer work—willing to work for nothing.' Think about your headline and then if you need to say something more, say it in two sentences."

Martin Turner, former Global Head of Events for Credit Suisse

If you're taking a creative approach to your resume, make the cover letter equally creative—in terms of both content and presentation. Include something that makes them want to click on the attachment and read more. Do something quirky with graphics and images. Think about creative mailings you receive in your email inbox; they're designed—they're not just boring old text. Which ones stand out to you and why? Just be careful not to go overboard and make it look like advertising or spam.

"Sometimes it's just simple things like finding out my name and personalizing the letter—you'd be surprised how many people don't even do that—anything that shows a little bit more thought. They might write, 'I read an article about X event that you did and that made me look into your company, and on your website I was really interested in X, Y, Z event.' I'm just looking for something that personalizes it and makes it less of a standard letter approach. Show me that you're interested in us as a company, rather than just applying to all the agencies for an internship."

Nicola Mosley, HR Manager, George P. Johnson

Follow up with a Phone Call

However you decide to approach an employer, you need to follow up. Don't just fire off a resume and expect them to get back to you. Chances are they won't. I'm amazed by how many emails I get asking for work or work experience—the majority of which, I confess, I don't get a chance to reply to—and only one in approximately 100 ever pick up the phone to follow up. Don't give up just because you didn't hear back from an initial approach. In fact, sometimes not getting an initial reply can be a good thing as it gives you a legitimate reason to pick up the phone and call.

Calling someone about work or work experience is a tricky thing to get right. Chances are, whenever you call, it won't be the right time. Also, you have to consider that, by calling someone up you are putting them on the spot—and most people don't like that.

In my opinion, there are two occasions when it's appropriate to call. The first is when you're reaching out to determine whom the best person is to approach in writing. This is a great opportunity to make a good first impression with someone at the company, without actually bothering them or taking up too much of their time. If you are polite and friendly, you might get into a conversation with them and they could end up giving you some valuable tips on who to approach, when the right time is, and how best to go about it.

The second occasion when it's appropriate to call is when you're following up on a previous approach made in writing. Most people would consider this a perfectly acceptable reason to call. I would suggest waiting three to five days after sending an approach in writing before following up with a call. They will either have looked at your resume, and can now give you some idea whether they have anything for you, or your call will remind them to look at your resume.

Personally, I would not advise calling someone if you haven't first made an approach in writing. Not only are you likely to catch them at a bad time, without having seen your resume, they probably won't be able to tell you if they have anything suitable for you. Now, there are exceptions to this of course. Some people admire a candidate who is bold enough to just pick up the phone and ask, like Charlotte Saynor's earlier anecdote about a work associate calling her about a job. However, I think that Charlotte is perhaps in the minority, or perhaps timing might have played a part in that situation—given that she knew she'd soon be needing some support. Unfortunately, I think there is a greater chance of getting off on the wrong foot by calling someone out of the blue without first sending in something in writing.

"Be persistent, but not annoying. You might apply one month and there's no vacancy, but three months later, there is. In reality, we don't bother going back through old resumes, we just look at new ones coming in. So keep up the communication."

Nathan Homan, Co-founder, Rouge Events

In reality, you might find you have to follow up more than once. Either because they haven't looked at your resume yet, or because they just don't have anything for you at that time. In either case, tell them that you're very interested in working for them and use it as an opportunity to ask when they would suggest is a good time to follow up again.

"Asking a potential employer when to follow up is always best. It shows respect and it gives them the opportunity to be honest with you. As a candidate, it also gives you a first look at what your chances are. If they say, 'don't call us, we'll call you' then you probably don't have a great chance with them, but if they say a couple of weeks or months, then it gives you permission to get back in touch."

Christopher Lee, CEO, ACCESS Destination Services

Remember to adhere to whatever time frame they tell you, or if you can't get that information from someone, be sensible about it. You need to keep on that company's radar by re-approaching them, but you don't want to become a nuisance. Of course, every situation is going to be different; there is no set time you should wait before re-approaching. You simply have to make a judgement call based on the feedback they give you. As a general rule, I would say it's fine to re-approach every few months unless told otherwise. Just keep further correspondence brief and only approach one contact within the company. Perhaps vary the method of approach too, so after you've sent your resume in and followed up with a call, you could maybe follow up again two to three months later by dropping that person a message via LinkedIn.

"There's a fine line between following up and maintaining a relationship, and just annoying the hell out of us. You know, some people email the CEO and copy on dozens of other people in the office because they've gotten hold of various emails. It's too much. It shows whether a candidate is business savvy if they know how to handle all of that properly. Being proactive is good and to be encouraged, but you've got to get the balance right"

Rachel Vingsness, Senior HR Manager, Jack Morton Worldwide

Ask for Advice

One of the best ways to develop a relationship with a potential employer is to target them for advice, rather than work or work experience. Approaching someone, at a company you admire and ultimately want to work for, and asking for 15 to 20 minutes of their time to pick their brains about the industry can be a great way to get your foot in the door. If you make it clear upfront that you're not asking them for work/work experience, it takes the pressure off, and you'll find that many are happy to help in this way.

The same principles apply as if you are approaching them for work, in that you need to do your research. You need to make it clear why you've chosen to approach them over another person or company; perhaps you discovered they were the lead planner on an event that inspired you, or they have the type of corporate career you aspire to. A bit of subtle flattery never goes a miss—as long as it's genuine—just don't go overboard! Be specific and try to demonstrate some depth of understanding. I get lots of emails saying, *'I love the creative events you do'* and I just roll my eyes because it tells me that they're focusing on the wrong aspects of the work; it makes them sound like amateurs. Don't focus on the 'front-end' creative; show me you understand the strategy *behind* the creative.

You also need to demonstrate your passion for the event industry by telling them about the effort you've put into getting experience. Send them your resume and in the cover note explain that you're trying to break into evening planning, explain where you're at in terms of getting experience, and ask whether they could spare 15 minutes for an informal chat about working in the industry. If you say something along the lines of, "*I know you probably don't have any suitable opportunities for me at [company name] but I'd really appreciate any advice you could give me personally that might guide me in the right direction.*"

"*Somebody gave me a break once, and I'm more than happy to do that for someone else. I may not be in a position to give someone a job, but I can sit down with them for a chat, get out the event guides and tell them who they should speak to, or which route to take.*"

Charlotte Wolseley Brinton, former Head of Events,
Rhubarb Food Design

Ideally, you want to try to get a face-to-face meeting, which will increase your chances of developing a relationship with them. To push for this, casually mention a time frame, i.e. 15 to 20 minutes, perhaps suggest 'over coffee' so that it comes across as informal, and definitely offer to travel to them whenever is most convenient, so as to minimize their level of commitment.

Not only will you probably get some great career advice, you'll also have a warm contact with a potential employer who you can then go back to when you do have sufficient experience. Depending on how well you get on, they might do a whole lot more to help you by introducing you to others, keeping their ears open for suitable work, or even offering to become your mentor. One of the contributors to this book, Charlotte Wolseley Brinton, former Head of Events at Rhubarb Food Design, remembers hiring someone who took this approach—even though, at the time, she didn't have a position available:

"She was so enthusiastic. She didn't even come in to ask about a job, she just said 'I want to sit down with you and talk about the industry because I'm really interested in getting into it. I don't know very much about it, I really like the idea of it because I love organizing and I'm particularly interested in catering, but I've only recently come out of university.' She just presented really well; she was eloquent, enthusiastic, well dressed, and groomed. She was honest; she didn't try to overstate her experience, so I found her a job because she was too good to pass up. I just felt she had the right characteristics and enthusiasm to be part of the company. Sometimes, despite having little or no experience, a candidate just really makes a great impression. Had she just sent in her resume to apply for a job in the normal way, I probably wouldn't have considered her because of her lack of experience. So, by being unassuming and asking to meet me for some advice really paid off for her!"

Charlotte Wolseley Brinton, former Head of Events,
Rhubarb Food Design

The candidate mentioned above clearly got lucky, but remember that she was straight out of university, curious about the industry, and so approached Charlotte before she embarked on her career path, to see if it was right for her. While you might want to do something similar before you start out in the events industry, I'm suggesting you use this tactic a little more strategically; once you've already decided a career in events is right for you. As a result, I would recommend that don't approach someone for advice in this way until you've already put a lot of effort into gaining experience yourself. A potential employer or mentor is far more likely to give up their time to help you, if they can see you've already made an effort to help yourself.

Informational Interviews

While approaching someone to ask for advice over coffee is a great way to target a senior person within the industry, this is very much an informal 'softly-softly' approach. You're not going in asking for a job, you're looking to develop a high-level contact that might be able to help you. Whereas, requesting an informational interview is a great way to reach out to a particular company that you wish to work for, and therefore is best employed as a sort of 'consolation prize' if you've already made an approach and find yourself being told 'we're not hiring right now.' It gives you an extra hand to play if you're faced with an initial rejection.

"If a company says, 'we're not hiring right now', it's not unprofessional to say 'I understand. Is it possible to have an informational interview, maybe just over the phone with whoever does your hiring, to better understand your company and what you're looking for, so I can prepare myself for when you do have a position available?' If you know what they're looking for, you can identify what experience you're lacking and go out and get it. Ask them 'what should I be doing in the meantime to position myself better as the right candidate?' It's very impressive when people take that step. If you find a company that is prepared to do that, and you make a good impression, it can often result in them saying 'go ahead and send me over you resume.' I definitely think it's a good tactic."

Christopher Lee, CEO, ACCESS Destination Services

23

Preparation You Must Do for an Interview

"You don't demonstrate passion by using big hand gestures and being effusive or dramatic. You do it by showing 'I did this, I read that, I taught myself this, I looked into that.' Passion is about showing that you've been proactive and that you're hungry for it."

Nathan Homan, Co-founder, Rouge Events

Throughout this book, I've stressed the importance of *showing* an employer your passion, rather than *telling* them. If you've followed my advice and acquired an impressive amount of on-the-ground experience, which you then used to get office-based work experience, your resume will already have shown an employer your drive and commitment. Before long, that will get you to the next stage, an interview. An interview is an opportunity for you to back up that drive and commitment by demonstrating your knowledge and understanding. Therefore, it's imperative that you put just as much effort into preparing for an interview, as you did getting experience.

Study the Company

"What really makes someone stand-out is when it's obvious they've studied my company. When they can talk about the values we have, or they recognize our accomplishments and says things like, 'I want to be part of the team that's voted one of the top 25 DMCs worldwide,' or, 'I believe in a company that has values like service, leadership, respect and integrity.' When people show they've really done their homework on my

organization, they understand our goals and objectives, or maybe they've taken the initiative to talk to one or two of my employees or suppliers—that really stands-out to me."

Christopher Lee, CEO, ACCESS Destination Services

A lot of job seekers seem to think that researching a company prior to an interview means looking at their website. However, most employers have much higher expectations than that. At a basic level, employers want you to show that you understand who they are and what they do: that you understand their core offerings, where they sit in the industry, what regions they operate in, which clients they work with, and who their competitors are. They'll also want you to know who their chief executive and senior management team are, their backgrounds, the company's portfolio of events, what they've done recently, and their achievements. However, there's a deeper understanding an employer is also looking for. They're not just looking for you to pay lip service, to look up past events or facts about the company and drop them into your answers. Employers are interested to see what you do with that research, how you relate to it, or apply it to your own situation.

Use the research you've done to communicate something about yourself and your understanding, either of the industry, the work, or the company. Don't just tell a potential employer how much you love X event that they did, tell them why—and don't just focus on the creative, that isn't what they want to hear. You'd expect the average person to evaluate an event based on the creative. As a job seeker wanting to work in event planning, you need to show that you were inspired by the bigger picture; the purpose, the process, the concept, how it communicated a key message, the values, the delivery, the technology, the methods used to engage the audience and, ultimately, the results—what was achieved? It's good to show an employer you've done your research by referring to the work they've done, but don't just leave it at that. Use it to demonstrate your own knowledge and understanding of the entire event-planning process.

Alternatively, you might have read articles written by employees of the company or noted talks and presentations they've given at industry events. Perhaps you've noticed the company is passionate about sustainability, or takes an active involvement in education and mentoring. Use what you've discovered to engage with them about industry-wide issues that they as a company, and yourself, are passionate about. It's always impressive when a candidate has a broader understanding of the company's values and ethos, rather than just focusing on the events they've done. It's also a great way to communicate who you are as a person, so they can see how you'd be a good fit for their organization.

"If someone says, 'I've looked at your website...' that's not really enough. That's just a given. They need to use that as a starting point for more in-depth research. For example, you can see on our website that we do Cisco Live, but have they then taken that further and checked out the Cisco Live website to really understand what that's all about? Maybe if they'd observed an event that we did and were able to compare it with a similar event by one of our competitors, then talk in a little more depth about which bits worked better on one or the other. It's about having that broader understanding of what the company does and how that fits in with other organizations and the industry in general."

Nicola Mosley, HR Manager, George P. Johnson

Follow Their Social Media

A great way to get a broader understanding of a company is to follow them on social media. Not only are these sites updated far more frequently than a company's main website, but the updates are often more varied and informal, with posts about current trends, employee achievements, news articles, and wider industry issues. Following a company on social media for a length of time will give you a much clearer idea about who they are as an organization, and may give you something topical to mention in an interview.

Understand the Issues Affecting the Industry

In addition to researching the company, it's important that you can also demonstrate an understanding of the issues currently affecting the industry as a whole. Over the past decade, there have been countless issues that have influenced and contributed to the evolution of the events industry—some good, and some bad. These include: the rise of formal training and education, the introduction of event management degree courses—and the knock-on effect that's having with graduates flooding the jobs market, the pressure for events to become more sustainable, the impact of digital, social media and new technologies, changes in licensing and health and safety legislation, and the effects of the economic downturn.

"In the depths of the recession in 2008 we were in the middle of the economic downturn, we had political scrutiny on meeting spending and social scrutiny on corporate excess. I had a candidate come for interview whose background was in social events. She kept saying things like, 'I'm so excited about this industry, I love doing big events, I've done a few big weddings and when I was in a sorority I did all our parties, I just really love special events, I throw great parties, and I want a job with you.' Here was someone who was completely oblivious that our industry was going through a really tough time and no one was throwing big events, hiring big named entertainment or using limousines. At the time, it was all about scaling back and paring everything down. Then here was someone telling me how excited they are about doing big parties. It was like, 'have you got any idea what's going on in our industry?'"

Christopher Lee, CEO, ACCESS Destination Services

If you want to stand out, show that you have an awareness of all the issues that have had an impact on the event industry, both in the recent past and those that are topical now. The event industry is constantly evolving and adapting to change, so you really do need to educate yourself on what's happened, what's currently happening, and what's expected to happen in the future. Most of which you can get from reading trade journals/websites and by signing up with associations such as ILEA.

Demonstrating an awareness and understanding of the industry will show an employer that you are truly passionate, and it's the kind of thing that will set you apart from dozens of other average applicants. Remember, employers are looking for the best; they might interview 10 candidates for one position. The more informed you are, the more impressive you'll be.

Equip Yourself with Relevant Local Knowledge

"If someone was coming to me for work experience for events that took place in London, then I'd probably say, 'can you tell me some great venues in London for X, Y, Z type of event?' just to see how clued up they were. If they were doing work experience for me, one of the tasks I might give them might be; 'we've got a cocktail party happening for 100 people on this day, can you do some research and find out what venues are available; hold them, get the contact, create a spreadsheet with all the options, then come back to me.' If someone's really tenacious and hungry for it, they'll already know what the top venues are for that employer's type of events. It's all information that you can research yourself at home."

Martin Turner, former Global Head of Events for Credit Suisse

Taking the time to research the type of venues and suppliers that a potential employer is likely to use for their events is really quite a basic level of preparation you can do prior to an interview. If you're going for an interview with a corporate firm, make sure you know all the 5 Star conference hotels they might use. Similarly, if you're going for an interview with a creative special events company, make sure you know which catering companies they prefer to use.

If you read the trade magazines, often when profiling an event they'll refer to all the specialist suppliers involved. From there, you can visit each supplier's website and get a feel for who they are and what they do. Before long, you'll start to build a little black book of suppliers and you'll get a feel for who they are, what they do, and which event-planning companies they work with.

The more knowledgeable you are, the greater impression you're going to make and, ultimately, the more useful you're going to be to that employer. You can even make a virtue of the research you've done in order to make yourself stand out:

"Every bit of industry knowledge you can acquire is going to help. We've had candidates say, 'I'm new to your city, but on my own time I went around and looked at all the major event venues and studied their websites, so I have a feel for which ones are suited to different types of events.' Or even better, if they can relate it back to our company by saying, 'I know you've used these three venues a lot so I downloaded their floor plans and studied their events brochure to familiarize myself with them in more detail.' If you can drop in information like that, it really indicates that this is someone who has made an effort to prepare themselves better for this opportunity, and things like that are always going to make you stand out."

Christopher Lee, CEO, ACCESS Destination Services

Familiarize Yourself with Trends and Technology

"In order for Jack Morton to keep being innovative, setting the bar high, and making sure we're at the forefront of our industry, we need to make sure we're keeping up with what's going on and current trends. So if a candidate comes in and they're already doing that, and saying to us 'have you heard about this campaign, or this website, or this supplier, or this new technology?' That can only impress. That's the sort of behavior that shows that you're truly passionate about this industry and what you want to do."

Dori Rodriguez, Senior HR Associate, Jack Morton Worldwide

In addition to researching the basics, such as venues and suppliers, demonstrate that you're knowledgeable about current and up-and-coming trends and new technologies. This is an area where younger people can really shine. Many employers rely on younger members of their team to keep them abreast of what's on-trend, or draw their attention to interesting discoveries that could inspire, or be integrated into, an event or campaign. Be the person who is tuned in to your surroundings and popular culture, who has an eye for all things new and original, and generally soaks up ideas and concepts that might influence future work. That demonstrates real passion and those type of people are a valuable assets to any team, especially in creative agencies.

"I love it when candidates talk about something new or up and coming—especially if it's something that I might not know about. It could be new event rental items, something they saw at another event, or some kind of next big thing trend that they feel is coming up."

Chad Hudson, President, Chad Hudson Events

Demonstrate Theory in Practice

"There's always academic reading they could do. Just Google 'event management theory' and a lot of books will pop up. If you're coming to an agency like ours, you should have identified that brand experience is one platform of events that we do, so come prepared having read Shaz Smilansky's book Experiential Marketing *and show me what you've learned from that. Find a case study in the media that brings her theory to life and talk me though it to show what you understand.*

Even if they came having read some of the old classic event management theory, which is very much process-driven—dealing with things like budgets, orders, risk assessments, and health and safety—and they could talk about that, that's also a good start. If you really want to get into events, then why aren't you reading that anyway? That sort of thing shouldn't be a chore. If you're not excited to research the industry you want to work in, then do you really want to do it?

A candidate might not have a huge amount of experience, but if they've made the effort to put together a presentation about something relevant, that shows how much they understand, I would definitely think well done for doing that."

Nathan Homan, Co-founder, Rouge Events

In the early stages of you career, one of the main purposes of an interview is for the employer to get a feel for how much you know and understand. If most of your experience to date is only in support roles, topped up by some office-based work experience, you can use an interview as an opportunity to demonstrate how much more you actually understand about the event-planning process—even if you've yet to experience some of it first-hand. You can do this by showing what background reading you've done on the theory of event management and/or marketing communications in relation to live experience. More importantly, you can show that you understand how this theory works in practice by relating it to actual case studies.

For example, you may not have had much involvement in large-scale public events or experiential campaigns. So take along a case study of one and use it to talk through the event production; how it was staged, what processes you think the organizers would have followed, or how you might have done something differently, in order to communicate your understanding. That would be particularly impressive. Especially if you're honest about it and said something along the lines of, '*I realize I still need to build up a lot more experience, so in the meantime I've been reading a lot of books about the theory of event planning/live communications and applying this to case studies of real events to further my understanding. I've prepared a short presentation about an event that really inspired me, which I'd love to talk you through.*' Not only does this show an employer that you're motivated to better educate yourself, it could also show them that you have the potential to take on more responsibilities in other areas of event planning, which might not obvious from the experience on your resume.

Therefore, my advice would be to look at what's missing from your experience and compensate with a case study applying theory to a real-world example. Then use this to demonstrate your understanding.

Prepare Your Story

"Something that's very important for me at the interview stage is, 'why Jack Morton?' Does the candidate really understand what we do, and do they have a specific passion for this type of work? Candidates that come prepared with 'my story', which explains why they've chosen Jack Morton, always impress me. I like it when they just have a clear way of explaining, in a chronological order, what their path has been, and what got them to where they are now. For example, this is where I went to college, this is how I got an interest for this type of work, that led me to this experience, which led on to this experience, and this is why I'm here now. It's almost as if I don't have to ask questions. They come prepared to tell me what they want and why they want it. For me, that explanation at the start of an interview is a huge plus.

In their story, I want to be able to tell that they did research and that they have a unique and special interest in Jack Morton. Pretty much the last thing a recruiter wants to feel is that this candidate is desperate for a job—any job, anywhere. I want to make sure this person is going to be passionate about the company they'd be joining."

Dori Rodriguez, Senior HR Associate, Jack Morton Worldwide

All employers will want to know why you want to work for their company in particular, and all too often they receive lame and generic responses such as, *'I love the creative events you do.'* Spend some time, prior to an interview, crafting a good response to this question. Your answer should tell them something about who you are, so that they can see a link between your passions and interests and the type of work they do. If you're going to comment on the quality of their events, reference a specific project that inspired you and relate it to something you're passionate about. For example, you might mention a car launch they did using 3D projection mapping onto the body of the car, and use that to explain how you're really interested in applying new technology in unexpected ways. Talk about what you think you can learn from working there, but more importantly, talk about what you think you can add to their organization. See it from their perspective; what can you do for them?

Once you've given some thought to how you're going to answer this question, relate it back to your own life and career path. Compose a coherent narrative that explains your background, inspirations, choices, experiences and the career milestones that have led you to them now—and express this in a clear, concise way to act as an introduction. If you can lead with that at the beginning of an interview, without the employer having to prompt you, it will give them a great insight into what you are all about and, hopefully, why you'd be a good fit for them.

Prepare a Portfolio

"I love portfolios; in fact I have my own. If you can present your experience in a visual way, it's so much more engaging. Create case studies for events you've worked on, include photos, floor plans and stage designs, if you've got a testimonial put that in too, and you can even demonstrate your ability to budget manage in a digital portfolio.

I'm pretty sure I got this job on the back of my portfolio. As it happened, they'd already interviewed a lot of people but they just didn't get a sense that any of them could actually deliver these big events. I'm sure they could have, but it just didn't come across. So I did a very comprehensive portfolio, with lots of color images and testimonials. I then talked through the entire process explaining what I did to influence each element e.g. 'this is the design for the stage set because it would allow us to do X, Y, Z' and 'we used a multi-interactive screen on this event, so we could have a fixed camera here.' I talked in technical terms and showed them printouts of schedules to show the entire experience from start to finish, so they could see everything that I was part of.

I think it shows real initiative to come with a portfolio, especially for a junior candidate, and it creates a talking point in the interview. If someone emailed me and attached a portfolio saying 'I'd like to talk you through this when we meet', I'm not going to say no to that!"

Sharyn Scott, Global Head of Events, Linklaters

Every contributor to this book encouraged the idea of taking a portfolio to an interview. Most event professionals think in a visual way, so it's entirely appropriate to communicate with them in this way at an interview. Visuals make it easier to engage someone; they bring the event to life and describe elements quicker and more accurately than words alone. It also gives the employer an opportunity to see your presentation skills in action.

Presenting your resume in the form of a mini-portfolio is a great way to catch someone's attention. However, for an interview, prepare a portfolio that goes into greater depth. You might create one slide for each event you've had a significant involvement in, to explain your role and demonstrate relevant skills. This is a great way to give an overview of your experience. If you've worked in support roles such as a waiter or crew, just consolidate these into one slide. There's no need to detail each one individually, just show that experience as a whole.

I'd then suggest picking one, maybe two, events to case study in more detail. In Chapter 19, I encouraged you to gather up as much information as possible while working onsite—such as production schedules, stage plan, set designs, floor plans, itineraries, agendas, and photos of the build and de-rig. Incorporate these into your portfolio to talk through your understanding of the event planning and production process. Ideally, you should case study the event you've had the most involvement with—perhaps from your office-based work experience—so that you can talk about the specific things that you did, in addition to the overall event production. You might start by outlining the broader event, explaining why things were done in a certain way, and then move on to explain how you fitted into that. However, if you're putting together a portfolio to make the move from onsite to office-based, then it's fine to profile someone else's event in which you might only have had a minor onsite role. In that situation, it's more about showcasing your overall understanding about event planning and production— maybe explaining the things you liked, what worked and what didn't, why you think certain choices were made, or what you'd have done differently—rather than just your actual contribution.

When choosing photos, include one or two that give an overall impression of the event to set the scene, but use the remainder as visual cues to talk through elements of the planning and production. For example, show pictures of the stage to discuss why certain technical production choices were made, or show the room layout in order to explain numbers, flow, and use of space. Be careful not to focus on just the superficial elements; it's not about showing the event from the guest's perspective, it's about showing it from the planner's.

"It's rare that applicants bring along portfolios, but I love it when they do. Even if it's not for events they worked on personally. They might have drilled down into the Olympics opening ceremony and discussed why they felt the different elements of the content were great. Not just 'oh it was exciting', or 'it looked amazing', but 'I can see why they used that staging technique', and 'I don't think this bit worked as well as it could have and this is why', or 'this is what I would have done to improve it'—to critically appraise it. That's pretty impressive. They're making an effort to show me what they understand. Also, the way they lay that presentation out becomes a talking point because I can see if it's smart and slick and if they're able to communicate well through presentations."

Nathan Homan, Co-founder, Rouge Events

Be Prepared to Think on Your Feet

"When I interview people now, even if it's just an informal chat and we're sitting in Starbucks, I always say, 'look at the space we're in now and if we were going to put on an event here, tell me how'd you'd do it; how many people could you fit it? Where would you put the tables? What would you think of? What do you think you'd need to pull it off?'"

Charlotte Wolseley Brinton, former Head of Events,
Rhubarb Food Design

It's not uncommon for employers to throw you an unexpected task in an interview. One of the requirements of being an event planner is to be able to think on your feet, respond quickly, and find solutions. So go into an interview primed and ready to demonstrate how you would deal with hypothetical situations.

312

24

What to Say and Do in an Interview

"You have to understand that when you're coming in to see us, you're going to have to do some work just to get the opportunity or even be considered for the role. It's very much a two-way thing. Sometimes people seem to think they just have to turn up at an interview and answer whatever questions we put to them. However, the candidates that we usually end up hiring are the ones who have taken it that step further and been proactive in the interview; they contributed something to the process."

Nicola Mosley, HR Manager, George P. Johnson

Interviews can be difficult there's no denying it. There is so much information you need to communicate, in a short space of time, to a complete stranger, all the while winning them over with your sparkling personality.

It helps to first pause and consider the purpose of an interview, which is:

- To demonstrate that you have the required skills, knowledge and understanding
- To demonstrate why you'd be a good fit for that organization

The first comes down to how well you communicate what you're capable of—what you've learned through study and experience. Do you understand what events, the industry in general and this company are all about, and do you have the necessary organizational, communication and project management skills to add something to their organization?

The second purpose is achieved by communicating the qualities an employer is looking for; which ultimately comes down to your attitude and personality. Are you a confident yet humble, professional, committed, resourceful, team player with a tenacious, enthusiastic, 'can-do' attitude?

Most employers place equal emphasis on both criteria. You may have all the right skills, but if you don't have the right personality to fit in, they're not going to hire you. Likewise, you may demonstrate all the right personal attributes and show potential, but if you don't have sufficient skills or knowledge, an employer is likely to think you're not yet ready.

In order to meet both criteria, you need to think very carefully about how you present both yourself and your experience in an interview situation. Don't leave it to chance. Be strategic and prepare your talking points in advance, so that what you say and how you say it illustrates the specific skills and qualities they're looking for.

Arriving for Your Interview

"Be on time. If you are late, it's a reflection on your time management and organization skills. It tells us you don't really care enough."

Rachel Vingsness, Senior HR Manager, Jack Morton Worldwide

This might seem obvious, but I was surprised how many contributors to this book mentioned it; which suggests it happens a lot. You should arrive early for any interview. It's not uncommon for employers to ask the receptionist to assess you from the minute you arrive, when you think no one is watching. If there's a table of magazines in reception, which one do you browse while waiting, *Vogue*? Or *Event Magazine/BizBash*?

Turning up early and being just as friendly, polite, and enthusiastic with the receptionist as you would with the interviewer, can only work in your favor. Acknowledge that you're a little early and tell them you're happy to wait. If it's a small company, you might want to strike up a conversation with the receptionist while you're waiting, assuming they're not too busy and it feels appropriate. If you make a connection, they might put a good word in or give feedback about how friendly you were. Employers will often be watching to see how well you speak to and treat other staff.

Appearance and Manner

"A lot of our clients are blue chip companies so it's important for a candidate to consider that when it comes to their own presentation; there's a business professionalism and formality they need to observe. They need to present themselves in a manner appropriate to our business by looking professional and presentable in a corporate way. Candidates should look like somebody that we could put in front of one of our blue chip clients."

Nicola Mosley, HR Manager, George P. Johnson

Being well presented and well spoken is essential. Often, an employer will be judging you based on whether you look and sound the part. Would they feel confident putting you in front of a client? You need to come across as a professional, and that means presenting and conducting yourself in a way that's appropriate for a business environment. Typically, that means adopting a more formal manner than you would at home or in a social environment.

• Appearance

In terms of your appearance, it's about being appropriately dressed; because that's one of the first things an employer will use to judge you. If you're wearing a suit, ensure it is business-appropriate; dark blue or grey—black is for security staff and funerals, not bright, shiny, or something you'd wear to a wedding. Make sure your shirt is a proper business shirt, immaculately pressed, and doesn't have a casual, wide, or button-down collar. Make sure the color and pattern of your tie is appropriate for business, tied with a traditional knot (not one of those silly oversized knots) and that the tip just kisses the top of the trousers.

Make sure your shoes are formal enough, the right color and have been cleaned and polished that morning. Your belt should match your shoes and the buckle should be slim and discrete—something you'd wear with dress pants, not jeans. No bright comedy socks, themed cufflinks, or sports watches. If you're a woman wearing a skirt, make sure it's the appropriate length for business, that you're wearing tights, and no open-toed shoes or boots. Make sure your coat and any bag is also appropriate for a business environment (no rucksacks) and that your phone, keys, bottle of water and any other personal accessories stay hidden inside at all times.

In terms of grooming, hair should be clean and worn in an appropriate, tidy fashion; tied back or up if need be. Men in particular, don't use too much styling product in your hair, definitely nothing that makes it look wet/greasy. Wear the absolute minimal amount of jewelry (wedding ring and small discrete earrings only) and when it comes to make up, less is definitely more. A bit of concealer/powder, lipstick (but no gloss), eye shadow in neutral shades, and a little mascara is sufficient. Do not apply makeup as if you're going out for the night. Absolutely no perfume/aftershave—it's not a date. Men, make sure you have deodorant on—but not so much that anyone can smell it through your clothes—and make sure your feet don't smell. Nails should be clean, trimmed/filed and neutral, eyebrows tidied and under control. Men should either be clean-shaven or if they have a beard, it should be neatly groomed, no one or two day stubble; it just looks scruffy. Teeth must be cleaned, flossed, and rinsed with mouthwash—and absolutely no smoking beforehand (the smell will always linger on your hair and clothes even if you do pop a breath mint in your mouth). And no chewing gum; it's common.

It might sound like a lot of attention to detail, but remember that is one of the skills an employer is looking for. Therefore, you need to project that in your appearance too. Show me; don't tell me.

This approach isn't just for jobs in a corporate environment either. Granted you might relax your style of clothes a little if you're interviewing for a cool, creative agency—that would probably love a hipster beard—but your presentation still needs to be immaculate. It's always better to be a little too formal than it is to be too casual. You can always apologize and make light of being too formal and people will forgive you. It's much harder to recover if you've turned up too casual and have to start making excuses for being under-dressed.

If you're at all in doubt about how to present yourself for a particular job, go and hang around outside their building and look at what the employees are wearing. Then take that level of formality up just a little—employees sometimes relax their appearance a bit once they're in a job, so you need to compensate for this and make your appearance a touch more formal than whatever you observe.

"I pay attention to body language a lot. A lot of times when I meet with someone, I'll get feeling immediately about whether it's going to work or not. There's just something about their personality that will stand out— their demeanor or the way they carry themselves, and whether they present themselves in a professional manner. You can get a lot of information from first impressions."

Chad Hudson, President, Chad Hudson Events

• Manner

"Often it's going to come down to the person and the personality. I'm more interested in people who I can put in front of the MD who can speak to people at all levels."

Martin Turner, former Global Head of Events for Credit Suisse

The way you conduct yourself and, perhaps most importantly, the way you speak, is key to how effectively you communicate. You have to be able to express yourself in a calm, confident, coherent, and articulate manner. Think about your energy levels as an employer will pick up on this as soon as you walk in the room; are you bright and awake, engaged and engaging, sparky and enthusiastic, cheerful and polite, smiley and responsive?

"Think about how you present yourself; remember that you're in an interview. I've had people come in and put their mobile phone down on the table—as if they might stop to answer a call at any moment. Another girl sat throughout the whole interview clutching a bottle of water. Every time she got enthusiastic answering a question she ended up shaking the water up and down."

Nicola Mosley, HR Manager, George P. Johnson

When you sit down, make sure you're sat up straight, not fiddling with anything (hair, rings, pens, water bottles), make eye contact, and don't put anything on the table (phone, sunglasses).

You also need to pay attention to the way you speak. Don't be too casual or overly personal. Speak in a clear, succinct and formal way—no 'umm's' or 'errrr's.' Don't ramble, go off at tangents, or leave sentences unfinished. Most importantly pay attention to your diction; avoid using slang or colloquialisms such as 'ain't', 'gonna', 'wanna' or 'innit' and definitely don't punctuate sentences with unnecessary phrases such as 'like' and 'you know?.' Make sure what you say is grammatically correct, for example, 'we were going' not 'we was going.' Be mindful of articulation errors too, such as substitutions (i.e. 'nuffink' instead of 'nothing', 'fought' instead of 'thought' and 'free' instead of 'three') and omissions ('av' instead of 'have'). And for the record, its 'asked' not 'arksed.'

One of the most common gripes employers have nowadays is that candidates often come across as far too informal, and therefore unprofessional. You really must pay attention to how you speak, I can't stress this enough. It's not a class thing, I'm not saying you need to speak with an affected accent; you just need to speak grammatically correct English in a formal way that's appropriate for a business environment. Keep in mind that an employer is looking to see whether you can be trusted to speak to clients or management without embarrassing them.

If you've never worked in a corporate environment before,

watch old episodes of shows like *The Apprentice* and see how the contestant's speech and behavior changes when they're in the boardroom; they sit up straight, are attentive, courteous, and succinct. It's that level of formality that you need to adopt.

Confidence

"Confidence is really important. If you come in for an interview, or you're volunteering onsite, and you're really nervous and quiet—and this does happen, particularly with young women—there's no way they're going to be able to stand in front of a senior partner and sell an event to them. I don't care how good their skills are, they've got to have confidence. That's where personality can really seal the deal and make or break it for a candidate."

Sharyn Scott, Global Head of Events, Linklaters

An employer needs to feel comfortable knowing you can take on the running of an event. To do that you have to project an air of confidence in order to convince them that you are capable of taking control. You need to be able to speak up, have a point of view, and express it in a calm and articulate manner. Don't make the interviewer have to force information out of you; take the lead. But know when to shut up too. Employers are looking to be reassured that you know what you're doing and can handle yourself in professional situations. We want you to inspire confidence in us by stepping up and taking just the right amount of control.

Tell Your Story

"Make sure you come prepared; that you've practiced your story and you're articulate about who you are, what you do, and what you want to do. Hook us in first, and then talk about all the other stuff like skills and experience"

Dori Rodriguez, Senior HR Associate, Jack Morton Worldwide

"They need to be telling a story, and a good story teller is going to go much further than someone who is having difficulty articulating their experience and what they're looking for."

Rachel Vingsness, Senior HR Manager, Jack Morton Worldwide

Find the right opportunity, at the beginning of the interview to introduce yourself with your story, as discussed in the previous chapter. Not only are you imparting facts; your background and what you want to do, it's about engaging the interviewer and demonstrating the essential communication skills an employer is looking for. It's refreshing when a candidate takes the lead at the beginning of an interview and articulately provides relevant information, without the interviewer having to ask. It sets the conversation up nicely and acts as a good introduction.

Demonstrate Industry and Company Knowledge

"I always think it's cool when people demonstrate a knowledge of the industry outside of Jack Morton; so they know who our competitors are or they can talk about certain campaigns or events that they were excited by—and it's ok if it's not one of ours."

Rachel Vingsness, Senior HR Manager, Jack Morton Worldwide

Part of 'your story' should involve explaining why you are drawn to work in the industry as a whole, and also for that particular employer. This is where you have a great opportunity to demonstrate the research you've done, by referring to what's going on in the industry, any events you've been inspired by, and the work and achievements of the company you're interviewing with.

Take Something to Present

"I always ask candidates to bring something with them to talk about, maybe their dissertation, or a team project that they've worked on.

Recently, I interviewed someone for a junior event co-ordinator role and they brought a portfolio of some events they'd worked on. Even at that junior stage, they'd realized that what they do is quite tangible so they could present it in an interview. Having something visual can help get the conversation going when someone hasn't got much work experience, so that I'm not just batting questions to them. If they can talk about something they've done, and there's a visual cue in front of them, then they tend to relax because they're starting to talk about something they know and they're much more engaged."

Nicola Mosley, HR Manager, George P. Johnson

"You have to remember that the people you meet sit in a lot of meetings. You need to stand out. What's really great is when people can bring the interview to life with some photographs or video footage. That gets the person engaged in the conversation and allows a candidate to take control of the interview."

Charlotte Saynor, former Vice President of Brands & Events, Fremantle Media Enterprises, and Head of European Events, Apple

As discussed in the previous chapter, I strongly recommend you take along a portfolio of events that you've worked on, as a visual way to communicate your experience and knowledge. When presenting a portfolio, remember that the photos, plans, and schedules are just visual cues. Don't just literally present them to the interviewer—you're not showing your holiday photos. Use each photo to demonstrate what you did, the contribution you made, what you learned, choices you/others made and why, and what you would do differently now.

Keep at the forefront of your mind that the purpose of presenting this experience is to communicate the skills and knowledge you have.

"Once, when we were hiring for event managers, we narrowed it down to our top six and brought each one in for an interview. In preparation, one of them basically planned out an entire hypothetical event and did a presentation talking through all the elements, such as why they chose that particular venue, how they designed the layout, what the menu

options were and why, all the interior design, and a budget. Coming prepared like that was really impressive; they showed initiative and used the presentation to show their understanding of events—and of course, they were the person we hired."

Chad Hudson, President, Chad Hudson Events

How you present is also key. An interviewer is going to be judging you on your communication skills, so make sure you present in a coherent, professional, and engaging manner—and remember to inject some personality. If you're not used to presenting, video yourself and watch it back to identify where you need to improve.

"Last year, the winner of The Eventice [UK event industry job competition] won a job with George P. Johnson which, for anyone straight out of college, is pretty amazing. Before he was announced as the winner, I was chatting to him as he needed to change the time of his train home, and he was worried whether it would cost him more money to get the later train. He told me he was a bit broke at the moment because he'd used his previous month's student loan to pay for a presentations skills course and to buy a new suit. He recognized he was bad at presentations, so he invested in himself, even though it meant he'd be struggling financially. I just thought to myself, 'well, you really deserve to be the winner because you've put yourself out to achieve it.'"

Liz Sinclair, Managing Director, ESP Recruitment

Demonstrate Commercial Awareness

"The amount of times people say things like, 'I really loved organizing my sister's wedding', and that's it. It just makes me roll my eyes. There's a whole industry out there filled with professionals using events and live experiences to communicate something and achieve business objectives. It's so much more than just putting together a nice party."

Nathan Homan, Co-founder, Rouge Events

When presenting your portfolio at an interview, it's important to establish early on that you have a commercial awareness. Demonstrate that you understanding that events are a communications tool, and therefore have a purpose and objectives that need to be met via creative solutions, with results that can be measured in order to demonstrate return on investment.

From my own experience, because my event company produces a lot of events with an emphasis on design, job applicants gush about how they love our work because it's really creative. That doesn't show me that they understand what it's really all about. People see my events for Elton John and talk about how beautiful the sets and decor were, but not once has a job applicant ever acknowledged that it's a fundraiser for his AIDS charity—and how that impacts the overall objectives. Yes, it has to look beautiful, but there's so much more that goes into a fundraising event. Ask me about how we market the event and sell the tickets—to ensure we attract the right type of people. Or how we need to sell advertising space in the program and get auction lots donated—and how we then have to make sure we've got the right type of people there who are going to bid on those auction lots. Ask me about managing a charity event committee, or providing value for money to justify a £3,000 ($4,600) ticket price— while still producing the event on a budget. Ask me about getting sponsorship to cover the production costs, making sure the event fulfils the sponsor's needs and objectives, and getting celebrities to attend without giving away free tickets, which would reduce the income raised. Or how we communicate the serious work of the charity, in a party environment, without killing the mood.

If someone asked me about those elements, I'd be far more impressed. It would show that they understand the purpose of the event; that the whole reason for staging a lavish party is to raise money, which in turn has a major effect on the choices made during the event-planning process. It also means that the success of the event is measured not just by which celebrities attended or how much media coverage there was, but by how much money we raised in relation to how much we spent. I expect guests to comment on all the front-end elements like the sets, menu, and entertainment— but if you're coming to me looking for work as an event planner you need to demonstrate that you are looking at it from a commercial perspective.

"We're always looking for candidates that have a slightly more strategic edge to them. The ones that have a broader understanding of why they're doing the event. They might tell us about a particular role they've done, and how that fitted in with the team or its purpose. So they're not just talking about what they did, they're setting the scene a bit; this is why I was brought in, this is what I was doing, this was the objective, and I worked with these people. Show that you understand what you're doing, but also what the people around you are also doing, why you're all doing it, and what it's going to achieve. Not that many people just starting out think like that, but someone who does really stands out. It's always interesting when you see that in somebody. It makes you think 'actually, they have a future' because they've already got a slightly deeper understanding."

Nicola Mosley, HR Manager, George P. Johnson

Describe Your Experience in a Coherent Order

If you look at case studies on an event company's website, they will often describe a project in four stages:

- The Brief; what they were asked to do
- The Objectives; what the project needed to achieve
- The Solution; what creative treatment was put in place to achieve those objectives
- The Results; what was achieved and how success was measured

When you discuss events in an interview, these are the key stages you need to refer to in order to show that you truly understand what events are all about. Be sure to present the information in a coherent order—one that mirrors these four stages of the event-planning process.

Start with the big picture information by giving an overview of the event, in terms of the brief and objectives. Then move on to talk about the solution; how the event was designed, planned and staged to meet those objectives. It's while explaining this stage that you have the opportunity to drill down into the detail; to demonstrate the contribution you made to the event, the skills you used and the knowledge you acquired. Then finally, pull back out to the bigger picture and finish discussing each event by mentioning the outcome. Explain what the results were and how these were measured.

Highlight the Core Skills and Qualities

When talking about your experience, always use it to demonstrate the core skills and qualities an employer is looking for.

Prepare in advance so that when discussing your contribution to each event, you can specifically highlight examples of organizational skills, budget management, time management, negotiation skills, resourcefulness, problem solving, accountability, managing a team, being a team player, customer-service skills, or being detail-oriented.

Go back to Chapters 15 and 16 and highlight all the core skills and qualities of an event planner, then find examples of these in your experience and use them as sign posts when talking through your contribution to the event.

Use Volunteer Experience

If the majority of your experience has been onsite at events, don't be afraid to use extra-curricular activities, student events, family events, and volunteer experience to demonstrate your project management and planning skills. It doesn't matter if it's not a professional event—or even an event at all—as long as you go into sufficient detail.

Interviewers are looking for you to demonstrate transferable skills. So, if you've project-managed a team climb up Mount Kilimanjaro or staged a student fashion show, turn it into a case study and use it to talk through every aspect of the planning process in detail. It's not about the event; it's about the planning.

"Presenting case studies makes it much easier for candidates to demonstrate their core skills. They can show me their ability to problem solve or execute a project on time. It doesn't even have to be an event. It could be, 'this is how I produced my final dissertation; this is what I did, this is who I spoke to and interviewed, this is how I compiled all this information, and then this is what it resulted in.' That's interesting for me, because then I can see that their brain works a certain way; that they're organized and they've thought about the domino effect.

It might be that you helped at your sister's wedding. So what exactly did you do? Did you run around behind the scenes to make sure the cake arrived on time? Did you create a budget and manage it all in a spreadsheet? Did you negotiate the venue hire contract? Those are the kind of things where you can tell stories to bring your experience to life. Maybe you helped on your company's staff Christmas party. If so, then the type of thing I'd be looking to hear is, 'I made a running order and handed it out to everybody'– that's great, that's music to my ears. Those are the things I want to hear.

Tell me about the systems and tools you used to manage that event so that you can demonstrate that you understand the domino effect and the process of planning a project. Because it is a process; there's a start point and an end point and it is how you get from one to the other that I want to hear about."

Sharyn Scott, Global Head of Events, Linklaters

Talk About the 'How' and 'Why', Not the 'What'

"Talk us through a project; was it with a team? If so, how did they divide the tasks? How did they produce it? Who was the leader? What role did they play? Where did they get the idea? How did they build upon it? How did they resource it? Where did they find the people? How did they go about keeping costs down? If they didn't have a big budget, how resourceful were they? How innovative were they with their thinking about how they could get things done? What was the event for? What

was the goal? Have they thought about those things? Rather than just saying, 'oh we do this event every year.'

Nicola Mosley, HR Manager, George P. Johnson

Unfortunately, many candidates have a tendency to focus on the end result when presenting their experience, when actually what employers want to hear about is the behind the scenes process.

Imagine the event was a cake you had baked. The guests are going to evaluate it based on how it looks and tastes, i.e. the end result. But an employer needs to evaluate your skills by hearing the story behind the cake. We want to know how or why you made it; how involved you were or whether someone else helped you. Whether the end result was a lucky fluke or whether you have the skills and talent to do it again—or whether you could also turn your hand to a pie or a tart. Or even whether, despite the cake looking great, you actually set fire to the kitchen in the process and massively overspent on the ingredients meaning that the end doesn't justify the means. To learn what you're capable of, we need you to tell us everything you did to make that amazing cake:

- Why did you make the cake? What was it for? What did you want it to achieve?
- Why a cake and not a pie?
- When choosing the flavor, did you consider the tastes of the recipients, or did you base it on what you like?
- How did you find out what the recipient likes?
- How did you research and plan it?
- How did you cost it out? Could you tell me how much it costs in terms of ingredients, equipment, labor, and power? What is the cost per portion?
- How is it going to be priced?
- How were you going to ensure value for money?
- Did you consider the nutritional content or possible allergies from ingredients?
- What ingredients did you use?

- What equipment did you use?
- How did you source these?
- What prep did you do?
- How did you plan the correct order of events?
- How did you monitor the process along the way?
- Did you taste it?
- How did you package and deliver the cake?
- Did you consider how it would be eaten? Whether utensils would be needed? How leftovers would be disposed of?
- How were you going to measure the success of the cake? Was feedback going to be anecdotal or were people going to score the cake/leave written comments?
- How were you going to evaluate whether the end result justified the money spent on making the cake?

Remember that you're interviewing for work as an event *planner*. So don't just show us the event, show us how you planned it and why?

"Even now I see senior people with lots of experience that come in for interviews and they don't use any of the language or terms that I'm looking to hear. I'm really interested in drilling down into the processes they went through. I want to know what tools they used, what documents they created, exactly how they managed everything. You need to think about how you can prove to me that you can do an event. Show me; what did you do and how did you do it? That's what I want to hear, and most people don't talk about their experience in this way."

Sharyn Scott, Global Head of Events, Linklaters

Define Your Role and What You Learned

"Candidates need to let us know exactly what they did; go into detail about what their role was, how that fitted in to the bigger picture and what they learned from it. Also what they would have done differently, because that will show an attitude to continuous improvement. We

recognize that somebody in the early stages of their career, in fact all stages of a career, needs development."

Fiona Lawlor, HR Director, Jack Morton London and Dubai

When discussing your experience, make a clear distinction between the event and your contribution to it. Discussing the overall event is a great way to demonstrate your broader understanding, but it's essential that you bring it back to what you actually did and what effect that had. So be specific. For example, if you were organizing transport you could acknowledge the potential knock-on effect if something had gone wrong. Then use that to explain what you did; *'I made a list of mobile numbers for the truck drivers so I could reach them directly if something didn't turn up', or 'I prepared a list of local taxi-cab numbers in case there was an issue with the coaches and we needed a plan B."*

You should also highlight anything that shows you took initiative, over and above the role that you were assigned. For example, *'the reception area became really overcrowded during check-in so I grabbed some spare ropes and posts and created a channeling system' or 'It started to rain, so I borrowed some umbrellas from the hotel concierge so we could walk guests out to their cars undercover.'*

"When they talk about their experience, I'm looking to hear specifically what they did and what they've learned; whether they've learned time management skills or customer-service skills for example. It's great if they can articulate what they've taken away from each experience that they think will add something to my business if I hire them."

Chad Hudson, President, Chad Hudson Events

Finally, when discussing your contribution always add something about what you learned from the experience. Don't just present the facts about what you did; demonstrate what you learned, or what you'd do differently in future.

"A candidate might say they worked on X event and were responsible for the guest list or delegate registration. I'd then be looking for them to use that to tell me what they added or learned, perhaps 'I suggested it might be much quicker doing it on an iPad; it looked more slick and professional and it got people in the room faster.'"

Charlotte Saynor, former Vice President of Brands & Events, FremantleMedia Enterprises, and Head of European Events, Apple

Results

The final stage when discussing events you've worked on, is to mention what the outcome of the event was—why it was a success or failure, and how that was measured. It might be measured by media coverage, an increase in sales, employee feedback, the amount of money raised, the type of people who attended, or any combination of factors. Showing that you've thought about the importance of measuring results and the return on investment is the final stage in demonstrating your commercial awareness—and, as a junior candidate, that will really make you stand out.

Realistic Expectations

"One of the hardest things I've found when recruiting is that people don't understand how many rubbish parts of the job there are. Stuffing name badges, then standing behind a desk handing them out, is a boring job, but you're the face of the event and the face of the company at that point, so it's a really important role. You need to be OK about handing out name badges and not feel that it's beneath you."

Sharyn Scott, Global Head of Events, Linklaters

At a junior/work-experience level, when it comes to talking about the opportunity on offer, you need to make it clear that you have a realistic idea of what the job involves. Show that you understand you're not going to be planning your own events anytime soon, that most of the work is going to be admin-related, and that you're fine with the mundane and menial 'grunt work'. One of the biggest problems employer's face, especially when dealing with college graduates, is that they have unrealistically high expectations. If a candidate has already organized some of their own events, perhaps for a charity or while at university, they often don't want to go back to the more menial support work. In the interview, show an employer that, although you're enthusiastic to learn and take on more responsibility, you're also humble and prepared to get stuck in or do anything. Show that you understand it involves long anti-social hours and unglamorous work; that being responsible for the guest list might mean standing outside the venue until 2am in the freezing cold arranging taxis. Or that event planning often means giving up your evenings and weekends, and you don't get paid extra for that. Or that you might have to leave home at 5am to be onsite for 6am.

"I would want to hear that they recognize that the events business is not a nine-to-five job, and that they're so keen on a career in the industry that they have no issue whatsoever about what hours they have to work—whether it was at the weekend or in the evenings."

Martin Turner, former Global Head of Events for Credit Suisse

Be the candidate who, no matter how much experience they have, is still 'up for anything.' Get your foot in the door by showing that you're prepared to do the menial jobs, then you can show that you're capable of taking on more. If you're willing and amenable, you'll be delegated more responsibilities and quickly move up.

"Volunteers often used to comment that they had no idea how much work went into an event until they came along to help out on the evening; that it's non-stop work with little or no time for breaks. Very often, we would start onsite at 7am and not finish until 3am the following morning, then have to be at the office at 9am. Anyone expecting a job where they can go home at 5.30pm shouldn't even consider it."

Farida Haqiqi, former Events Manager, The British Red Cross

Personality

"At entry level, so much of it comes down to personality, being well presented and proactive. If you don't have much experience then you've got to sell yourself on your personality and attitude. In an interview you need to come across as warm, outgoing and be able to build a rapport quite quickly."

Liz Sinclair, **Managing Director, ESP Recruitment**

Interviews can often be quite cold, formal, and unnatural situations, so it's important to find ways to get your personality across. You have to try to relax into it and be yourself, rather than put on some sort of act, or try to be the person you think the employer is looking for. Sometimes it's the little things you say in an interview that give a glimpse of your personality and resonates with an employer—and this just may be the thing that clinches it for you. Employers are looking for a connection, something that makes them think, 'yeah, I think we'd get along, they're the type of person I could see working alongside me.'

Charlotte Saynor, former Vice President of Brands & Events for FremantleMedia Enterprises and former Head of European Events for Apple, recalls a time she was interviewing a candidate who stood out because of the way she expressed her personality.

"In the interview, I asked her, 'what do you find challenging?' and she said:

'I believe you can find a solution to most challenges; you can ask someone for help, or identify the resources to fix it. You can also try to learn something that you don't understand—apart from physics—don't get that, will never get that.'

That made me laugh and I immediately thought, 'she's interesting, she's quirky.' It was a serious answer to the question, and she also injected a bit of her personality in at the end, but the key thing was she answered the question. It wasn't one of those smarmy answers like, 'What are your weaknesses?' 'Well sometimes I'm too much of a perfectionist.'

Later on in the interview I asked her how she got her last job and she said 'I talked someone into it in the pub.' It was honest, which I liked, but the key thing was that she talked someone into it so she was demonstrating that she could negotiate."

"Personality doesn't mean being hyper, bubbly, and outgoing all the time—you don't have to be the life and soul of the party—just have certain level of confidence and be able to communicate well."

Fiona Lawlor, HR Director, Jack Morton London and Dubai

All too often, people make the mistake of thinking that in order to show your personality you have to be energetic and outgoing. But actually, employers don't want too many people like that, as that can soon get on everyone's nerves. In fact, one of the qualities that kept coming up when I spoke to contributors was calm. Employers are looking for event planners to be calmly in control.

"Wall flowers? Next! You don't stand a chance. But you also don't want to be too gushy or overbearing either."

Nathan Homan, Co-founder, Rouge Events

The other thing to be wary of is cockiness. When you're trying to convince an interviewer that you have the necessary abilities and experience, it can be very easy for confidence to cross the line into cockiness. When I was a judge on *The Eventice*, the UK competition to a win a job in the event industry, I had to watch dozens of introductory videos that applicants had submitted. I remember taking an instant dislike to one candidate because of one little thing she said in her video. When recapping a handful of events she'd worked on, she said something along the lines of 'so, three of the top events of the summer....which I just happened to organize' adopting a faux-modest tone. It was just one throw-away line in her video—which she probably didn't intend to sound the way it did—but I came away with the impression that she thought she knew it all, which annoyed me. As such, I automatically put a mental cross against her name, because there were plenty of other candidates who came across as far more humble.

"I like confidence, but I also like an openness to learn. I don't like it when someone gives the impression that they think they know it all. For as long as I've been doing this job, I still find myself learning something every day. I've had new hires that come in and they don't want to hear any kind of constructive criticism, they get defensive."

Chad Hudson, President, Chad Hudson Events

Employers don't want you to come in bragging, thinking you know it all, or telling us how fantastic you are. I'd be so much more impressed if someone said, *'although I have a degree in event management I'm prepared to start at the very bottom and do anything.'* It's far better for you to show us what it is you've done in a humble and understated way—just present the facts without a commentary—and leave us to make our own judgement about how impressive that is. Show us; don't tell us.

Ask Intelligent Questions/Give Intelligent Answers

"What always impresses an employer is when, not only are you really prepared and you know everything there is to know about them, but also that you ask intelligent questions that are really relevant. They want to hear that you know what you're talking about and understand the work they do. So, for example, 'I read in an article that you're going to open an office in China, how do you see the Chinese market developing your business over the next five years?' It shows that you've done your research, that you understand what they're trying to do, and that you're interested in their business. Compare that to when they ask a candidate whether they have any questions and they just say, 'no, not really.'"

Liz Sinclair, Managing Director, ESP Recruitment

Always prepare a handful of questions to ask in an interview. If you want to make an impression, it's simply not an option to say no, when asked if you have any questions. Use the research you did into the current issues facing the industry and relate it back to their business, or demonstrate that you've been following them as a company by referring to something their CEO has said in an interview, blog post or at an industry talk. The key here is to ask questions that are relevant and intelligent. It's an opportunity for you to show some depth; show that you're tuned in to broader industry issues, that you're have a commercial awareness, and you've given some thought to their company in particular and their place in the industry.

"I expect a candidate to come armed with some really good questions. I like the interview to be 50/50. I like it when they demonstrate that they've read up on the business and they use that as the basis for questions. That instantly gets me on side. I don't expect them to have all the information, but to show that they've tried to find out what they can and they're using the opportunity with me to get more information. Then, if they respond and tailor the rest of the interview around what I've told them, that shows they can think on their feet."

Charlotte Saynor, former Vice President of Brands & Events, FremantleMedia Enterprises, and Head of European Events, Apple

The same applies to how you answer questions. Make sure your answers are also intelligent and relevant. It's not about saying what you think they want to hear, but just being sensible with your answers and making sure they're appropriate for a professional job application. When I was judging *The Eventice*, the finalists were asked to give a presentation about something they are passionate about. One of them chose to do a presentation about how much she admired Kim Kardashian, and immediately the judges, myself included, rolled our eyes. Now, I'd like to believe that candidate was intending to make a convincing and intelligent argument about the power of a branding; how a person with no discernable talent can harness sufficient media attention and public interest to create a brand, and then license that brand across a range of commercial products made by others. Unfortunately, that wasn't how it came across.

Compare that to another example recalled by Rachel Vingsness, Senior HR Manager for Jack Morton Worldwide:

"Once we have a shortlist of candidates, we bring them altogether to

spend a day at an assessment center. Part of that day involves them preparing a three-minute presentation on anything they want. Some people bring in props to use and it's always interesting to see how they use those.

One person—who incidentally, we ended up hiring—sticks in my mind because she stood there and emptied out her purse. Then she told a story about everything in her purse, why it was important to her, and what she uses it for. What was clever about it was that she managed to tie everything back to her work, her experience, and finally, what she would use it for if she worked for Jack Morton.

Typically, people come in and talk about their favorite summer vacation with their family, so 'this is what we did and here are some pictures.' Emptying her purse was such a different approach and very simple, but it told a great story and really got a message across about how she would add value to the organization."

The lesson in both these examples is to consider the audience you're speaking to. Make your answers relevant to the situation and use them to demonstrate a level of intelligence.

What Not to Say

"It really annoys me when people ask about money and salary. You'd be surprised how many times someone has said, 'to be perfectly honest with you, money is a big driver for me.' That's just not what I want to hear. It might be true for a lot of people, but it's something that should be kept back, at least in the first round of interviews when you're looking to make a good impression."

Dori Rodriguez, Senior HR Associate, Jack Morton Worldwide

"One of the real turn-offs for me is when we ask the candidates if they have any questions for us and all they ask about is the hours of the job or 'when can I start?' I find it hard to believe that you don't have any questions about what the role involves or what it's like to work at Jack Morton. That probably shows that you're not thinking strategically."

Rachel Vingsness, Senior HR Manager, Jack Morton Worldwide

While you might genuinely want to find out about the hours, salary, or benefits, just park those types of questions until later. If they're interested in you, there might be another round of interviews to follow before they offer you a job. Alternatively, someone from HR will probably contact you. If they're going to offer you a job, there will definitely be other, more appropriate, opportunities to enquire about all the practical details. However curious you are, don't lead with that in a first interview and risk coming across as someone who's only concerned with getting paid and what time they'll finish, otherwise you might ruin your chances.

Follow Up

"My old boss told me a great story about how she went for an interview very early on in her career for the position of Head of Travel at a large fashion brand. Toward the end of the interview, she asked the guy, 'what are you looking for in a person that would make you hire them for this role?' He told her that he wanted someone who was really going to knock his socks off. So, after the interview she went straight to a department store and found a pair of socks made by that particular fashion brand, and sent them to him with a thank you note saying 'thank you so much for the interview, it was lovely to meet you, please keep the enclosed because if you hire me you'll need them.'"

Martin Turner, former Global Head of Events for Credit Suisse

Granted, you might not have the opportunity to follow up after an interview with a bold, creative gesture like this, but you should still follow up. Very few candidates do, but a simple email or handwritten note thanking them for the opportunity is a very nice touch that will make them remember you—which might help if you're just one of many candidates interviewing for a position.

Summary

- Use the interview to demonstrate:
    - That you have the required skills and understanding
    - Why you'd be a good fit for that organization
- Arrive early, make an impression with the receptionist
- Be well presented and well spoken
- Be confident, but not cocky
- Take the lead and tell 'your story':
    - Who you are
    - Where you're coming from
    - Why you're passionate about events
    - What brought you to this company
    - Refer to specific events and the work of the company
- Take a portfolio to present your experience
- Present in a coherent and articulate manner
- Talking about your experience:
    - Demonstrate a commercial awareness; introduce each event by referring to the brief and objectives
    - Describe the solution; how the event was designed, planned and staged to meet those objectives
    - Define your role
    - Explain your contribution; citing examples of the core skills and qualities
    - Explain the process you went through and the tools used
    - Explain what you learned and would do differently
    - Refer to the outcome; what the results were and how these were measured
- Demonstrate realistic expectations of what the work involves
- Find ways to communicate your personality
- Ask intelligent questions, give intelligent answers
- Don't talk about salary, benefits or hours
- Follow up after the interview.

25

What You Need to Demonstrate Once You Get an Opportunity

"Once you get an internship, you then need to prove that you do have the skills and qualities we thought you had during the interview process, and that you can put those to good use here at Jack Morton. Show us that you're a team player; show us that you're flexible and that you'll do anything it takes to get the job done because the client always comes first. Show us that you're professional with clients, and that you're very organized and driven."

Rachel Vingsness, Senior HR Manager, Jack Morton Worldwide

Being offered work experience, an internship, or even an entry-level position is just the beginning. If you've demonstrated some potential by being proactive, driven, and committed, and that's resulted in someone giving you a chance, the next step is to prove yourself. Make sure you continue to demonstrate all the core skills and qualities that they glimpsed in the interview. Be professional in how you speak to clients and colleagues, show them that you're resourceful, that you're a team player, and that you're driven and hungry to learn. Show that you're detail-oriented, that you can negotiate and problem solve, and that you have organizational and project management skills. They might have seen examples of that in your previous experience, but now you have to demonstrate all of that in action. Show that employer that they were right to take a chance on you.

Just because you've landed a work placement, don't take your foot off the accelerator. Your employer will still be assessing you, and your performance will determine whether they offer you future work. Continue to apply the same drive and persistence that got you there in the first place. Exceed expectations, over-deliver, and make yourself indispensable

Be Proactive

"Our most successful interns are really proactive; they don't just sit around and wait for someone to tell them what to do. They either identify something that needs to be done and do it, or ask if it needs to be done. Alternatively, they're constantly checking in saying, 'is there anything you need me to do?', 'can I help you with that?', or 'I know that you have a meeting at 11am, do you want me to sit in and take notes for you?' They're someone who can identify things that need to be done before they have to be asked."

Dori Rodriguez, Senior HR Associate, Jack Morton Worldwide

When you're on a work placement, be sure to demonstrate initiative. Show that you're resourceful, can work autonomously, and just pick things up and run with them. One of the problems employers often face with work experience candidates/interns is that they have to spend so much time briefing them or explaining how to do something, that they spend all their time managing someone else and end up thinking it would have been quicker just to do it themselves.

Demonstrate to an employer that they can delegate tasks to you. They should be able to say to you, *'We're working on a family-friendly festival and we need to set up an area with entertainment for children. There's a budget of $5,000, come back to me with options and full details'*, or *'We've got 25 people that need to arrive at this conference by 9am, they're coming from different parts of the country, work out a budget and the logistics.'* Those are the type of entry-level tasks that you should be able to do on your own.

Remember that you're there to support the event planner

and the rest of the team; to help them deliver their events more efficiently. So constantly push yourself to take on more, over and above what's asked of you. This is your opportunity to show what you're really capable of. You want to leave an employer with the impression that you made a definite and valuable contribution, rather than just being the person who helped with some admin.

Be a Team Player

"Going the extra mile on projects will make an impression. Be that person who, when you've done your work, is asking the rest of the team if there's anything you can help with. Or, before you leave at the end of the day, make sure everyone has everything they need."

Fiona Lawlor, HR Director, Jack Morton London and Dubai

It's not only about how well you do the work; just as important, perhaps more so, is how well you fit in. If you're not totally proficient in the job at first, most employers will cut you some slack. They'll recognize that you still have time to learn and develop—better still, they might be prepared to teach you. However, if you don't fit in with the culture of the organization—because you don't get stuck in, have a bad attitude, or don't go out of your way to support the rest of the team—then they just won't keep you around.   Employers won't cut you any slack when it comes to your attitude.

Be friendly, treat people well, support the team, and be enthusiastic—especially when it comes to the long hours and grunt work.   Don't be that person who rolls their eyes and sighs when they're asked to stuff gifts bags, set up tables and chairs, or print-off name badges. Recognize that employer is giving you a break, that you're starting at the bottom, and that even when you're a senior event planner, there will always be times when you'll have to stuff gifts bags, set up tables and chairs, or print-off name badges. Event planners don't have

341

the luxury of being divas—because it's usually their job to service the actual divas: the clients and guests.

Get Involved

"Those individuals who are willing to go the extra mile always stand out. They sign up for organizing our social events, such as the staff summer party, or get involved in our charity committee. It's the people who are always there at the front of the queue when we need something doing, that stand out. Those people come in and do a great job, but they also really want to be part of Jack Morton so they get involved in other areas of the business. It's about being part of the team, part of the company, and seeing it as more than just a job. That's key: you really want to help and be part of the Jack Morton team."

Fiona Lawlor, HR Director, Jack Morton London and Dubai

If you're hoping to get a job with a company at the end of an internship or work experience placement, you need to show them that you're committed beyond the day-to-day aspects of the job. Prove that you have a genuine interest in their company—that you want to work for them, not just anyone— by getting involved in other activities they do. Show them; don't tell them.

"I don't want someone who just comes in and does their job; I want people who get involved. I want people to ask questions and make suggestions—which is why we like to hire outgoing people who have ideas and want to contribute them."

Chad Hudson, President, Chad Hudson Events

My Route into the Industry
Starting as a Volunteer

From volunteering at the American Film Institute, to producing the reveal of the largest LEGO model ever built in Times Square

Marie Davidheiser, Senior Vice President, Director of Operations, Jack Morton Worldwide

Marie's route into the industry is a great example of someone recognizing that they need to start at the very bottom, and being prepared to volunteer in order to gain some initial experience. The turning point in Marie's early career, when she first started working for Jack Morton as a freelancer, came as a result of networking and contacts; proving that any personal introduction—no matter how vague a connection—can open doors far quicker than sending our resumes in the traditional way.

Marie studied at film school Northwestern University, with a view to starting a career in film editing. *"Then I realized you sit alone in a room all day long. So then I thought, 'OK maybe I'll produce films instead, that's so cool.'* While at film school, she started organizing the wrap parties after each film shoot. *"Since I was a kid I've always been the type that was making lists and organizing things, so it was sort of natural to me, and of course it was fun so I thought, 'OK maybe I'll be an event planner instead.'"*

After college, Marie went back home to Los Angeles where she grew up and, being a film major, decided to contact the American Film Institute (AFI) and ask them if she could volunteer.

"For me, it was that typical post-college experience of 'how do you get your foot in the door? You just volunteer.' I did some research into what events the AFI does throughout the year and found out who ran their volunteer program. Then I just emailed them to ask if I could volunteer at one of their events. I just offered

to do whatever, I said 'I'd be quite happy to just take tickets from people as they arrive, whatever I can do to help.' It was a 'cold call' email. They take hundreds of volunteers each year, so I was just part of the masses, but I think a lot of their volunteers are people who are not necessarily career searching. I just knew I wanted to be in the events world, so what better way to experience it than jumping right in on the ground floor. Once I'd started volunteering, I worked on developing a relationship with their event director. I said to her, 'look, I've just graduated and have more time on my hands than most of these volunteers and I'm looking to do more.'"

As a result, Marie began to get involved in organizing the volunteer database to keep track of others who had enquired, then scheduling which roles should be assigned to them and organizing gift bags to distribute at the events. The work wasn't particularly complicated and it involved a lot of cold calling. Although the tasks were administrative, she still felt as though she was learning about event planning. However, it was the people and the organization, she acknowledges, that really kept her engaged—and the excitement of putting on an event for the American Film Institute. The events included screenings, talks by directors, and premiere parties, so she also got some experience of working with celebrities and all the issues that go with that.

"I didn't volunteer for all that long, maybe a month or so, and then they started to hire me as a freelancer, so I was paid an hourly rate. It wasn't full-time work. It was just whenever they had an event, maybe once every two weeks or so. In between, I did all sort of other jobs, from temp work to babysitting, to keep the money coming in. During that time, I also worked on a small film festival run out of El Segundo, California, which I came across on Craigslist. I would take lots of little jobs to get experience, as I didn't know if I wanted to work for a big company or a little company. The film festival in El Segundo was essentially one person, so I sort of became his assistant which was great experience."

After about a year of freelancing, Marie felt she needed to commit to a full-time job. *"Probably because of some pressure from my parents!"* She came across an events assistant job on Craigslist, which involved being part of the development office at a non-profit health clinic that organized approximately six big events each year. The goal was to raise money for the clinic, so they were fundraising events, but the clinic had links to the entertainment industry, which appealed to Marie because of her background at the AFI, and this, ultimately, is what she believed made her a good fit for the position.

"Working on those events I got to meet various presidents and executives from companies like E! Entertainment, Warner Bros and Sony. As a non-profit, we were able to tap into their networks and contacts to throw these great parties. We did events such as a 1,000-person gala at the Regent Beverly Wilshire Hotel, golf tournaments, poker tournaments, lunches, art auctions—and my favorite—a wine and food tasting on the backlot of a movie studio. That's where I got my basic event-planning experience, and later learned it was ten times harder than regular event planning because the events had to make money; you have to raise it before you can spend it! Now of course, I work for a large agency and we often have big budgets, but doing those fundraising events really gave me a good grounding and taught me that 'a dollar is a dollar' and we can always save and figure out how to stretch the value."

She stayed in that position for approximately a year, before deciding to move to New York. *"I moved with two suitcases, no job, and no apartment. I said to myself 'I'm going to New York!', so I got there and quickly figured it out."* Before leaving for New York, she started doing some research on websites like BizBash to figure out who the big companies were and which ones were headquartered in New York.

"Then my uncle put me in touch with someone he knew in New York, who it turned out was a headhunter. When I met with her, she asked me who I wanted to work for and because I'd done my

research, I was able to reel off a few big companies I'd heard of, including Jack Morton. She immediately said, 'Oh I know someone at Jack Morton', and she gave me someone's details and told me to email them. So I emailed the person to say hi, and she immediately said, 'are you creative or production?' To which I replied 'I guess I'm production....' It turned out she was in fact a senior vice president of creative, so she redirected me to the HR department. We never actually met. HR called me in for an interview and I ended up being offered a freelance production co-ordinator role working on the Bank of America account. It all happened very quickly and because the senior vice president of creative had passed on my details, they assumed she was recommending me and they actually had no idea the two of us didn't actually know each other!"

> Often, introductions can carry more weight than is perhaps intended. If someone introduces you, no matter how tentative your relationship, it is often interpreted as an endorsement or recommendation. So never under-estimate the power of contacts, however vague. Always thoroughly scrutinize your network of contacts to see if someone can provide an introduction before making a 'cold' approach.

After working freelance for Jack Morton for three months, the Bank of America account moved to another agency. However, being freelance, Marie was encouraged by the client to move with them to their new agency C2 Creative (now GO! Experience Design) where she ended up working 'perma-lance' on a long-term freelance basis, for two-and-a-half years, with clients such as National Geographic and TV Guide, as well as Bank of America.

> If you're good at your job and work on developing relationships throughout your career, when people move on—whether its colleagues or clients—they will often think of you when an opportunity arises. The events industry is all about networking and contacts.

"Once you're connected to a company it's important to maintain that relationship, so I kept in touch with Jack Morton and all the production leads. They'd often invite me back to work on projects as a freelancer but I was often booked on other jobs so I didn't really have the opportunity to, but we kept in contact over the two-and-a-half years that I was at C2. Part of this industry is really about managing your relationships with people, keeping contacts informed of what you're up to, and making sure they feel as though they haven't been blown off just because you're not available to work for them at the time."

After two-and-a-half years of working freelance for the other agency, Marie put a call in to Jack Morton to see if they had any work. It turned out they had a project for her, so she talked to the account director and within five days was back at Jack Morton working on a relatively small project for what would eventually become their largest New York client, Verizon.

"I initially went back to Jack Morton freelance for about six months. Then, as I was building up the team and the account, my bosses approached me and said, 'you're developing into more of a manager role and we want this account to grow and for you to help lead that business, so you need to be full-time staff to do that.' To be honest, I didn't really want to be staff at first. I liked the freedom of being freelance, and you can often make more money that way, so I was a little reluctant to give that up at first, but then I realized it was a great opportunity. So I went for the opportunity and became full-time in March 2008—and I've been here since. I worked on Verizon for another three years, and then I moved off Verizon and onto other clients such as Samsung, Walmart, Kimberly-Clark, American Airlines, and Lego—which included producing the reveal of the largest LEGO model ever, built in the heart of Times Square. Then in 2013, I was promoted to Director of Operations."

26
Conclusion

Being an event planner can be a hugely rewarding career; despite the long anti-social hours, the impossible demands from clients, and the fact that there is never enough budget for what you want to do. The truth is nothing quite beats the buzz you get from problem solving and coming up with innovative ideas, the anticipation you feel during the build, and the final rush of seeing the client's and guest's reaction to months of your hard work coming together in an amazing live experience. When you do that for a living, month on month, it's almost impossible to imagine feeling satisfied in any other type of job.

The great thing about the event industry is that, at this stage of its evolution, it's still accessible to anyone. Unlike most other professions, you don't need formal qualifications, education, or training. What counts is experience. As long as you have drive and commitment, the right personal qualities, and can develop the necessary core skills, you can go out tomorrow and get an entry-level support role. From there, you can work your way up the career ladder to become an event planner.

However, it's essential that you go about it the right way and with the right attitude. Don't sit at home sending out resumes cold. Get inside the industry, at the most basic support-staff level, and network from within to work your way up. Be strategic. Decide which area you want to work in, then research and truly understand that sector. Study each event you work on, and soak up every detail you can onsite in order to learn and better educate yourself about planning and production. Connect with people onsite, develop relationships, and use those contacts to create opportunities to move up the career ladder. You'll have far more success this way than if you just sit at home sending out resumes, and the great thing is, it's entirely within your own control. If you're prepared to make the effort and inconvenience yourself along the way, the entry-level opportunities are there. The only potential barrier to entry is the level of commitment you're prepared to put in.

One final piece of advice I'd like to share is to be realistic. It takes time to carve out a career in events. As you'll have read in the case studies, neither the contributors to this book nor I went straight into a job as an event planner. We all started in lesser positions; some as volunteers, some as support staff, others in entirely different professions, and worked our way up. Sometimes it happens quickly and a 'lucky break' can speed up the process, but for the most part, it takes time. Time that you need, to learn and develop your skills and contacts along the way, so that when you do eventually become an event planner, you'll be a good one—because you've put in the groundwork.

27

Final Advice from the Professionals

To close, I asked each of the contributors to this book what one piece of advice they would give to someone looking to start a career in the event industry. So, over to them:

"There's a ton of variety in what I do and within, specifically, event planning. There are so many different industries and positions that you can explore. My advice would be to follow whatever interests you have and follow your passion. Think through what your passion is. If you love fashion, then target the events that are going on in the fashion industry. If you love sports, find a sports marketing firm. If you love food, find a caterer/restaurant/event facility that you can work in. Every day you'll work with people and elements that excite you. Event planning is one thing, but you'll love it even more if you can do it within a field you're interested in."

Marie Davidheiser, Senior Vice President, Director of Operations, Jack Morton Worldwide

"If you can, get some experience that pays; be that at a hotel, caterer or staffing agency—anything that gets you working at events – do it! You've got to love hard work and the rewards that this brings. You've got to be passionate about detail and relish the opportunity of working long hours under pressure. You have to truly care about each and every event you work on and genuinely want it to be the best possible experience for all of your guests. It's not some great mystery about how to get into events; simply put, be prepared to start at the bottom, work hard and be enthusiastic, no matter how dirty or mundane the job given to you. If you have got the right characteristics and personality you'll soon get spotted—all senior event managers always need junior staff that they can rely on to get the job done well and on time. You'll quickly earn their respect and if you keep your eyes and ears open you can learn a

tremendous amount just from observing what's going on around you— and not just the practical stuff about how an event is built and fits together; in time you'll hopefully begin to understand how to create atmosphere, energy and excitement too."

Nathan Homan, Co-founder, Rouge Events

"Do a lot of volunteer work. Charity events are a great place to start. I was Vice President of the student union and organized all those events, but really it comes down to wherever you can get involved; music festivals, stewarding—it will all help you get an insight into the back stage goings on."

Grace Nacchia, Event Director, George P. Johnson

"Be tenacious and don't be put off by doors closing. Try every avenue and use every opportunity. Maybe get your foot in the door by working at a supplier, venue, or a staffing agency—there are many different areas of the industry you can use as an entry point. Don't worry about getting stuck in one area, or starting out in an area you don't really want to stay in, because you can always transfer and move around. Just concentrate on getting as much experience as you can."

Charlotte Saynor, former Vice President of Brands & Events, FremantleMedia Enterprises, and Head of European Events, Apple

"You have got to understand what event planning is really all about. You're not going to be sitting on a flight going to a 5 Star hotel having a lovely time. You might be on a flight sometimes, but it will be late at night, after a full day in the office, you'll be tired, hungry, and your feet will hurt. It involves long hours; you've got to give up your weekends sometimes, evenings often, and you don't get paid extra for that, it's just part of what we do.

There are some great rewards though. If you like the sense of achievement involved in delivering a well-executed project, then you're on the right track. If you don't like early mornings then you're probably not in the right industry; you've got to be onsite at 6am when you're doing a conference, and you've got to be the one who's bright-eyed bushy-tailed, smart, and coherent—and you can't have been drinking the night before. Everyone else is having a good time when they're onsite; they are there to party, but you're there to make sure everyone goes away with the most amazing experience—that's your job and unfortunately that means that behind the scenes you're running around like a headless chicken making it all work. If you understand that and you're still passionate about it, if you really understand the core skills and can demonstrate what they are, then you're probably heading in the right direction."

Sharyn Scott, Global Head of Events, Linklaters

"You need to be proactive and really put yourself out there. Get as much experience as you can. Networking is also so important when developing your career in the industry. Working in event management is hugely rewarding, you just need to put in the time and effort."

Lisa Simmons, Project Manager, EAME Events,
Goldman Sachs

"Don't expect it to be a glamorous job, but expect it to be a really exciting career. There's not that many careers where you get to see your work regularly come to life and have other people experience it first-hand. But you've got to really want it; be ambitious and hard working. If you're all of those things, you should do well in events. Go that extra mile, be proactive to get experience, and you'll do well. "

Liz Sinclair, Managing Director, ESP Recruitment

"If you've already got a full-time job, how much of your personal time are you willing to sacrifice? Are you willing to work six to seven days a week to get where you want to be? Because that's what determination is all about. If you think that you can just coast along and someone's going to offer you an event job, forget it. You have to sacrifice.

My suggestion would be to go and sign up with a staffing agency. Why? Because if you work on events at night and at weekends you are going to get phenomenal venue knowledge and you'll start to get an understanding of the dynamics involved in delivering food and beverage to a whole crowd of people—and often in a VIP situation. You're going to make contacts and you'll see what it means to be at a film premiere, a product launch, or a private party. I'm not suggesting you do it forever, but go out there and get the experience.

Another thing that I think would be good to do is sign up with a host/ess agency to work on events. Go and be a host/ess on Formula

One events or on a T-Mobile roadshow for six weeks around the country—that's how you'll start to get event experience. Trying to knock on the door of an event agency, having not demonstrated that you've even tried to get experience, is just not the way to go.

Also, look out for the exhibitions that are related to events like The Wedding Show and Square Meal. Go to them, walk the floor, and meet people. Get some business cards printed for yourself that just have your name and contact details on them and network—get people's telephone numbers, get out there, and make it happen."

Martin Turner, former Global Head of Events, Credit Suisse

"Try and find the best suppliers in the industry and hound them for work experience, it doesn't matter what area of the industry, as long as they're the best. It could be a venue, caterer or if you're prepared for more physical labor then maybe production. Personally, I think catering will give you a much bigger picture of the overall event and it's easier to cross over into event planning from catering."

Charlotte Wolseley Brinton, former Head of Events,
Rhubarb Food Design

"The only way you're going to really understand the process of event planning is to get your hands dirty and get involved. Every event business can use some extra hands onsite during a conference or event. Dollars are being spent on temporary help at all these events. Put yourself out there and volunteer. Get in touch with your local convention and visitors bureau and see how you can help. I would also highly recommend taking some kind of internship. Making a few more bucks and advancing to a higher level will all come later if you work hard—and you play nice in the sandbox on your way up!"

Bill Jones, Vice President, Managing Director, Events,
The Channel Company, formerly UBM Tech Channel

"Get some experience; maybe volunteering with a charity, or if you're at university organize an event there, just so you can experience what it's like and whether you enjoy it and have a passion for it. It's really hard work but very rewarding, so get as much experience as possible before you decide this is the career for you."

Fiona Lawlor, HR Director, Jack Morton EMEA

"It comes down to three things:

1. *Educate yourself about the industry; either formally or of your own accord*
2. *Gain some level of experience; either volunteering or through part-time work*
3. *Be persistent; realize that it's not personal when someone says, 'we're not hiring.' It doesn't mean they don't like you. Don't limit yourself to just one company, or one interview.*

Realize that it's a marathon, not a sprint. Careers are built in years and decades, not weeks and months. So where you begin your career is not going to be where you end up. You may not get the ideal first position, but you'll gain experience and the opportunity to better assess where you want to be for your next job. Don't live or die by that first job, in most cases it's just a stepping stone."

Christopher H. Lee, CEO, Access Destination Services

"Don't be afraid to start somewhere just to get your feet wet. You'll learn so much along the way about who you are, what you have to contribute to the industry, and where you want to take your career.

Be open to all different types of experiences and thinking of yourself in various roles, not categorizing yourself as solely an operations or a sales person. Most likely, where you start is not where you will end up, and the most seasoned and knowledgeable professionals are those that have been open to learning everything they can from each experience offered.

Always go the extra mile for your colleagues and clients, it won't go unnoticed or unappreciated, and may be just the thing to take you to the next level in your career."

**Jennifer Miller, DMCP, Partner & President,
ACCESS Destination Services**

"Be open to all different types of experiences, because you never know what path you're going to take, who you're going to meet, and how those experiences are doing to contribute to your career in event planning. Be open, take things as they come, be proactive, and most of all don't give up."

Rachel Vingsness, Senior HR Manager, Jack Morton Worldwide

"Getting an entry into the event industry will require you to commit to hard work, but be tenacious, professional, and open to opportunities and you will find your way in."

Nicola Mosley, HR Manager, George P. Johnson

"Get as involved as you can; be it through volunteering or internships, and start as early as you can—as soon as you realize this is something you want to do—so you can get as much experience as you can."

Dori Rodriguez, Senior HR Associate, Jack Morton Worldwide

"If you want to be a charity event planner, do as much research as possible on all the charities that interest you. Make sure you understand their work and their fundraising strategy, including how much of their fundraising is done through events and what kind of events they run. Offer to volunteer at any or all of their events so you become a known face to the event planner and the team. Whether it's in the office or onsite, be punctual and willing to do whatever is asked of you—and show plenty of initiative. The worst thing you can do is sit around waiting for someone to give you work. If work experience doesn't lead to a job straight away, make sure you keep in touch with the events team to let them know you are around whenever they need extra help—and keep volunteering to build up experience in the meantime. When an opening comes up, you'll likely be one of the main contenders for the job."

Farida Haqiqi, former Events Manager, British Red Cross

"Try to take an internship somewhere, whether at a corporate client or with an event production company—or even with a supplier; anywhere that you can learn how events are done from the inside and take that knowledge on with you to your next position. Also, read up on the industry, whether that's trade publications or books that explain the theory of event planning—anything that enables you to absorb knowledge and connect with what's going on in the industry. Try to know what the current and up-and-coming trends are, what's in fashion, and what's influencing the industry. There are so many different things that you can be influenced and inspired by. That type of knowledgeable 'plugged in' attitude will come across well in job interviews."

Chad Hudson, President, Chad Hudson Events

My Route into the Industry

Starting in Catering

From selling printer cartridges, to working on events for HRH Charles, Prince of Wales

Charlotte Wolseley Brinton, former Head of Events, Rhubarb Food Design

Charlotte is a great example of someone who started her career as an event planner at a catering company, and then used the opportunities and experience she gained to eventually start her own special events company. Despite having little experience of organizing events when she started, by working as a planner for a catering company, she was able to learn everything there is to know about event planning and how the industry works.

"Working as an event planner at a catering company you're exposed to every part of the event. If you're looking for a way into the industry when you don't have much experience—that's the way to go."

I've worked with Charlotte on many events over the years and I think it's worth pointing out that she is incredibly well spoken, turned out, and articulate. She has always presented herself impeccably, in appearance and manner, and has the ability to deal with people at all levels. Learning about her route into the industry, and her subsequent progression, I suspect her communication skills and personality have probably been a significant contributing factor in the opportunities she has been offered and, ultimately, her success. When she had little experience, I don't doubt that it was the confident and professional way she conducted herself that won her certain jobs. Keep this in mind when you read her journey below, as these are skills that anyone can develop for

> *themselves and, although it might sound like very basic advice, you'd be surprised how important appearance, manner, and personality are in service-oriented jobs such as event planning. When a job seeker is young and inexperienced, it's even more important that they come across as confident and professional.*

Charlotte admits that it took her a long time before she realized what she wanted to do career-wise, and as a result, she was 31 years old by the time she took her first job in the industry, working for a small private venue called 30 Pavilion Road in London. Prior to that she had started out, aged 18, working as a switchboard operator after leaving school in South Africa. From there she was promoted to a sales manager role, selling printer cartridges and 'uninterruptable power supply systems' *"Not exactly a glamorous start!"* She then moved to London and began temping as a secretary working for investment banks such as Goldman Sachs, Lehman Brothers, and Credit Suisse.

Interestingly, it was while working on a temporary contract as a personal assistant to one of the directors at Credit Suisse that she had her first taste of event planning, albeit in a small capacity, by organizing hospitality events for her boss, such as corporate skiing trips and evenings at the ballet and opera. Although these might seem like a very basic level of event planning, organizing anything for senior executives (and their high-net-worth clients) in leading financial institutions is invaluable customer-service experience. Investment bankers, or any senior executives for that matter, generally have extremely high expectations when it comes to service and there's typically no margin for error. In fact, when I was looking to hire a PA myself, I specified that they had to come from a City background because I knew from my time working in events for Credit Suisse that City PA's are of a particularly high caliber and can be relied on to get things done. Therefore, I don't doubt that these jobs probably helped give Charlotte a confidence and professionalism when dealing with senior people, that later helped her to get her first job in the event industry at 30 Pavilion Road.

Event-planning companies also have clients who are senior executives or high-net-worth individuals. If a candidate looking for work is articulate, professional, and has experience of dealing with senior executives—regardless of whether that's in the events industry or not—then the employer may feel comfortable putting them in a client-facing role, so that's going to be a huge advantage.

Don't underestimate how experience of working in a corporate environment, and dealing with senior executives and clients, can be a valuable asset to employers in the event industry. If you have that experience, however unrelated it might be to events, be sure to highlight it.

From temping as a PA, Charlotte then took on the role of Business Development Director for a UK charity, Macmillan Cancer Support. The charity were looking to stage a fundraising initiative based on a classic TV comedy game show from the 1970s and 80s called *It's a Knockout*, which featured teams representing a town or city completing tasks in absurd games, generally dressed in large foam rubber suits. In this case, the charity were planning to have teams representing different City firms, such as banks and law firms, so Charlotte was able to leverage her experience of working for investment banks at the interview stage, along with her background in sales. She also believes her attitude at the interview contributed to her getting the job. *"Macmillan asked me why I wanted this job. I remember saying 'I love what the charity stands for, I know I can do it, and I know I can do it well.' You just have to have that essence of confidence and demonstrate that you can make a contribution."*

After her job at the charity, Charlotte then took a year off to take a cooking course, and then worked for six months as a chalet girl in Verbier in the Swiss Alps, before going to work as an assistant to an interior designer. It was while working for the interior designer that a friend told her about a job opportunity at a small private venue called 30 Pavilion Road that was looking for a general manager.

30 Pavilion Road is a country-style townhouse in Knightsbridge—a very upmarket area of London—that is used for dinners, cocktail parties, weddings, and small meetings, conferences and seminars. The venue is known for its classical Georgian décor and very traditional atmosphere, which in turn attracts a very traditional, conservative, and affluent clientele. The décor is very grand, which is why most people choose to hire it as a venue. The majority of the event-planning duties, after selling the venue itself, are focused around the banqueting requirements (in fact, the venue is owned and operated by a catering company). Being able to cite experience working for senior investment bankers, an interior designer, and as a business development director for a well-known charity meant that Charlotte was able to demonstrate that she could deal with senior people, understood the importance of the aesthetics of the venue, and had experience in sales-based roles. *"I think I just fit the type of profile and background they were looking for. Their clients were quite traditional and so I was able to show that I was used to dealing with those types of people."*

At the interview, she was also able to talk about her interests, which included a great love of food—for which she'd taken a cookery course—entertaining, and interior design, all of which were in line with that of her prospective employers. *"You've got to want something quite badly. I loved the venue, it was a lovely house, so it was an easy sell once you got people in the door and I know I can sell. A lot of the event industry is about selling, if you're not selling a product you're selling yourself and building relationships. I think they could feel my passion and drive."*

Although the job at 30 Pavilion Road was technically Charlotte's first position in the event industry, it was actually her next role that would truly set her on her career path to becoming an event planner.

Although Charlotte might feel that she got into the industry late, she's a great example of how you can get into event planning if you're looking for a change of career. You don't have to start straight out of college. In fact, by coming into it a little later, Charlotte was able to go into a more senior position as the general manager of a small venue. I suspect one of the reasons she was hired by the venue was that, by being a little bit older and having worked in a number of professional environments, including investment banks and a national charity, she was able to conduct herself in a more professional manner— which was just the type of candidate they were looking for.

After leaving 30 Pavilion Road, a friend recommended her to a public relations company that was looking to hire someone on a short freelance contract to help them organize a party for *OK! Magazine*. During the planning stages, Charlotte asked five different catering companies to submit quotes for the catering. She was particularly impressed by one caterer, Rhubarb Food Design, and fixed up a meeting with one of their event planners, Caroline, which resulted in her hiring them for the event. While Charlotte was working with Caroline and planning the event, she made a point of telling her that she was just working on this project as a freelancer and that if they (meaning *Rhubarb Food Design*) ever needed any extra staff to let her know. This passing comment would later prove to be a defining moment that would influence Charlotte's career path, and it underlines the importance of networking and putting yourself out there. If you're trying to get into events, you'll have far more success by getting out there, meeting people, and taking a proactive approach to get the most out of every opportunity.

Remember that every person you work alongside is a contact that could help you find future work.

Following the death of Princess Diana, *OK! Magazine* decided it would be inappropriate to go ahead with its party and so the event was cancelled, leaving Charlotte—who was working freelance—out of a job. She used the opportunity to take a holiday, but when she arrived home there were several messages from Caroline explaining that she was about to go away to work on another big event and asking whether Charlotte would be interested in filling her post at Rhubarb Food Design for three months. Charlotte went in to meet the owner of the company, Lucy, on a Friday and started working for them on the Monday. *"I went in on a three-month contract and ending up staying for four years."*

There's a great lesson to be learned here, not only about the power of networking, but also to remember that whatever role you are doing in the event industry, you are constantly auditioning for your next job. Perhaps without even realizing it, all the while that Charlotte was planning the OK! Magazine party and working alongside Caroline, she was demonstrating her skills and abilities. So, when Caroline was looking for someone to recommend to her own boss to replace her, she was able to testify to Charlotte's suitability, and a recommendation like that often opens doors.

On her first day working at *Rhubarb Food Design* Charlotte went, with the owner Lucy, to a meeting about a big event they were planning a few months away. It turned out the event was Andrew Lloyd Webber's 50th birthday party and they were meeting with his wife, Madeline.

"After the meeting, Lucy turned to me and said 'right, I would like you to work on this with me.' Having had almost zero experience organizing events, apart from running a venue, I went from 0–60 in a heartbeat. Suddenly, from not having a job on the Friday, here I was four days later running Andrew Lloyd Webber's 50th birthday party! It was a huge leap of faith from Lucy in me."

After a very short period, Rhubarb Food Design asked Charlotte to become their Head of Events. As they were a very young company, Charlotte was given a lot of opportunities that perhaps she might not have had working at a larger company—including the chance to work her way up very quickly.

Sometimes it pays to try and get work experience with a small company because there's often more of an 'all hands on deck' approach, which means you won't just be confined to one particular role.

After four years working for Rhubarb Food Design, Charlotte had amassed a huge amount of knowledge, experience and—perhaps most importantly—contacts, and felt she was ready to start her own event-planning company, Event Fusion.

"I knew I wanted to do the whole thing; to have more input in other areas and manage the whole event, that's why I moved on. By that point, I'd been exposed to all the different areas that go into event planning; venues, catering, back of house, logistics, staffing, lighting, decoration, and working with clients. So it just felt like the right time to do my own thing."

My Route into the Industry

Starting in Venue Management

*From managing event bookings at a castle in Italy,
to producing conferences and conventions for IBM, Shell,
and Ferrari throughout Europe, Asia, and the Middle East*

Grace Nacchia, Event Director, George P. Johnson

Throughout this book, I've explained that when it comes to the hiring process, having the right attitude, personality, and people skills is just as important as having the core project management skills. After getting a taste of the event industry by working as a venue manager, Grace's first significant role as a planner came as a result of her people skills, a strong work ethic, and her proactive approach to building and maintaining relationships.

At university, Grace studied European Business with Italian, and specialized in marketing. The course included a one-year placement working in research and development in the marketing department of Olivetti in Italy. After graduation, she returned to Italy and took various temporary jobs, such as teaching English, before taking a job with an historic castle venue.

"I was their internal representative looking after their event bookings, such as weddings and car launches. It wasn't even advertised as an event role as such. I didn't really understand that's what it was going to involve until I got the job—it was a little vague and I was 22. I didn't really know what I wanted to do so I just took this job at this beautiful castle venue."

The best thing to do is just get into the industry in some shape or form, don't worry too much about whether it's exactly the role you want. In this case, Grace ended up in a

> *venue manager role which provided her with a great introduction to the industry. Once in, it's far easier to build on that experience by networking with the people you meet in order to move sideways or upwards in the industry. Just think of it as a necessary stepping-stone to get to where you really want to be.*

The work at the castle was very process-driven. Grace was involved in taking the initial booking, and then she would talk the clients through all the planning and logistics, before handing the event over to the operations team to run it on the day. As it was a small company, she found it very easy to learn how the entire process of event planning worked. *"Before I even realized it, I was in a profession and had started on a journey that led me to the type of events I'm doing today."*

After a while, Grace decided to move back to the United Kingdom where she re-connected with a recruitment agency that she'd used to find temporary work throughout her college years. Over the course of her four-year university course, she'd developed a good relationship with the recruiter by always being open to work.

"I was so up for earning any kind of money during my degree that I became quite reliable, and I hardly ever turned down work they offered me. I always made myself available, especially during the summer holidays, regardless of the job. So they really got to know me—and if there's anything I've learned during my career, it's that it's all about relationship building."

Not long after she moved back to the United Kingdom, having told the recruitment agency she was looking for work, they contacted her with an opportunity.

"The lady called me up and said, 'I've got a great opportunity for you. I know this company really well, and I've got to know you really well over the years, so I'd like to put you forward for an interview. I just think you'd get on well with them.' I asked her what the job was and she gave me this overview of an account

manager position running exhibition trucks. I thought it sounded interesting, I didn't really have a clue what it involved, but I just went to the interview anyway."

This is a great lesson in the importance of networking and developing relationships. Even before she knew she wanted to work in events, Grace had adopted the right attitude by being professional and accommodating with potential employers. As a result, she was able to develop a relationship with a recruitment agency, one that she maintained over several years. That relationship then paid off a few years down the line when, because of her personality and professional attitude, the agency thought of her first when an opportunity came up. That's exactly the type of relationship–based approach that makes up the majority of hiring in the events industry. So, be professional with everyone you work with—even when it seems like they might have no connection to where you want to be; you never know where that contact might end up working in future.

"I met the two directors of the company at the pub, it was all very informal, and they said they were just looking for someone who was the right fit for them; that personality was key. They said, 'based on your work ethic and what we've heard about you from the agency, we just feel you'd have the right personality and attitude for this particular client, because the client is quite difficult. Whatever you need to know, we'll teach you.' So in a way, I really did fall into events by accident."

Although Grace's new employers were happy to teach her, the experience she had as a venue manager in Italy shouldn't be underestimated. In that position, she was essentially project-managing bookings and events. Although it was her personality and attitude that ultimately

> *landed her the job, I don't doubt that experience would
> have given her new employers the reassurance that she
> had the necessary core skills to apply to their roadshows
> business. It's all about transferable skills, which is why
> working in one area of the events industry can often be
> used as stepping-stones to another.*

Grace accepted the job and founded herself working for a small live events company called EMS Worldwide. At the time, they only had two clients, Sony and Royal Bank of Scotland. Her role was to manage the touring exhibition units for Sony, who used one of the largest exhibition trucks in Europe to tour the United Kingdom, along with a demonstration unit that toured different towns and cities. The Sony *'Jaminator'* touring exhibition, a 40ft mobile unit housing hundreds of products, such as TVs and laptops, would be taken on the road to different events in support of their local dealerships, with the objective of boosting sales. EMS Worldwide would provide an entire team of staff trained in Sony products, and the individual dealers would hold special events, while Grace managed everything from booking the sites and handling logistics, to working with each dealer's site-specific promotions. She also went on to work on the company's other account, The Royal Bank of Scotland, where she was part of their annual awards conference execution team.

"The amount I learned from working for a very small company—there were only four of us—was immense. David, one of the directors who gave me my first opportunity, really taught me everything I know. He said to me, 'I can teach someone whatever I need to teach them, but I can't make someone have the right personality', so he made a decision to go out and look for the right personality type that would fit with his client. Obviously, it was a junior role; it was hard work, it wasn't highly paid, it was stressful and sometimes I'd think 'wow I get paid very little for doing so much.' But then I'd look at what my friends were doing, and how boring their jobs were, and I'd realize that my job was

pretty fantastic because I got to go to lots of places, do site visits around the country, go to food tastings, travel abroad, and meet interesting people."

When looking for work experience, it's definitely worth weighing up the benefits of working for a small company over a larger agency. In a larger agency, you'll likely end up working on one small aspect of the event, whereas in a smaller agency you'll probably be able to take on more; so the experience you gain can be far richer. I would certainly recommend approaching smaller, reputable, companies in the early stages of work experience to practice the basics, before then moving on to seek experience with a larger agency, which might add more credentials to your resume.

Unfortunately, after about 18 months the company went into liquidation, but one of the directors went on to start another company called EMS Live and asked Grace to come and work for him.

"Another great thing about working for a small agency is that you're a lot more involved in everything. It taught me a commercial awareness and the importance of chasing a purchase order, because I knew the financial status of the company and I knew that I couldn't commit to any contract with suppliers if we didn't have a guarantee of the money coming in. It was the 'all hands on deck' approach, where you learn so much about how everything connects and the implications of something not being done properly—which is just the most perfect training for events."

After a further 18 months, Grace decided to move on and took a six-month contract at a marketing agency that dabbled in events. The agency was quite keen to get her into their events department full-time because of her experience working on large touring exhibitions, but she didn't feel it was a good fit for her and decide to look elsewhere when the six months was up. She then interviewed for an event manager position with George P.

Johnson, an opportunity that also came via a recruitment agency. There, she started on their dedicated IBM team working on conferences and exhibitions (aka conventions) for all the different software groups within IBM, such as Lotus. After a year or so, she moved up to a senior event manger position which, although a similar role, involved more negotiating with venues and other suppliers in order to provide value to the client.

"After four years, I felt like I needed something different because the same events were coming around each year and I just felt like I needed to see what else was out there. George P. Johnson was the only large agency I'd worked for and IBM was all I'd known for the past four years. So, again through a recruitment agency, I got a job as a senior project manager for Imagination where I spent two years working on events for Shell and Ferrari. It was mainly exhibitions [conventions] that I worked on. Shell had a global exhibition program that was rolled out around the world, so I went to places like Qatar and Bahrain, and for Ferrari I worked in Italy a lot. I loved my time at Imagination but it was quite different to George P. Johnson, so when I was ready to move on I really just felt like I wanted to come home, and for me George P. Johnson felt like home and I've been here ever since."

Index

Made in the USA
Las Vegas, NV
14 December 2021

37658181R00224